SPEAKING OF THE UNIVERSITY

Two Decades at Vanderbilt

ALEXANDER HEARD

Chancellor of Vanderbilt University, 1963–1982

SPEAKING
of the
UNIVERSITY

TWO DECADES AT VANDERBILT

Alexander Heard

VANDERBILT UNIVERSITY PRESS

Nashville and London

Excerpt from "The Hippopotamus" in COLLECTED POEMS 1909–1962 by T.S. Eliot, copyright 1936 by Harcourt Brace & Company, copyright © 1964, 1963 by T.S. Eliot, reprinted by permission of the publisher; in the United Kingdom by permission of the Eliot estate and Faber & Faber, Ltd.

This publication is made from recycled paper and meets the minimum requirements of American National Standard for Information Sciences—Permanence of Paper for Printed Library Materials. ⊗

Library of Congress Cataloging-in-Publication Data

Heard, Alexander.
Speaking of the university : two decades at Vanderbilt / Alexander Heard.—1st ed.
p. cm.
Includes index
ISBN 0-8265-1264-X (alk. paper). — ISBN 0-8265-1265-8 (pbk.: alk. paper)
1. Vanderbilt University—History. I. Title.
LD5588.8.H43 1995
378.768'55—dc20

94–48422
CIP

Manufactured in the United States of America

for Jean

Contents

Foreword

I HAVE KNOWN ALEXANDER HEARD for many years, as Chancellor of Vanderbilt University, as Chairman of the Board of the Ford Foundation, and in connection with a number of educational boards on which we served together. I especially remember a fruitful meeting we had in Bogotá, Colombia, in February of 1969. We were both attending a meeting on higher education in the American republics, but I was mostly concerned with an urgent message from President Richard Nixon that needed an immediate reply. Chancellor Heard generously set aside his schedule and worked with me for two hours in his hotel room drafting a response. I was most grateful for his help and ever after followed his career at Vanderbilt with growing interest and admiration.

During the years of student unrest, I spoke at his university and readily sensed the sustained analysis and skillful attention that he gave to the sources and issues of campus disturbances. Many of the selections in this volume reveal his remarkable rapport with faculty and students, which made it possible to maintain a free and civil platform for discussion at Vanderbilt throughout those difficult years. Also clear is his understanding of and effective attention to the myriad less dramatic demands that burden university chief executives.

During Chancellor Heard's tenure, Vanderbilt grew and

prospered, adding three schools to the seven it already contained, constructing three dozen new or radically enlarged buildings, conducting two highly successful fund-raising campaigns, doubling its enrollment, and increasing its annual budget tenfold. That extraordinary record of accomplishment has contributed significantly to Vanderbilt University's long and distinguished history.

What follows in this engaging volume is not a simple reprint of past speeches but rather a carefully chosen selection of excerpts that deal with the issues, opportunities, and difficulties of university leadership. In the history of twentieth-century American higher education, especially the troubled and challenging decades of the 1960s and 1970s, few leaders have been as effective, courageous, ethically consistent, or influential as Alexander Heard. This instructive book will remind us all of his many achievements, of his great good humor, and of the exemplary clarity of his thought and words.

Theodore M. Hesburgh, C.S.C.
President Emeritus,
University of Notre Dame

Preface

FROM TIME TO TIME IN PUBLIC REMARKS at Vanderbilt, I cited, in what I hoped would be an opening felicity, "Jean Heard's Law." My wife had formulated it earlier when we lived in Chapel Hill. It declared, "A speech should be two-thirds as long as it was." On occasions, when Jean was present, she corrected, "You mean half as long as it was."

This banter gave the audience at least temporary comfort, but how long the comfort lasted would depend on what followed, including how long it followed. I once used it at the opening of an address as president of the Southeastern Conference, on January 20, 1972, at the Park Plaza Hotel in Orlando, Florida. About ten minutes into the great speech—which was delivered in a cavernous ballroom that swallowed the university presidents, faculty chairmen, athletic directors, coaches, and sports writers clustered together in the center of the large acreage—a telephone rang in a distant corner. Without a moment's hesitation, a healthy young fellow proclaimed, loud and clear, "That's Mrs. Heard."

I have prepared this book ever aware that the phone might ring. Its contents are drawn from the texts and notes of some 880 speeches of which I have record that were made while I was chancellor of Vanderbilt University, from February 1, 1963, to June 30, 1982. Excerpts or summaries, and in a rare case or two the full text, have been drawn from seventy-six of the speeches. They were selected in part to illustrate the range of subjects and variety of audiences embraced in the total. A few jokes and other diversionary material were left intact, but space limitation, if not superior judgment, made it wise to stick to the subject. In each case I have added orienting comments to give a sense of the context of the talks. A book drawn from speeches is not, however, a full history, nor is it an autobiography. These speeches were functional, intended to increase understanding, to generate rapport and support among diverse constituencies of Vanderbilt. They were rooted in a philosophy of university education, but it was an applied philosophy, not an abstract one. Many selections must be viewed as illustrative—especially so the reports to the regular meetings of the joint faculties and the Faculty Senate. The language is preserved as delivered, with an occasional minor adjustment for clarity. The selections are arranged chronologically.

During the past few decades, a general preference has evolved for use of the term *black* or *African-American* instead of *Negro* or *colored* when referring to the nation's largest historic racial minority. Here, I have let the terms stand as I used them at the time. Similarly, I have let stand my original use of inclusive terms such as *mankind* and *men* when the reference is to all people (e.g., all men are created equal).

Some categories of remarks have been omitted, among them talks on political science subjects (my academic field), speeches about the history or future of Georgia (my native state), remarks to audiences at the University of North Carolina (my alma mater), speeches made as a trustee of the Ford Foundation or as a director of Time Incorporated, most memorial service tributes, and all reports on foreign travel. The focus is on Vanderbilt in particular and on higher education more generally.

I would be remiss if I did not confess that one outstanding regret has pervaded my preparation of the volume. It is simply impossible to acknowledge adequately my debt to a large number of persons for their crucial roles in the life and work of Vanderbilt during my time in office and later while preparing this book. I assume that anyone would automatically appreciate my grateful indebtedness to the successive presidents of the Board of Trust—Harold S. Vanderbilt, William S. Vaughn, Sam M. Fleming, David K. Wilson, and E. Bronson Ingram—to my predecessor, Chancellor Harvie Branscomb, and to my successor, Chancellor Joe B. Wyatt, but a chancellor is daily dependent on hundreds of others in all reaches of the institution, and my gratitude also goes to each of them too. I think especially, but not only, of Ralph and Lulu Owen, without whom we would not have the Owen Graduate School of Management, and of David K. and Anne Wilson, without whom we would not have the Blair School of Music.

I will delay for the moment my particular appreciation of the abundant contributions to Vanderbilt's welfare made by Sam M. Fleming, former president of the Vanderbilt Board of Trust. Those remarks, which appear in chapter 11, were made at a dinner honoring him that was given in 1982 by presidents of the Alumni Association. But I must say here, at the outset, that without his persistent initiative and ever-present generosity this book would not have appeared.

A word about alumni clubs. My record of texts and notes for meetings of Vanderbilt clubs shows that I spoke on 112 occasions in fifty-two places. The files of the University Alumni Office, however, record, in the ten most visited cities, eighty-one alumni gatherings, of which my tabulation includes only forty-five. The remarks at alumni meetings were so numerous and repetitious that I have included only one here. Talks to alumni normally embraced a report on the "state of the university"—enrollments (including numbers from the local area), important developments in each school, important grants received, innovations effected, traditions preserved, honors received, matters of special interest in the locality of the meeting, and always athletics. I would express appreciation to local alumni for services to Vanderbilt, would recognize any prospective students and their parents, and the parents of any current students who were present, and acknowledge significant local developments. Although I took pains not to tell jokes used previously in the same community, I was not overjoyed when a person came up after one meeting to say he had attended a similar gathering in St. Louis the previous month and had very much enjoyed Oscar Wilde's comment about Niagara Falls the second time around. ("It would be more impressive if it flowed the other way.")

Universities have been evolving in Western culture for centuries. In the United States they have changed in ways that radically affect their daily operations and the parts played by those who make up the university, most importantly the faculty, administrative personnel, and trustees. In 1887, William T. Magruder, Vanderbilt's professor of mechanical engineering, found himself responsible not just for teaching and research but also for construction of a new mechanical engineering building and maintenance and modification of other buildings on the main campus, as well as at the Medical Department located elsewhere in Nashville. Now many powers and responsibilities that formerly fell to members of the faculty have devolved to hands of the administrative staff, and the duties of the latter have become increasingly specialized and delegated. Chancellors no longer periodically journey to the bank to clip coupons of the University's investments as did Chancellor Kirkland, who was Vanderbilt's head from 1893 to 1937. Higher education, especially advanced universities, Vanderbilt among them, has inevitably grown in diversity and complexity. No longer, alas, can a Vanderbilt chancellor easily know the names of all the faculty and of their spouses and of most of the students.

The increasing complexity and deepening divisions of knowledge, and the consequent development of subspecialties, have been accompanied by increased sources of funding for research and by the heightened mobility of faculty within the broad academic society. Circumstances encourage the orientation of faculty members more narrowly toward their academic disciplines than toward their academic institutions. Although far from true of all faculty members, the rising frequency and range of travel of faculty in the normal course of their work has expanded both their outlook and their associations, for some making the university more the place where one works than the institution one is committed to serve.

The evolving conditions of university life inevitably change the climate in which leadership labors, a fact borne in on me before taking office when I read everything I could find to learn the history and nature of Vanderbilt. And of course the processes of change do not stop.

Most activities in a university continue one year after the other: attracting students and seeking to enhance their educational experience; engaging and seeking to satisfy the needs of faculty; seeking to provide the increasingly sophisticated support systems they require, of which libraries and computer centers are but two; recruiting and improving the performance of other staff; renovating old and constructing new buildings; caring for and improving the campus; raising money; investing financial assets; and endlessly more. These form the myriad operational and developmental decisions that are essential to a complex, diversified institution. One year flows into the next, but as I look back over the years that concern this book, they can be divided into three moods.

The four years from early 1963 to early 1967 were relatively calm, both on the Vanderbilt campus and in our relations with the larger community.

The years from 1967 to the early 1970s saw the trend toward campus unrest, which was already rising across the nation, come to Vanderbilt. That aggressive condition commanded the continuing attention of faculty, students, trustees, alumni, financial supporters, and everyone else, but most directly it challenged the University's responsible administrators. In the course of this period, between 1966 and 1970, a $55 million fund drive was successfully completed.

The years from the mid-1970s to 1982 saw important steps in institutional development, including construction of a new hospital and Light Hall in the medical center—among some thirty-five major construction projects between 1963 and 1982—and the addition of Vanderbilt's ninth and tenth schools (with their own important physical plants), the George Peabody College for Teachers and the Blair School of Music. A fund drive from 1977 to 1981 raised $181.4 million.

Naturally, the subjects of speeches I gave over the years often reflected the particular circumstances of the university and of the nation at the time. Although a university's nature and needs have tenacious continuities, exhibiting themselves in different guises under changing circumstances, the increasing size and diversity of a developing institution like Vanderbilt had obvious consequences for its leadership. To function not only as a college president, with special attention to undergraduates, but also as the chancellor of a diverse and advanced university, both of which I considered it my responsibility to be, became increasingly challenging.

Although broader perspectives and lessons may be present, what follows pertains primarily to a particular period in American higher education and to the specific university it was my good fortune to serve from 1963 to 1982.

SPEAKING OF THE UNIVERSITY
Two Decades at Vanderbilt

Arriving
1963

NOT LONG AFTER IT WAS ANNOUNCED that the Heards would be moving from Chapel Hill in North Carolina to Nashville and Vanderbilt, I met a friend on an elevator in nearby Durham. He felicitated me on the appointment, and then mused, "I always thought you would go into politics." "I just did," was my reply.

Universities comprise many constituencies on each of which, at one time or another, in one way or another, they depend. They do not depend on them for ultimate survival, as the virtually nonexistent mortality rate among universities testifies. Yet the chief officer of a university has constituencies *for* which in one way or another he or she is held responsible, including rambunctious students, outspoken faculty, sometimes recalcitrant employees, and always, it seems, losing athletic teams. At the same time, he or she has constituencies *to* which in one way or another he or she is expected to be accountable, sometimes including parents and donors, and always including alumni and trustees. There are also local, state, and national public officials, regulatory and accrediting bodies, campus neighbors, special interest groups, and abundant others who can make a chancellor's life demanding and who always make it interesting.

Among all these constituents of university leadership, the

faculty is the most important. Without the faculty there would be no students, no scholarship, no community services rendered. I was therefore alert on my first day in office, Friday, February 1, 1963, when Vice-Chancellor Rob Roy Purdy spoke of the special meeting of the combined faculties that had been called for the following Tuesday, February 5, in Underwood Auditorium of the Law School, to meet the new chancellor. After expressing enthusiasm for the courtesy shown, I inquired whether I should perhaps say something. Mr. Purdy, like the rest of us, did not relish bearing heavy news, but I can still hear him saying politely, but with clear anxiety, that my new faculty colleagues were expecting "something rather formal." I learned then a lesson confirmed many times during the next two decades: I would never have all the time desired for preparing a speech.

I set aside the intervening Sunday afternoon to work alone in the new office at this maiden effort. The telephone soon rang. Calling was Vanderbilt's (and my) ranking local trustee, Mr. O. H. Ingram, the valuable vice-president of the Board of Trust, who thought there were sights we should see and matters we should discuss. We saw and discussed immediately, with benefits to me, and let the speech-writing temporarily slide.

When I retired in 1982, I was pleasantly surprised that the faculty committee charged to arrange a ceremony said it wished to have that first speech reprinted in a formal limited edition, as a gift to be presented at a special faculty convocation to be held April 28. The full speech went as follows:

I am deeply conscious of the great privilege that brings me before you this afternoon at the beginning of the tenth decade in the life of this famous university. I am proud to be your faculty colleague. I am honored to be your chancellor. And I am already enjoying my part in the most important secular task of the twentieth century—our common mission of sustaining and advancing a significant university.

A vital synthesis of need, vision, and resources gave birth to Vanderbilt University. I am much aware that its regional service has been large and tangible, that its national stature has been recognized, and that its international outlook is established. The tradition has been long, often tumultuous, always dynamic, and I am happy to join you in it, I hope without losing a single step.

The historic achievements of this institution under the imaginative and indefatigable leadership of my friend Harvie Branscomb are widely known, and better known to you than any. As a citizen, I am grateful to him for his services through Vanderbilt University to our nation and our world. I am also grateful to him for his cordial friendship, and cooperation without stint, in recent months. If I ever have a claim to boldness in this life, it is the willingness to follow in his wake.

This willingness may be styled boldness, rather than folly, only because of you who sit before me at this hour, and because of the grace that has favored this university with a devoted and sagacious Board of Trust. My confidence in your and their understanding of the nature of a university and of the conditions necessary for its proper operation gives me a cheerful heart for the tasks that lie ahead.

And as I look ahead I realize that I am already vastly indebted to Vice-Chancellor Purdy for his aid of many kinds. I appreciate not only his diligence, loyalty, and sane judgment—all of which are abundant—but also his good sense of humor. Education is a serious business, and we shall ever treat it so, but *we* mortals err if we take *us* mortals as seriously as we take the causes for which we work. Even with all the high purposes we gravely pursue, and despite the tragic sadnesses that lie about the world, man may be saved yet by the divine joy of humor. I propose that you and I shall have a good time during these coming years. He who laughs often lasts.

I want to talk among ourselves for a while this afternoon inside the Vanderbilt faculty family. I will not presume to speak with you so soon about specific objectives I hope we can reach together. Rather, I would speak about how, in my view, we must go about determining what to do, about how we must go about doing it, about the yardsticks by which we should measure ourselves, and especially about your part in these matters—all toward the general goal of making Vanderbilt an increasingly significant American university.

The broad and inherent obligations of modern, complex universities in the United States are known to most of us, if not always understood fully everywhere in our society. In these institutions, we inquire into the nature of man and his environment. We transmit to others a portion of what is known, and believed to be dear, or believed to be useful. We train in the application of knowledge. We seek to stir and develop human minds and even to touch human hearts. Altogether, the modern American university as an institution is the central thinking organ of our society and as such is laden with responsibilities both grave and precious. How such an institution is governed affects all men, both inside and outside the universities.

A university is above all a community, a community of teachers, investigators, practitioners, students, alumni, trustees, supporters of all kinds, who in all their disparateness are bound together ultimately by the common interests of intellect and the common purposes of learning. Among the essential components that all together make up the university community, the central element of transcendent importance is the faculty. The ultimate success or failure of an institution is registered most readily in the quality of its faculty. The eminence or disappointments of Vanderbilt University will always be reflected first, and most durably, in the successes or failures of its faculty, of you.

This is true, most obviously, because the quality of faculty determines the quality of instruction. It determines the quality and quantity of significant research performed. And by these qualities it determines the kinds of students who come to us and later go forth from us, and the sentiments of esteem and affection they carry with them the rest of their lives. And in this day of grants and contracts and mounting respect for scholarship throughout the entire American community, in the long run the quality of faculty performance more than anything else affects the flow of financial resources to the institution. After all, individual faculty members do the frontline educational work, which is the end product and the only legitimate objective of a university.

For another reason, however, the destiny of Vanderbilt University rests more in your hands than in the hands of anyone else. True universities are basically self-governed by their faculties. I would like to speak about two phases of this self-government, about two ways this self-government comes about.

One phase is formal, organizational. The procedures and forms of faculty self-government are often legally established and clearly visible. In another setting, I myself have been a part of these and made vigorous use of them. I know their values and accept their purposes, and it goes without saying that the chancellor of this university will do all he can to strengthen and perfect and make use of the official systems of faculty participation in the government of this institution.

The other phase of faculty self-government is quite different. It is also more important. It grows from the simple, essential fact that faculty members enjoy extraordinary independence in the performance of their duties and in the ordering of their professional lives. They do not enjoy total independence, of course. But they—you, we—do enjoy greater autonomy in fulfilling professional obliga-

7

tions than do officers of corresponding significance in any other type of social organization. This independence is, in fact, the distinctive feature of a university as a type of administrative organization. The origins and values of this relative independence do not require explanation here. Certain implications of the condition, however, do need to be emphasized.

Whether individual faculty members intend it or not, or even know it, the facts of faculty autonomy result in a crucially important kind of faculty government of a university. The real quality of an institution—its vigor, its competence, and the directions it takes—stems at heart from the training, skill, energy, initiative, originality, dedication, and vision of the individuals who make up its faculty. Within extremely broad limits—wisely and loyally maintained by those with ultimate legal responsibility for the institution, our trustees—what faculty members do and do not do is determined largely by them alone. And when they individually, each in his own way, determine how they will spend their time, they are exercising the most significant privilege and are engaged in the most important acts of university self-government.

I have often said that the most important thing, the really important thing, a university official does is to select and retain faculty. If he does these two things successfully, everything else takes care of itself. This is true, but university officials must also seek to create the conditions in which a faculty will realize its full potential.

One such condition is a sense of identity between the faculty member and the destiny of his institution—a feeling, for example, that these things I have been saying about the self-government of a university are actually, in his case, true. I have had enough experience in the development of universities to know that durable institutional achievements must be rooted deep in the interests and competencies of the faculty. Innovations not in harmony with these tend to languish. Innovations that grow from them easily become part of the organic whole of the institution, and they endure.

Arriving, 1963

It is my purpose in the years ahead that we shall counsel together as one in developing and advancing the important missions of this university. I could not, if I would, chart our course alone. I will not be reticent in asserting myself, but neither will I be reticent in asking you to assume the responsibilities of full partnership in providing the impulses, in deciding the directions, and in supplying the vigor for what we are to do. As I have observed the government of true universities, in the achievement of educational missions the chief executive is in the end far more dependent on his faculty colleagues than they on him. And that has always seemed to me to be a reasonable as well as an inevitable proposition.

From these conditions many consequences flow. Two I would emphasize.

I am an old Navy hand, but in an educational institution I see little use for the convoy system, the system by which all parts of an institution must proceed at the pace of the slowest part. I have never seen a great university that was a well balanced university. The dependence for institutional vigor on widely decentralized and inevitably uneven faculty energy and ability necessarily produces uneven institutional development.

Moreover, the great opportunities inherent in unmonitored faculty independence impose tangible personal obligations on all who enjoy and take advantage of this independence. The obligation to produce successfully in the classroom, in the library, in the laboratory is a first obligation. But there is also another obligation in the conduct of the affairs of our self-governing university community, an obligation of good academic citizenship, if you will, an obligation to exercise mature and reasonable judgment, to maintain good cheer, to focus on the significant and ignore the petty, to act with sophistication, recognizing that this is seldom a world of absolutes but rather a world in which great men have always done, and only done, the best they could with what they had. In a university, the exercise of self-control is the surest way to avoid control by others.

Speaking of the University

Every organization needs yardsticks by which to measure its progress. Self-governing organizations, especially, require ways of informing themselves whether they are succeeding in their missions.

The criteria of success in universities are not always stated explicitly. This is so in part because the proper diversity of objectives of universities complicates the task of doing so. Nonetheless, in these early days of thinking out loud together, I want to offer you four broad, long-range standards for the judgment of our university performance. In naming them, I do not suggest that these are all there are, nor that Vanderbilt presently either meets or fails them, but rather that in the years ahead we should measure ourselves by them. One of these standards pertains to the students we teach. One pertains to the research we do. One pertains to our place in the contemporary world. And one pertains to the sights we set for ourselves in our work. They are all connected with each other, but they are all quite separate in the educational values they emphasize.

One proper test of the performance of a significant university, I would urge upon you, is the extent to which its graduates become constructive leaders in *varied* phases of our national life.

A significant American university will attract, admit, and educate a diversified student body. Moreover, effective teaching sharpens native talents, inspires originality, and frees young minds from conformity, all in the end stimulating individuality. The product should be university graduates who gravitate to positions of leadership in *many* sectors of our nation's life. I have noted with pride that illustrious alumni of Vanderbilt have included YMCA secretaries along with bank presidents, college professors as well as corporation chairmen, religious leaders as well as military leaders, journalists as well as lawyers, and among these and others a rainbow of political, social, and economic beliefs. I have discerned with pleasure that there is even a beautiful singer among them.

The educational values reflected by this diversity are abundant.

Arriving, 1963

Students are educated by other students as well as by faculty members, which means among other things that a diversified student body is an essential ingredient of a rich, invigorating, and sophisticated educational atmosphere. Beyond this, however, the unity of our society is deepened, hence the service of our university broadened, if some who lead its different parts have shared an educational experience in common.

The stature of a significant American university can be measured in important part also by the volume and quality of its faculty's research. This criterion is appropriate to a university. It is not applicable to many other types of educational institutions, including some institutions of higher learning. But original intellectual inquiry is an essential requisite of the kind of institution we call a university.

As I understand the history of universities, the thread that runs through the university as a distinctive kind of institution in the Western world, in all its varied forms, across eight centuries, is the thread of inquiry. The famed medieval centers of learning in Salerno, Bologna, and Paris are often called the forerunners of the modern university. Salerno became a school of medicine. Bologna arose for the study of law. Paris arose for the study of theology and what was called the arts. In these settings, training was demanded for the professions of medicine, law, and theology. Training meant leading students to the ancient works, also to the then newly discovered or newly rediscovered works, and to the commentaries upon them. The human mind cannot expound information about the human being and about his surroundings, nor offer interpretations of the meaning of this information, without examining what he professes for its consistencies and without comparing it with what is professed by others. Once this is begun, inquiry and reflection begin. And even in these earliest antecedents of the modern university, within all the shackles operating on the medieval mind, hand-in-hand with teaching and training went inquiry.

Colleges and other institutions bring the student to beauty, or thought, or skill, or maturity. They teach; they train. Sometimes their object is the whole man and sometimes just his hands or his feet or a sector of his brain. Universities do these things, too, and we do them here at Vanderbilt, but the addition of exploration to exposition defines the unique role and one essential responsibility of a university.

Vanderbilt is a university. Occasionally I hear someone use the phrase, "research-oriented university." This phrase to me is redundant. A university is by definition research oriented, and so one measure of our success in fulfilling our mission is the volume and quality of the research of our faculty, and the ability and productivity in research of their students.

The stature of a significant American university can be measured, also in part, by the relevance of its teaching and investigation to the environment in which the university functions. The origins and histories of the ancient universities I have just mentioned, and of all universities, including those in our own country, reveal that universities have always by their nature been functional institutions, institutions that render services to the society that supports them. Sometimes these services are directly utilitarian, as in the training of physicians, lawyers, farmers. Sometimes these services are less so, especially in our own time when great value is granted to liberal education and to pure research. In pure or basic research, the immediate purpose may simply be to satisfy the curiosity of an inquirer or to test an abstract hypothesis or to elaborate a theory, the application of which is not the concern of the investigator, or at least not yet. But even here, at bottom, is the unarticulated premise that in this way man will better and faster add to his understanding of himself and his environment. And so, too, liberal education is cherished for its utility in developing wise and versatile citizens and leaders.

No university of my acquaintance has ever functioned in the abstract. A true university is an organic part of the society in which it lives, and a register of its achievement is its relevance to that society.

Arriving, 1963

This university is part of an important metropolitan area, Nashville; of a distinctive political-social-geographic region, the South; of an embattled nation born in a revolution of its own and now seeking to live in a world inflamed by the revolutions of others.

Every university has a unique relationship to its environment. It will necessarily play a distinctive role. A university that succeeds at least in part in identifying the distinctive role it can and wishes to play improves its opportunities for effectiveness. I shall not today attempt to define the present missions or to recommend to you the future missions of Vanderbilt University. But I do say that great universities are conscious of their objectives and that these objectives are of crucial relevance to the social context in which the institution functions.

Finally, the stature of a significant American university—regardless of the distinctive missions it may seize for itself—must be measured by the highest standards of national and international judgment. As applied to our universities of historic regional importance in the South, among which Vanderbilt is conspicuous, this is as much a matter of attitude and point of view as anything else. There are at least three aspects to a university's intent to guide itself by universal standards.

In choosing its faculty, in admitting its students, in exchanging ideas, in rendering its services, whatever they may be, it will view the nation as its campus and the world as its proper concern.

In appraising its own performance, it will accord itself first-class citizenship in the community of universities and compare itself only with the best that exists anywhere.

In governing itself, its mood will be one of continuous self-assessment, of alertness to innovation in far places, of receptivity to needed change, of long-range vision, of pioneering without fear, of dedication to the goal of superiority in all that it does, of always showing the worst that is in us to ourselves and the best that is in us to others.

And so our years together begin. I have waited to the end to tell you that I, too, know that nothing is possible without the freedom we call academic. I join you and your trustees in protecting it for you, which is protecting it for all who love and have a stake in this university, for without this freedom there is no university.

Leadership in a university is a many-splendored thing. You and I share it together. I will do my part and you will do yours and this noble institution will prosper.

❧

Two days after addressing the faculty, I spoke to a student convocation. I had come to the campus wanting to do what would be sensible to establish an early rapport with the student body. As a student at Chapel Hill, nearly three decades earlier, I had deeply appreciated the friendship of the president of the University and his wife. And I had been constructively stimulated by extensive participation in student extracurricular activities. Such, I knew, was not for every student, but I also knew that for some it opened doors to learning and opportunity. At Vanderbilt I wanted to encourage as vigorous and diversified an extracurricular life as possible. I also wanted to do what I could to encourage rapport between students and the new chancellor whom fate had bestowed on them.

As a symbolic act, I invited a group of student leaders to have coffee at nine in the morning on February 1—my first formal appointment—in what was then a place of student gathering, the Gold Room on the first floor of Alumni Hall. Tom Abernathy, president of the Student Association, Linda Armstrong, president of the Women's Student Government Association, and Patty Lewis, president of the Women's Residence Halls Council, were among the students present.

That first spring, Jean and I held a picnic for student leaders

at the University house where we were then living—105 Lyn-
wood Boulevard—and in subsequent years invited students to
at least one picnic each year at the University residence. For
a while we had a large picnic for sophomores in the fall, and
eventually settled on a picnic at the beginning of the academic
year for entering first-year students. Similarly, that first spring
we held four faculty receptions in the University house. All
faculty members, and their spouses, including the clinical faculty of the Medical School, were invited to one or another of
them.

My first formal remarks to assembled students, on February
7 in Neely Auditorium, emphasized my knowledge that they
were the first and principal reason we had a university, that they
had voluntarily become an essential component of the Vanderbilt University community, and that most of them—ideally all
of them—would remain part of that community the rest of
their lives.

Vanderbilt University is a community ... and in a way it is a
more meaningful community than a home town, for all of us chose
to come to it voluntarily. The Vanderbilt community is made up
not only of students and faculty and staffs of many kinds. It embraces also parents, alumni, trustees, supporters, benefactors and
beneficiaries of many types—in fact all on whom the institution
depends, all who feel bound to it or who benefit directly from it.

What this campus gives to you and what you give to it during
your years as a student remain ever afterward. . . . Your lasting citizenship in the Vanderbilt community makes you a ... partner ... in
sustaining and advancing a significant American university, . . . the
most important secular task of the twentieth century.

I emphasized that in addition to its first mandate, undergraduate instruction, their university was an institution of
many missions, obligations, and opportunities:

Speaking of the University

This university, like all true universities, is also obligated to explore the outer rims of knowledge toward the eternal objective that man may better understand himself and his environment. It is also obligated to indicate the relevance of new knowledge to the problems that plague men in our times. It is obligated to provide forms of professional training when it is qualified to do so and the needs are great. Taken altogether, a university is a central thinking organ for our whole society. . . .

A university education should stimulate and equip men and women to seize the personal and public problems about them and to work toward their constructive solution. Whether or not we shall be able to master our environment, including our man-made environment, will be the ultimate test of the success or failure of the American university system of which Vanderbilt is a part. This environment is defined in important part by all the problems foreign and domestic that scream at us daily through the news. I ask myself whether we are doing all we can to equip ourselves to handle these problems, whether you individually are doing all you can to equip yourself for the serious business of living, of living in a perplexing world in which the desire for peace so often brings war, in which the desire for freedom so often brings enslavement, in which the values men cherish on some parts of our globe clash with the values men cherish on other parts of the globe, in which material welfare and cultural opportunity are so unevenly distributed that men are willing to sacrifice the interests of the whole of their group or country or society if they cannot have what they consider their proper share in it.

I also stressed in this first meeting with those who were the University's first reason for being that education is not a passive process, that success or failure rests with students themselves. It was they who must take the offensive with enthusiasm, vigor, toughness, and persistence. There were abundant tragedies in the human record, from ancient times to our own century, but sources of hope and of obligation also abounded in the world of 1963, which included the goal that educated persons like Vanderbilt graduates would also be socially constructive, effective citizens.

❦

Before I took office on February 1, random reports of campus matters inevitably seeped through. I had heard, for example, that Professor John Wahlke, whom I knew as a fellow political scientist, was being tempted by an offer from another university. I had also been told that David Howell Jones, director of the Vanderbilt University Press, had been invited to accept another position. I had consulted enough locally to want to keep them both. I asked each to come by, separately, on February 1 for a talk. Eventually we lost Professor Wahlke and kept Mr. Jones.

In the early weeks after arriving on campus, I asked to visit all the rooms, attics, basements, playing fields, tunnels and other areas on the campus, and the astronomical observatory six miles to the south. It was too much to invade every fraternity, dormitory, and hospital room, and every surgery, but colleagues cooperated, sometimes a bit bemused, and I met many people I would otherwise not have met so soon, or perhaps at all, and I learned and saw much that later became useful, including, but not only, when reviewing proposals for building modifications and additions.

As part of a larger community orientation, I visited the president of each of the other twelve colleges and universities in Nashville. I wanted to get a feel for their institutions and to assess what our enterprises had in common and whether there were modes of cooperation that should be instituted or could be improved. A spirit of cooperation was in fact fostered. A council of presidents was formed and met periodically for several years. A later extension of this effort took the form of the Nashville University Center. Vanderbilt led in organizing the center in cooperation with Fisk University and Meharry Medical College, both historically black institutions, and George Peabody College for Teachers and Scarritt College for Christian Workers, Peabody being immediately across Twenty-first Avenue and Scarritt a block farther away, and both sharing the Joint University Libraries with Vanderbilt.

As Vanderbilt was the most conspicuous university in the city, there was inevitable curiosity about the new chancellor. I was alerted, even before arriving in town, of the need very soon after arrival to address the Rotary Club of Nashville, which was declared by its members to be the most prestigious civic club in the city and whose president, Dan May, was a Vanderbilt trustee. This I did on February 25 in the Hermitage Hotel. I spoke under the title "A University and Its Community." With the thick typed manuscript before me, visible to all, I set out to address a number of the relationships between the two.

One of the prices of public speaking, even on serious subjects, is the audience's constitutional expectation that it should be entertained or, at a minimum, humored. I explained that I had the stack of manuscript that all could see to keep me within the allotted time, but its presence reminded me of verses called "Lines Composed in Fifth Row Center," which I then recited:

> Of all the kinds of lecturer
> The lecturer I most detest
> Is he who finishes a page

And places it behind the rest.
I much prefer the lecturer
Who takes the pages as he finishes
And puts them on a mounting pile
As the original pile diminishes.
But best of all the lecturer
Who gets his papers in confusion
And prematurely lets escape
The triumphant phrase, "And, in conclusion. . . ."

There are connections of many kinds and intensity between universities and the rest of society, and I dwelt on several of importance between Vanderbilt and the metropolitan area of Nashville and Davidson County: Vanderbilt was the largest private employer in the area, annual expenditures through University channels exceeded twenty million dollars a year, often one-third of the construction under way at a given time in the area was at Vanderbilt, tens of thousands of patients were treated annually at Vanderbilt Hospital, artistic and intellectual activities at the University enriched community life, and more. I emphasized the relationship between an area's level of living and the industrial development it could attract and hold, the importance of advanced research activities to industrial location, the bearing of vigorous research-oriented university faculties on those research activities, and the conditions necessary for such advanced universities to exist.

In those years the significance of Harvard and M.I.T. to the development along Route 128 near Boston, of Stanford to much-noted developments in the so-called Silicon Valley and Palo Alto, and of the evolving achievements of the Research Triangle area in North Carolina could be cited to illustrate the synergistic relationship among advanced university capabilities, sophisticated research, and economic development. The point was not necessarily that Nashville could or should match these other areas in achievement, but that for it to advance at its optimum rate it needed a first-rate university. And I had seen and heard enough among important people of Vanderbilt and Nashville to make me expand on the concept that a first-rate university could only exist and prosper in a climate of intellectual and political freedom. So I said to the Rotarians:

Unless faculty and students have a confident freedom in which to investigate the unfamiliar, to speculate on the uncertain, to assert the novel, to practice innovation—unless they are secure in doing these things to the best of their ability—they cannot perform well the magnificent university missions of discovering, transmitting, and applying knowledge, of stimulating originality and loyalty to high purposes. Without this confident freedom that they are in fact a part of a true university—for only an institution enjoying this freedom can be a true university—the best of faculty and students will not come, and those who do come cannot, after they get here, do well what they came for.

The presence of this working condition is fundamental and essential in fulfilling the opportunities and obligations of university research, itself fundamental and essential to the optimum economic and social development of our part of the nation. And of course beneath all this runs the deep fact that the preservation of educational freedom is necessary for the preservation of political freedom.

I remind you today of the importance of these conditions of educational freedom to our common destiny only because all of us, inside universities and out, need constantly to be aware of it. A consequence of this freedom, if it is exercised—and if it is present in a true university, it will be exercised—is that a university campus is a lively place hospitable to debate and controversy. It will hear many points of view (some of them strange), from many sources (some of them odd), on many topics (some of them major, many of them minor). Most of these points of view never reach your ears or mine. Occasionally some do. The peculiar ones that we agree with we usually let go without notice. Occasionally some of the other peculiar ones startle us. When they do, we need to remember that differing points of view are inevitable and desirable in a university at work.

. . . [It] is our nation's democratic doctrine that if an idea is false it should be exposed, and if an idea is dangerous it should be understood. Weak ideas that you or I may not agree with will not prosper in the open air nor in free debate. And certainly if we know anything from the history of this century it is that strong ideas cannot be beaten by attempting to deny them circulation. You as men of practical affairs know that the only defense against a strong idea that one does not like is to have a better, stronger idea that one does like and to be able to interpret and advocate it effectively. Because it is a major function of a university to foster the development and circulation of ideas, we can be sure that over the years on its campus will be heard both weak and strong ones, both familiar and unfamiliar ones, both popular and unpopular ones.

But ideas there will be, and the more creative they are the truer the greatness of the institution and the more productive and economically valuable will be the investigations and intellectual innovations—that is, the research—that it produces. And the more significant this research, the greater the university's gift to the common welfare of this community with which it shares so much of its heritage and so many of its hopes.

❧

During the spring of 1963 I spoke on a number of other occasions in Nashville. Colleagues and alumni were patient with my view that I should learn something of the home scene before venturing to speak across the land, especially when alumni clubs would be the audience. During April and May, I spoke to a dinner of Vanderbilt's Alpha Omega Alpha Honor Medical Society, to a senior convocation as graduation approached, at the commencement exercises of Peabody College, and to the men of St. George's Episcopal Church (where our family were communicants). Sundry other occasions called for remarks, including the visit of President Kennedy to Nashville when he spoke as the University's guest, celebrating the ninetieth anniversary of its founding, in Vanderbilt Stadium on May 18.

Throughout, the welcome to the Heards by the University and the larger community was extraordinarily generous. In June, Jean and I calculated that since our arrival in February we had met for the first time over two thousand persons.

My first speech to the Annual Alumni Assembly, a large luncheon meeting on June 1 in Rand Hall on the campus during reunion, provided the first exposure to most of the gathered faithful. I had learned very early that a good fellow to listen to, to have on one's side, was Madison Sarratt, retired vice-chancellor, who had been at Vanderbilt since 1916 and liked the title Dean of Alumni, so I said:

I have told some of you of Mr. Sarratt's compliment to me after I had been around a couple of weeks. He had been watching the new lad with some interest, and then one day in introducing me to someone he said, "I've concluded this young fellow is going to be a great help to me in running the University." I repeated the story a few weeks later in Mr. Sarratt's presence, I suppose in a spirit that suggested I considered it a great joke, and he observed, I thought rather piously, "Well, I was right. You have been."

I later closed the speech with a word of comfort: "Madison Sarratt gets to his office early and he stays late, and if he didn't this young fellow would find he couldn't run the University without him."

In the course of the luncheon remarks, I reported on the President's recent visit, spoke of the long-range Vanderbilt Planning Study just getting under way, invited contributions of memorabilia to the Vanderbilt University Archives we were in the process of establishing, acknowledged members of the class of 1913 who were back for their fiftieth reunion, and pointed to the need for the University to plan ahead. I also emphasized two matters of major substance.

The first of which, however it might be phrased, was simple. Vanderbilt would find it increasingly difficult to accept as students all qualified applicants among alumni children. I cited increases in the size of the college-age population (estimated to increase 40 percent in the next seven years) and in the proportion of them wanting to go to college.

In these circumstances, universities necessarily apply standards of admission that differ from those they employed in earlier times. Vanderbilt, along with most of our best public universities and all of our best private universities, has found that entering students possess increasingly high academic qualifications.... We cannot be certain what the future will hold, but I suspect that three factors will be influential.

First, I doubt that Vanderbilt will expand in size sufficiently ... to eliminate the need to be selective in admissions.

Second ... we will continue to try to find improved criteria for admission that will recognize the importance of many different characteristics of mind and personality in determining potentials for intellectual development and for leadership in our society.

Third, it is inevitable that Vanderbilt will continue to receive applications from many students whose interests would be better served elsewhere. Fathers and mothers with more than one child know how much children differ from each other. I have four and I can testify. There are great differences among educational institutions just as there are great differences among children. Just as children are neither better nor worse simply because they are different from one another, colleges and universities are neither better nor worse just because they differ. The mounting specialization of higher education in our country increases the importance, and the ease, of putting a given student in precisely the best location to fill his unique combination of requirements.

Not all alumni with children whom they wanted admitted to Vanderbilt would be comforted by these remarks from a newcomer.

The other subject that I addressed at some length was the increased role in university education of the Federal government:

Universities have become the principal institutions in our society—short of government itself—through which we seek common national purposes. Our nation cannot arm for war, plan for peace, seek prosperity, or get to the moon, without the sustained and integrated aid of the university system of this land.

Inevitably, industry and government have turned to the classrooms and laboratories of the universities for help in doing the things that must be done. Wise universities render these services when doing so will help them better achieve their own basic educational missions. The better the university, the more it attracts outside funds, through grants and contracts for teaching and research purposes, and the better use it makes of such money.

Money from our national government, going into universities, has been of great and will be of increasing importance. During the fiscal year now ending, Vanderbilt University has received over $5 million from this source. This is small compared with many universities, but it constitutes something like one-fourth of our annual budget.

Having said that I believed such public funding would increase, I hastened to explain that this development in no way diminished the need for generous private financial support from traditional sources, including the faithful now listening.

First, to qualify for a grant or contract that will bring money to a university for an educationally useful purpose, the university often must bear a part of the cost of the new activity. Sometimes it must undertake to carry the full costs after an initial period.

Second, grants and contracts almost invariably provide money for specific purposes, not for the general support of an institution. Moreover, these outside funds help to finance graduate teaching and research much more than they help to support undergraduate education. The need for the general financing of the institution remains.

❧

In preparing for my first commencement on June 2, 1963, I learned that Vanderbilt took pride in awarding every diploma, for both undergraduate and advanced work, individually, and that it was difficult for undergraduates to get permission to be absent from the exercises. Vanderbilt formerly had a conventional commencement address, but after one especially famous visitor had spoken at inordinate length, my predecessor, Chancellor Branscomb, decided that no more visitors would be invited. He, as chancellor, would say words of hail and farewell to the departing graduates, but lasting no more than about ten minutes. We continued the practice during my twenty commencements.

For my first commencement, on the Library Lawn, I asked

Chancellor Branscomb to march at my side in the long procession and to sit on the stage, and at the end of the ceremony I spoke as follows:

I have felt presumptuous making the award of this year's degrees. If a chancellor is an academic parent of the sons and daughters of alma mater . . . my tenure of one semester at Vanderbilt, during the eight semesters most of these ladies and gentlemen have spent earning their degrees, makes me at best a one-eighth parent. I would proudly claim the whole host entirely as my own, but the other seven-eighths of a parent sits watching, and I think if it were not for his generous spirit I could detect an affectionately possessive gleam in his eye. I am glad, however, that . . . he is very much with us tonight.

This is my first senior class, and it will always remain so to me, but Chancellor Emeritus Branscomb has a greater claim to this class, and also to those senior seniors who have received graduate degrees this lovely evening of a rare day in June. Those of you who have strolled about the campus these last few days, and also those of you who have done so these last few years, have seen in the walks and buildings and trees, and in the faces of young and old, the harvest of many academic generations. But most of what you have seen has been the work of Mr. Branscomb.

Nearly three-fourths of Vanderbilt's living alumni were graduated during his sixteen years in office. And during these years he brought to this campus as we now find it an ever-restless momentum, a giant's vision, and two-thirds of the buildings, nine-tenths of the faculty, and all of the students. So, this night, like all the nights ahead, is Mr. Branscomb's night, too.

You who have been graduated tonight have really only one obligation to this institution. This is to behave in the years ahead as educated men and women. You remain part of Vanderbilt as a member of our university family. This membership continues to carry other responsibilities and other opportunities. But none of these exceeds in its grandeur or in its rewards the behavior of an educated person. An educated person follows high and serious social purposes, effectively and honestly. You and I and all of us live in a world of revolt—not just in a world of change, but in a world of revolt—a world in which the question is not whether there are to be revolutions, but, rather, what kinds of revolution there are to be. The question is not whether we can preserve the past, but how we can shape the future. The sagest philosopher and the sharpest operator will both know that the future of mankind is indivisible, and they will both know that there is no lasting glory and no lasting gain for the few that does not include the many.

Our friend Chancellor Branscomb is ... an ... example of an educated person. He has followed a sense of mission with singleness of goal and with many well-cultivated resources. Through these many years his mission has been a public one, higher education. And his goal has been a greater Vanderbilt University. His resources have embraced imagination and skill, dignity and humor, courage and integrity, energy, and, more noteworthy than any of these, a marvelous wife.

It is your obligation to possess for yourself such resources as these. Mr. Branscomb is an educated man in action. I can wish no better for you than that you shall do as well as he does by your fellow men and by the causes you hold dear.

Our devotion and deep concern follow you wherever you go.

☙

I knew that followers of Vanderbilt's intercollegiate football and basketball fortunes constituted a major University constituency in Nashville. Many of the fans were Vanderbilt alumni, but to significant numbers of others Vanderbilt's was the city's team. The constituency was vocal, had two newspapers to keep it stimulated, revered a long tradition (that was also long past) of winning football teams, and included a large portion of the active and financially supportive local alumni. It was clear that much curiosity, and no little anxiety, about the new chancellor's understanding of intercollegiate athletics accompanied his arrival. "What does he *really* think?"

Jack Green had been engaged as the new football coach. His first season would be the fall of 1963. Basketball performance had been encouraging. I delayed speaking publicly about athletics until a meeting of the Vanderbilt Quarterback Club at the Noel Hotel on September 23, 1963. I had, however, shown the colors with enthusiasm before that. All six Heards had attended a basketball game in Memorial Gymnasium shortly after our arrival in February, the event celebrated by bright lights and motion picture cameras. (I was disappointed to learn that the cameras came from the Vanderbilt Office of Alumni and Development, not from a news-sensitive commercial television station.) In my first fifteen years in office, I routinely attended home basketball games whenever I was in town, and Jean also attended many of them. Later, especially after Emmett Fields came to Vanderbilt in 1977 as president of the University and himself attended as many games as possible, I missed more of them, often while touring the country for the $150 million fund-raising campaign.

Jean and I also regularly attended all home football games. One of the rare exceptions was the Alabama game in 1969 when I was away attending parents' weekend at Woodbury Forest School in Virginia, where one of our sons was a student. It was an extraordinary night. We beat Alabama. Gerald Ford, less than five years before becoming president of the United States, had sat with Jean in what we were pleased to call the chancellor's box (ten chained off seats in the open air). My absence led not a few experts to suggest that it would be good for the Chancellor to miss some future games, too. Jean's and my plan was to go to at least one out-of-town game each year. We went to Knoxville several times, to Memphis, to Atlanta, to Lexington, Kentucky, and elsewhere, but somehow, every other year, the Tulane game tended to be chosen.

In my first talk to the Quarterback Club I spoke on "Athletics at Vanderbilt," emphasizing that:

Athletics at Vanderbilt are a part of our educational program. Our athletic programs are means to educational objectives just as are our other curricular and extracurricular activities. Everyone knows that what is done in the classroom is done to achieve educational purposes. Likewise, extracurricular student enterprises that are sponsored or encouraged by the University are sponsored or encouraged to serve educational objectives. Student self-government, student publications, student religious associations, and student participation in debating, in drama, in organized discussion groups, and in many other undertakings outside the classroom, are part of our total educational effort. So it is with our athletic activities, both those that form part of a student's required curriculum and those that a student undertakes voluntarily.

Viewing student athletic activities broadly—both required and voluntary athletic activities—we seek at least four educational objectives through them. These four goals make up part of Vanderbilt's unending effort to bring forth individuals who are significantly more mature and better equipped for their lives ahead than when they came to us.

These objectives are:

First, healthy bodies. A Greek philosopher once said, "He who has health has hope, and he who has hope has everything."

Second, the capacity for constructive recreation. The faster the world spins, the more important wholesome diversion becomes. I'd rather have the boys (and the men) on the links than in the taverns.

Third, the capacity for synchronized, cooperative action with others—team play, or teamwork, we sometimes call it. And,

Fourth, the capacity for competition under pressure. The strains and psychology of rivalry and achievement are significantly alike wherever they are found—on the tennis courts or in the law courts, in writing a track record or writing a book.

The primary goals of a college or university are intellectual goals. The general development of the individual, however, is also an aim of colleges and universities like ours. Attainment of the four objectives I have just cited . . . contributes . . . to the development of the intellect, to the development of the personality, and to the development of the total personal effectiveness of our students.

I have myself, in much younger years, taken part in four different competitive sports, and I know personally something of their value.

I then addressed the state of the physical education curriculum, intramural sports, recreational sports, the five less-publicized intercollegiate sports, and the two much-publicized intercollegiate sports. It was the last of these, of course, that the Quarterback Club most wanted to hear about.

Remembering that football is the only sport with a quarterback, there was little I could tell the Quarterback Club about the state of our spectator sports, football and basketball. I acknowledged the imperative to win more, thanked the club and its president, Willie Geny—he himself having been a famous Vanderbilt football and basketball star—for the club's significant financial support, and pointed out that while the two squads engaged 125 students the previous year, and 119 appeared on other Vanderbilt intercollegiate teams, some 1,750 students took part in Vanderbilt's intramural competitive sports.

Arriving, 1963

Then I asked, what of the future? That, of course, was what everybody had been asking, for months. I reiterated the four educational objectives that should be served by a university's athletic programs—healthy bodies, capacity for constructive recreation, capacity for teamwork, and capacity for competition under pressure—and said,

> I do not believe that any part of our athletic program at Vanderbilt, including our participation in intercollegiate athletics, is justified unless it serves those goals for our students. I know full well that much of the enthusiastic interest in Vanderbilt basketball and football stems from the immediate excitement of seeing, or wanting to see, a winning team. And I know full well that the interest of many people in the University's general welfare is made more robust by their particular interest in basketball and football. But as your chancellor it is my responsibility to you to keep educational objectives in the forefront of all that the University does.

> This means to me at least three things.

> Academic standards must be kept high for all Vanderbilt students. Vanderbilt athletes have been and will be required to meet our regular standards of academic performance.

> Intercollegiate athletics must not receive so much emphasis in the University's affairs as to divert the University from its primary educational mission of instruction. As basketball and football have evolved in the United States over the past half century, they have become primarily spectator sports for nonstudents, as opposed to participant sports for students. On some campuses, preoccupation with intercollegiate athletics has at times become so pervasive that it has deflected the attention of students, faculty, trustees, and friends from the principal purposes for which the institution was created in the first place. This will not happen at Vanderbilt.

> It seems to me manifest, moreover, that an institution like ours—with severely limited financial means compared with other

universities of comparable academic standing in the United States—should not divert its resources from primary educational purposes to support spectator sports merely to entertain itself or its friends. Vanderbilt has not done this in the past and we shall not do so in the future....

Insofar as athletics are concerned, I have been listening rather than talking since coming to Nashville—and I assure you that in eight months one can do a lot of listening about this subject. I have concluded that my views about a university intercollegiate athletic program, and about what Vanderbilt's own posture should be, are in accord with the considered, sober views of most of those whom I have heard, on the campus and off, who address themselves seriously to these matters.

In later years I sometimes spoke among administrative colleagues, trustees, and other friends of a fourth function of a university that goes along with the traditional three, teaching, research, and public service. Public entertainment was the fourth function I mentioned. That is demanded of all publicly supported institutions and most independent ones. Why not, I asked, acknowledge that reality at Vanderbilt and take one of two approaches? We could create an explicit curriculum in intercollegiate athletics, with a Bachelor of Athletics degree to be awarded, when earned. Some precedent for that existed in physical education programs around the country. Alternately, we could join others in sponsoring acknowledgedly professional teams, like the commercial teams in many sports in cities across the nation and around the world. Players could be, but need not be, students. The first approach was routinely deemed outside Vanderbilt's tradition. The charitable among those who heard the second thought the Chancellor surely had a peculiar sense of humor.

Arriving, 1963

✣

The University held a formal ceremony on October 1, 1963, on the Library Lawn, to install the new chancellor in office. Some asked why "installed" instead of "inaugurated." I have always thought that inaugurations should be confined to policies, programs, and presidents of the United States.

The visiting speaker was Nathan Pusey. He was the president of Harvard, which I described in my remarks as America's oldest and the world's greatest university. He had come out of gratitude to Harold Vanderbilt, president of the Vanderbilt Board of Trust, a Harvard alumnus whose unanticipated generosity, at the very last minute, of approximately $2.5 million to his alma mater a few years before had put "A Program for Harvard College," a drive for $82.5 million, over the top, to the great relief of President Pusey.

In my own remarks, I emphasized the centrality of undergraduate education among Vanderbilt's missions, but then spoke, as I had before and would again, of a *university's* obligation to inquire and explore:

As I read the history of universities, now stretching across eight centuries in the Western world, the thread that runs through the university as a distinctive social institution, in all its forms in all the centuries, is the thread of inquiry.

Colleges and other educational institutions may bring the student to beauty or thought or skill or maturity. They teach and they train. Sometimes their object is the whole man, sometimes just his hands or a sector of his brain. Universities do these things too, but it is the addition of exploration to exposition that underlies the unique opportunities of a university. And if an institution is to be a university, it must provide the conditions under which this exploration can take place. The thread of inquiry has no meaning without freedom to inquire, and freedom to state the conclusions of inquiry. There is no inquiry without freedom, and no university without both. . . .

The most driving force of our time is scientific inquiry and the technological development it spawns. The most compelling need of our time is cultural and political accommodation to the consequences of scientific change. The most pervasive aspiration of our time is for greater human freedom in many forms. The university, as an institution, is more an ultimate source of scientific change, more an ultimate hope for coping with its consequences, and more itself dependent on a climate of freedom for all, than any other secular institution in our society. More than any other, the university is now the central thinking institution of our society—more an explorer, more an inventor, more an interpreter, and more concerned with the outcome and meaning of it all.

Beyond these things, the university is also the ultimate wellspring of educational advance, of educational advance at many levels, for many purposes, all around the globe. The watchword of the future everywhere is education—education in how to read and write, education in technical skills, education in professional proficiencies, education in the arts and science of government, education for a richer inner life, education of every kind. And always men look eventually to the university as the chief source of educational goals and of the means to them. Wherever peoples aspire to prosperity or to power or to independence or to more effective self-government or sometimes just to happiness, they search through education. Everywhere on our planet education is marching. At the head of the procession is the inquiring university.

Then I emphasized the contemporary reach of university influences, including those of Vanderbilt, on all contemporary life:

Arriving, 1963

The United States cannot arm for war, plan for peace, seek prosperity, maintain domestic tranquillity, or go to the moon, without the freely inquiring universities of this land. It makes a difference what kind of university Vanderbilt chooses to be. . . .

For me, Vanderbilt's spirit of mission holds more than one can really ever say, but it also holds much that one must never fail to say. A sense of relevance to our times infuses it. A comprehensive vision enlightens it. The will and adventure of leadership inspire it. The style and joys and emotions of life concern it. And the spirit of mission belongs in all of us, to be of fullest meaning to any of us. . . .

For our country, the most tenacious and important issue of our time is the struggle of American Negroes for a fuller freedom. I am proud to follow the leadership of the Vanderbilt Board of Trust in its voluntary decisions, taken before my time, that qualified students shall be admissible to all of Vanderbilt's schools without regard to race or creed. . . .

There is necessarily more, however, to a true university's role in this compelling matter of our time. By definition, a university must be a place where anybody's plea for a fuller freedom can be calmly heard, fairly debated, and conclusions about it stated freely. The more perplexing a public issue is, the more significant to society is this inherent responsibility of a university.

University faculties . . . have an essential dependence upon a climate of freedom for themselves, if they are to achieve personal and professional fulfillment. I find it appropriate when, in consequence, university faculty members have a special understanding of the drive by other persons for the fuller freedom they need to achieve their personal and professional fulfillment.

Many aspirations for fuller freedom hinge in the end on opportunities for a fuller education—more education and especially better education. With their special resources, universities have obligations to aid however they can in creating wider educational opportunities for all citizens. . . .

Speaking of the University

In the complex combination of universities that constitute the American university system, each university, on the Charles or on the Cumberland, has its unique bundle of qualities—its heritage, its resources, its special opportunities and obligations, its hopes— a unique bundle of qualities that defines its own role. . . .

Vanderbilt has enjoyed the unbroken interest and the important support of the citizens of Nashville since its founding. We cherish our union with its inhabitants, and it will bind us closer in the years ahead. We are grateful, too, that Vanderbilt's sons and daughters, and those who support her in a myriad of essential ways, are strewn across the land and in many lands around the globe. Our interests wherever they may be are indivisible: to be a university.

Toward the end I expressed admiration for Vanderbilt's trustees, in whose councils I had found that "our hopes are hung to the stars." Especially important was the wisdom and generosity of Mr. Vanderbilt, of whom it could be truly said, "More than one Vanderbilt has founded this university." I declared that our university knows

that life is a many-splendored thing. Our first concern is the human intellect but our main concern is the human being. We seek to fathom not truth alone, but goodness and beauty, too. In its view of man's needs and hopes, a university must be universal.

TWO

🌱

A Placid Time
1964–1965

T HE SEVEN SELECTIONS IN CHAPTER I
were chosen from forty public speeches made in 1963
of which I have record. There were forty-four such in
1964 and forty-five in 1965, from which the eight in chapter 2
are drawn. In these first three years, full texts exist for slightly
less than half the total—the others having been delivered from
outlines or notes. This is true also for the whole period, 1963–
1982.

The selections in this chapter illustrate local audiences: the
Junior League of Nashville, the Commencement Exercises of
Scarritt College, the Nashville Area Junior Chamber of Commerce, and, on the Vanderbilt campus, a joint dinner meeting
of the Women's Panhellenic Council and the Interfraternity
Council, three student convocations, and the exercises unveil-
ing a statue to Harold Vanderbilt.

The Junior League of Nashville has long been associated
with the Vanderbilt Medical Center. In 1964 it operated an independent Junior League home for children with clinical problems. It had close and important Vanderbilt relations, especially with Vanderbilt's Departments of Orthopedic Surgery
and Pediatrics. It was one force that led later to creation of the

enormously important Children's Hospital of the Vanderbilt Medical Center.

I was asked to speak to the members of the Junior League at their headquarters on Abbott Martin Road on February 14, 1964, and spoke about education, saying, "Whether we have children or not . . . we all have more at stake in education than in any other common endeavor. In dealing with such a subject, I hold that we should show the best that is in us to others and the worst that is in us to ourselves. . . ."

In the many remarks about the importance of formal education that I made over the years, and about the crucial role of education in personal and societal development, I worked from an underlying assumption that people are not made happy or virtuous or wise by intellect alone. But enhancing human capacities and realizing human aspirations depend in our time on personal qualities that we seek to improve through education. I usually spoke from that viewpoint, as I did this day to the Junior League, making three initial points:

First, the role of formal education in contemporary society is of stunning new importance. You have, I hope, heard that fact stated before, but the point needs to be understood widely. The prosperity of Tennessee and the welfare of its citizens . . . demand it.

Second, despite the vast strides that have been taken and the progress made, gigantic tasks lie ahead.

Third, the tasks are common tasks, falling upon all of us—those of us directly involved in education and those who are not.

I then went on with a message that was not always welcome but was in my view always important.

A century ago, the United States could fight a war, settle a continent, build a railroad from ocean to ocean, and run its burgeoning economic system with relatively little dependence upon the institutions of education. Immense national objectives were sought, and achieved, by a population that was more than 20 percent illiterate, contained only a handful of college graduates, and, in 1864, seven Ph.D.'s.

Since the end of this last century, public demand for education has reflected a revolutionary change in the function of education in our society. The proportion of the nation's population enrolled in secondary schools was seven times as great in 1960 as in 1900. The proportion enrolled in institutions of higher education was fourteen times as great. The proportion of the adult population going to graduate schools was twenty times as great in 1960 as in 1900. . . .

Whether a student goes to college or to graduate school is no longer a decision affecting his welfare alone. The nation now depends for almost everything it does on a formally educated citizenry. We are increasingly dependent on educational institutions to produce technical skills, professional abilities, the potential for highly specialized on-the-job training, and the capacity to cope with the public and political problems that beset modern nations.

The nation's dependence on highly educated citizens is shown in the requirements of public and private employment. In simplest terms, lack of education and lack of employment go together. The unemployment rate is five times higher among persons whose education stopped after high school than it is among college graduates. It is ten times higher among persons with less than five years of grade school than it is among college graduates.

And do not think the revolution in education is confined to America. Since World War II an immense expansion in education has occurred in other nations, too. . . .

National military strength, local economic prosperity, personal equipment for living . . . are hinged, in our times, to education.

I reported how we in Tennessee and the South were faring. Despite marked effort, that was not well. Despite recent improvements, Tennessee's expenditures per pupil in average daily attendance ranked forty-seventh among all the states, and Tennessee's average teachers salaries ranked forty-third. In higher education the situation was similar.

Tennessee has within its borders one of every fifty-one persons who reside in the United States.

Tennessee has within its borders, however, only one of every fifty-seven college students in the United States.

There were granted within Tennessee's borders only one of every eighty-seven doctoral degrees awarded by the graduate schools of the United States in 1960 and 1961.

And during this same period, Tennessee institutions granted only one of every one hundred and thirty doctoral degrees in the natural sciences, those vital academic disciplines that affect directly industrial growth and economic prosperity.

For the optimum well-being of a state, the number of students in its colleges, and the number of graduate degrees conferred within its borders, need not, necessarily, constitute precisely the same proportion of national totals as does its population. Nevertheless, knowing what we do, I can assure you that the discrepancies in Tennessee are reasonable indicators of need.

Our needs are confirmed by national ratings of academic quality of many kinds, and the informed judgments of serious and friendly people. I do not hesitate to paint a realistic picture, for all of us, in education and out, must understand the immensity of the work to be done in Tennessee in higher education in the years ahead.

Let me give two examples that indicate the size of this task. When I made a check two years ago of five hundred and ninety-nine highly honored members of the National Academy of Science, I discovered that only twenty-one of them lived anywhere in the South, and only two in Tennessee. Of 481 members of the American Philosophical Society, perhaps America's most distinguished learned society, there were only seven Southerners and no Tennesseans. . . .

Despite the progress made . . . we can properly conclude . . . that the per capita educational income of Tennessee, at all educational levels, is too low. The per capita economic income is also too low, and the combination of the two plights poses a heroic challenge for our state and our people.

Our problem is really the problem of our whole Southern region. We need to lift ourselves by our own economic and educational bootstraps, and this is painfully hard to do. . . .

I think it is clear that Tennessee education requires extraordinary help if it is to advance at the rate required by the interests of the state. I think it is also clear that the main burden of what must be done will always rest within the state. The best investment a community can make is in the education of its youth. Public and private investment in education will yield greater profits, and will yield them longer, than any other investment a state or its citizens can make.

🌢

During my first year at Vanderbilt, I encouraged student initiative in creating more intellectually vigorous extracurricular activities. On April 18, 1964, I spoke about this to a joint banquet of Vanderbilt's Women's Panhellenic Council and its Interfraternity Council in the Memorial Room of Alumni Hall.

University chief officers can learn two facts very early. One is that their administrative and faculty associates seldom receive the full credit they deserve for constructive contributions to the institution's life. The chief officer welcomes their successful achievements with gusto, and often may garner unearned credit from them. If equity is needed, however, it may be found in a companion second fact: when matters not of the leader's direct making go wrong, there ought be no shirking of responsibility for them. Both these conditions encourage university chancellors to hope for wise and skillful colleagues. In speaking on this occasion to the leaders of Vanderbilt's Greek chapters, I paid a deserved tribute, saying that aside from the students themselves, I had found that "the most important individuals to the processes of student self-government are the Dean of Men and Dean of Women and their associates," referring to Dean Sidney Boutwell and Dean Nora Chaffin. I tried always to remember their importance and that of their successors in later years.

My remarks on this occasion asserted the conviction that "the important rationale and the important opportunities and obligations of student government are educational. It is their educational functions that justify their existence on a university campus."

The chief function of a liberal education in the United States is to prepare persons for life in our self-governing society. Your training in self-government on this campus is an explicit educational objective of this university. With all the many reasons campus institutions of student government exist, this is the main educational function that justifies their existence. One learns by doing. This is not the only way one learns, but there is no substitute for the practice of self-government in learning the subtle and complex art of operating successfully a democratic society. Only by participation in practical affairs can one develop the human and intellectual capacities required. These required capacities are many—among them the faculty of creative thought, a receptivity to innovation, a respect for differences, a sense of humor, the ability to collaborate and cooperate, the ability to see ahead, to plan ahead, to accommodate to sudden catastrophes, the skill to express one's views effectively, the talent to discriminate between the false and the true in others, the development of enough confidence in oneself to permit one to have proper confidence in others, the wisdom to know when to follow and when to lead.

In pursuit of these objectives through the student government of our campus, I have obligations to you, and you have obligations to your fellow students. The campus is a great laboratory of self-government. It will not run itself. Student government will not automatically succeed by some mystical process—no more than will the government of the United States—unless many heads and hands work consciously at it. . . .

My obligations to you are at least three in number.

First, to guarantee to you freedom to operate within the agreed-upon rules that govern us. You can be sure that while I am your chancellor this campus will be a place of intellectual freedom. I will also protect and encourage your right to exercise fully the independence of all kinds that you enjoy under our student constitutions and codes and other regulations that all together make up what might be called the Campus Constitution.

My second obligation to you is to remain receptive to your initiatives for changing the rules and, in fact, to feel a responsibility myself to take the initiative when I see improvements that seem possible. I will seek to broaden the latitudes open to you and to respond sympathetically to your own ambitions for extending them.

My third obligation to you is to insist, in all that all of us do, on standards of quality and performance worthy of Vanderbilt University.

Your obligations to yourselves are, first, to use the freedoms that you have; second, to abide by the rules that are in effect, and if you think they should be changed to move for their amendment through the orderly processes provided for doing so; and, third, to insist, in all that all of us do, on standards of quality and performance worthy of Vanderbilt University. . . .

During the previous year, I noted, there had been many instances of student initiative in creating or enhancing activities of educational value to the University, among them Faculty Fireside visitations, Great Decisions discussions, the Freshman Orientation program, Parents Weekend, Impact, the efforts of Bill Featheringill, president of the Student Association, to form a new national organization of student governments, a Mock Republican Convention, and improved activities of Greek Week. I expressed the hope that student reports being made as part of the Vanderbilt Planning Study, launched some months before, would exhibit the same energy and inventiveness that had been increasingly displayed in extracurricular life. And then:

As I listen to discussions on the campus of student freedom, and of the presence or lack of independence in the various agencies of student government, I often feel there is a lack of basic comprehension of the nature of freedom. Let me speak of this a moment. There is no such thing for anybody, anywhere, as total freedom. I cannot have total freedom as a citizen or as a chancellor. You cannot have total freedom as a citizen or as a student. Such independence as I have, and such independence as you have, in our respective roles in this university, derive, to be quite technical and legal about it, from the Board of Trust of the institution, and beyond that from the charter under which we operate and the state of Tennessee that granted it. . . .

The performance expected of particular agencies of campus self-government, and the precise limitations imposed in various ways upon the conduct of all of us associated with Vanderbilt, are the products of many factors. . . . The rules we live by, the discretion that you enjoy and that I enjoy, are modified from time to time. We at Vanderbilt have the means to propose modifications in student government, to evaluate the proposals and to give them effect. But campus freedoms, like freedoms in any self-governing society, will always be limited in some ways. . . .

We are embarked on a joint undertaking together. . . . As we face the tasks along the way, all of us must take care as we form opinions and make decisions. We can really do these things only after seeking in all ways possible to learn the relevant facts and understand the relevant circumstances. In my time here, there has been and there will be no censorship of student opinion by faculty or administrative officers. In what you say and write as you practice self-government, and in what I say and write in discharging my responsibilities to the University, we share the obligation to avoid inaccuracies, incompleteness, misrepresentation, and bias. I hope that we can approach all our opportunities in the spirit of a man who once faced many of his own, the President of our nation who visited our campus last May, when he reminded us, "It is better to light a candle than to curse the darkness."

The Board of Trust took an important initiative at its 1964 spring meeting. For the first time it elected a woman as a trustee: Mary Jane Lowenheim Werthan, Lady of the Bracelet in the Vanderbilt Class of 1929. I had learned soon after arriving at Vanderbilt that Mrs. Werthan's long and conspicuous record of civic and university service, and the respect and affection in which she was held, made the choice for this pioneering role an obvious one. From the outset she served Vanderbilt as a trustee with notable effectiveness, not least in addressing sensitive social issues. Her election was followed in later years by the election of many more women trustees.

45

Speaking of the University

By the time of her election in 1964, the United States was launched on a social revolution of first magnitude: the latest phase of the long fight for racial equality. President Eisenhower called the civil rights issue "the nation's most critical domestic challenge." Families, organizations, and communities—including the Vanderbilt community—were often deeply divided by the controversies that emerged and the personal, organizational, and governmental issues and decisions that had to be addressed.

When the president of Scarritt College for Christian Workers, Vanderbilt's neighboring Methodist graduate training institution, invited me to speak at its commencement exercises in Wightman Chapel on May 28, 1964, I thought the occasion suitable for comment on what was clearly the most important and divisive domestic controversy of our time. Scarritt had been receiving students from and sending graduates to countries all around the world for nearly three-quarters of a century. It was a significant pioneer in religious education, and its long international and multiracial traditions gave it an educational experience of direct relevance to the times we were in. I spoke about "A Continuing Condition."

The demand for education around the world springs from deep torrents of human aspiration. Whatever the origins, a great awakening has occurred. Individual men seek freedom from disease and poverty and ignorance. Individual men seek personal fulfillment of many kinds. Groups of men, small and large, organize themselves as politically independent nations. Men want self-government for themselves within these nations. Individuals and nations alike seek status among their peers in this competitive world where we all now live within sight and sound of each other. These and their associated trends add up in scope and depth to the most fundamental societal readjustments in human history. And education is intertwined throughout, as cause and as consequence.

Something else is intertwined throughout, too. This is the striving of persons of many races to overcome handicaps and achieve greater fulfillment. Consciousness of racial identity permeates the world and often forms part of the motive forces that enliven the aspirations of individuals and groups and nations. And so a college that is both international and multiracial in its traditions is functioning in the mainstream of the contemporary world. . . .

In years like these, on a campus like this, on a day like this, I think we are obligated to deliberate among ourselves on the great human striving that stirs up so much that is noble and so much that is ugly in our society. . . .

I want to note . . . three important characteristics of the current situation in the United States.

First, I believe it a mistake to think that the incentives at work would be wholly gratified if all forms of separation based on race were eliminated. More is involved . . . than the ambition to overcome legal or de facto separation of races. . . .

There is a deeper aspect of this matter . . . that I do not see discussed. I believe that the aspirations of persons for *general* social advance are also involved. If all prejudicial practices of every kind disappeared immediately, both in form and in substance, there would yet remain other differences associated with color. Differences in education and economic standing and social status, and more, would remain.

. . . [T]hose who would look ahead must recognize that social and economic deprivation are associated with color in many places in the United States. It seems possible that general social remedies will increasingly be framed as demands for racial justice, or even as demands for racial reparations, because of past practices. No realist will assume that Negro aspirations for *general* advancement will easily be satisfied.

Speaking of the University

This leads me to what I think is a second fact of the situation. We . . . are faced by a continuing condition. We often tend to look upon demands and disturbances, problems and solutions that grow from social motivation, as transient. Sometimes some of us think of them, quite understandably I believe, as disruptions of normalcy. Indeed, they have been. But a hard-eyed appraisal of the recent past and of the probable future can lead only to the conclusion that the social, economic, and political demands that spring out of consciousness of color will be with us continuously for years to come. . . .

The ambitions of colored peoples have been ignited all around the world. These ambitions are part of immense social trends beyond the reach of individual persons. Students of ethics, of philosophy, of anthropology, of sociology, of education, of religion, of history, which Scarritt students are, know this. We are not dealing simply with the initiatives of energetic, or ambitious, or misguided, or dedicated persons who happen to have interested themselves in questions of racial equality. In the broad social trends that are at work—these trends whose origins extend far back in our history— if certain individuals were not active, then others would be. And so I think that, whatever a person's set of personal values and hopes, he can only realistically expect that a public concern with racial ambitions will be a continuing condition.

There is a third aspect of the situation that I think detached observers could agree upon, although perhaps not all who comment on current events do. . . . [T]he drive for general betterment and for equality is widely supported among American Negroes. *Newsweek* magazine, which would have no reason, I think, to distort the case, looked at this matter last summer, using a nationwide poll conducted at its behest. *Newsweek* published the following conclusion on July 29, 1963:

> The wave of protest . . . has won the allegiance of vast majorities of Negroes wherever they live and whatever their age

or economic lot. Its leaders are militant partly by choice—and partly because they have no choice.

... To say that vast majorities of Negroes, in the South and outside it, support the general wave of protest is not, however, to say that all Negroes agree unanimously on ends or means. Deep and conspicuous divisions have become evident within the last year among leaders and followers over objectives and tactics. But this should not, I believe, lead to the conclusion that any significant numbers of Negroes in the United States are content with their lot. The point here is not whether they should or should not be, but whether they are or are not. ...

In your years ahead, as in our nation's years ahead, we can all pray together for one personal quality of consuming importance to us all: patient tolerance of differences. Individuals, groups, nations require a patient tolerance of differences if we are to resolve the burdensome problems that beset all men everywhere. Indeed, it may be right to say that we require this patient tolerance if we are to survive at all. In the work that you yourselves go to, at home and abroad, you may have no greater chance for service as Christian Workers than to encourage this quality in all of God's children whom you touch.

❦

It was Vanderbilt's custom for the chancellor to speak to entering undergraduates and their parents each fall at the beginning of the orientation period for new students. I was always startled at the large number of parents on hand, almost as many, it would seem, as there were students. Three decades earlier my own parents had visited my undergraduate campus once, at commencement.

No prudent chancellor would exaggerate the impact of a

first-day speech on incoming students, students variously excited or confused by the new adventure. But while I had their captive attention, I would try on opening night to advance some thoughts that I hoped some would find stimulating and that some, perhaps, might remember.

In the early years, as I did on September 10, 1964, in Neely Auditorium, I would acknowledge that I was something of a new arrival myself and would reassure the more recent arrivals that the place was truly hospitable.

Take a look around and you will see that buildings, as well as students and faculty, are among the newcomers to Vanderbilt. Some of the classrooms you go to will be in use for the first time this year. They signify the steady intellectual growth and material change of the University, in step with growth and change in the nature of our world's knowledge and, in fact, in the nature of the world itself. You, yourselves, will contribute to Vanderbilt's growth and change by much that you bring to the campus—by the questions you ask, the goals you set for yourselves, the activities you undertake, the rewards you reap for yourselves and this institution, on the campus and later. Vanderbilt is most of all the people who inhabit it, and you are now a valued portion of these.

We hope you enjoy yourselves in many ways. Vanderbilt has its traditional campus frolics, and I have the impression that we do not lack opportunities for joy. Be it known that it is Vanderbilt's official policy that you shall have a good time—but remember that the roads to pleasure, excitement, and satisfaction peculiar to a university are chiefly intellectual. We are in a serious business, and the fact that we go about this serious business with good humor and good cheer ought not to mislead. . . .

We do many things of value at Vanderbilt, but the greatest of these are the opportunities we offer you for your personal development, especially for your intellectual development—the opportuni-

ties we offer you to educate yourselves. You will find three characteristics running through these opportunities, three objectives or
standards that we seek for the campus and that we seek for you. We
are deeply serious about them, and we believe that our nation and
our world must also be deeply serious about them.

First, there is such a thing as good sense, as dependence on reason, as using one's head—such a thing as applying the skills, values,
and perspectives of the intellect to the problems of life. We believe
in learning to use one's head. That, my friends, is a hard thing to
do. For it means knowing oneself well enough to curb emotion with
reason; it means applying oneself diligently enough to overcome ignorance with knowledge; it means having the vision to choose the
long run over the short haul. . . . We live in a world of danger and
crisis, and this will be the nature of our world as long as you and I
shall live. The most profound and important truths in life are sometimes the simplest, and here is one of them: minds educated in the
fullest sense are essential if our world is to endure. You and we together must do our part.

Now, secondly, a university is not a university unless it keeps itself relevant to the society it serves. Vanderbilt is a great regional
institution. It is also, however, national in the goals it sets and in the
standards it uses to judge itself. We consider the nation to be our
campus, and the world to be our proper concern. Our region, our
nation, our world are beset with massive difficulties and with massive opportunities for greatness. These difficulties and these opportunities you will find treated in the classroom and out—sometimes
in their immediacy, sometimes in the long perspective of the human
experience, sometimes indirectly or by implication—but always everything done in a university relates ultimately to the lives you lead,
and will lead, and to the welfare of the society of which we are all part.

I then spoke about the importance of the university as a
place of freedom and of the value to Vanderbilt and its stu-

dents of recent public discussion programs on the campus—
the previous spring on "The South in Transition" and the one
the year before on "The Democratic Responsibility"— which
had brought to student audiences a large number of diverse visitors: governors and senators, corporation presidents and
union leaders, integrationists and segregationists, Republicans
and Democrats, poets and novelists, Americans and foreigners,
and the President of the United States.

Then to the third of three opportunities Vanderbilt offers
its students to enhance their personal and intellectual development:

Essential to the educated mind and to enlightened citizenship is
the third matter of Vanderbilt's deep concern, integrity—integrity
in the sense of honesty, integrity in the sense of accuracy, integrity
as unfaltering respect for logic and the conclusions to which logic
leads. . . . [I]ntegrity in an individual, like freedom in a society, is
not acquired at one time and place, once and forever after. The
struggle for personal integrity, like the struggle for political freedom, is eternal, and they are both necessary for the happiness of the
human estate.

We at Vanderbilt believe in student self-government. You are
asked to accept the responsibilities of the honor system. You are
asked to discipline yourselves and your fellow students in maintaining honesty in examinations and in other assignments. You have
grave obligations under this system, for through it, and through
you, are developed the sinews of reliability and common trust that
bind a society together. If we cannot trust each other, and the institutions of self-government set up to help us trust each other, we are
lost. This is true on this campus and throughout this life.

This theme was expanded by emphasizing the obligations
of honorable and educated persons to be honest in the largest
sense of accuracy:

A Placid Time, 1964–1965

Inducements to carelessness and casualness abound when problems are complex and difficult to solve. Then comes the greatest temptation to intellectual laziness, to take the short cut, to ignore the demand for painstaking investigation and logical thought. Then comes the great temptation to draw unjustified inferences, to impute motives, to leap to conclusions—instead of sticking to the sober tasks of the educated mind and gathering facts, evaluating them carefully, and interpreting them with logic and responsibility.

I ended by reminding our new students that many of their predecessors, our former students, had become persons of fame and large achievement in almost all human undertakings, and all had started as they were starting that night. I read famous lines written by one of them, Donald Davidson, just retired after forty-five years on the Vanderbilt faculty.

> Morning was golden when from one high tower
> The cool bell stirred its bronze and rang the hour.
> Trees were all April to our youthful mood,
> And sun lit golden Morning in the blood;
> For what is Morning but to tread old ways
> Where other steps have trod, and measure days
> With eager touch as for an ancient door
> That willingly swings as it has swung before?
> Where youthful feet have passed and yet will pass
> Morning abides on trees and tower and grass;
> And Morning rules where voices murmuring
> From April windows summon up the Spring.
> Old paths may change, new faces light old walls,
> Morning will still be golden in these halls.

❧

In my undergraduate years at Chapel Hill, much emphasis was placed on the educational importance of the student honor system in developing self-reliance and personal integrity. Conduct was not perfect there, but I took the obligations of the system seriously. During my sophomore year, in fact, I reported the cheating I observed by two students and gave testimony at their Honor Council hearing.

I was consequently impressed to learn that the Vanderbilt Honor System was begun in 1875, the year University classes were begun. I often spoke to a special freshman convocation that addressed honor at Vanderbilt. The remarks were sometimes printed in a special leaflet, as was true of those made to a freshman convocation in Neely Auditorium January 5, 1965.

I enunciated a theme that I often emphasized:

[The Vanderbilt Honor System] is more important to your education than any program of courses the University could possibly offer. And this importance is permanent, for integrity in an individual, like freedom in a society, is not acquired at one time and place, once and forever after. The struggle for personal integrity, like the struggle for political freedom, is perpetual.

Integrity is a commitment to honesty, a commitment to accuracy, a commitment to logic. Honesty, accuracy, logic all require honor, the honor we seek through our Honor System, the honor of which Shakespeare spoke in King Richard II:

> Mine honor is my life; both grow in one;
> Take honor from me, and my life is done.

A moving story records that when Sam Houston was dying—he who had been president of the Republic of Texas and the only person to serve as governor of two states, Tennessee and Texas—

his wife took a ring from his finger, a ring given him by his mother fifty years before ... that carried the creed his mother said must ever shine in the conduct of her son. . . . Engraved on the inner surface was one word: "Honor".

The tradition of honor has run long at Vanderbilt. Half a century ago, one of our faculty members recalled that on a morning like this one, a quarter of a century before that, the venerable [Landon C.] Garland, Vanderbilt's first chancellor, appeared at a convocation like this one, and announced that a Vanderbilt graduate, whose name he withheld, had sent back his diploma. The graduate had returned it with the confession that in a single examination he had used forbidden help. Although he had never been suspected, and years had passed, he had never found peace of conscience. He therefore returned his diploma and asked that his name be stricken from the roll of alumni, and that public announcement be made of his confession. He preferred public disgrace to living longer with the secret knowledge of his dishonorable act. Chancellor Garland said that after much thought he had decided that the young man's repentance and suffering constituted sufficient atonement for his error, and he urged that the alumnus retain his diploma. But the young man would not consent. Then the Chancellor held up before the student audience the diploma and said, "but I have cut the name out and the secret shall die with me."

This son of Vanderbilt had erred, but having erred, he could not rest until he set the matter right. He had to set the matter right because he had found honor, had found honor within himself, the only place honor can live.

I told other episodes of honor from Vanderbilt's history. Bachelor of Ugliness was the strange appellation conferred early in the University's life as the highest honor that could be conferred on a male undergraduate.

If you look at the early records you will find that no Bachelor of Ugliness is reported for 1909, simply the notation, "no election."

They had an election that year, but the winner, who received an overwhelming number of votes, learned that some of his supporters had voted twice. He declared it no election. His friends argued that even allowing for the duplicate votes he had without question won by a wide margin. But no, he said, it was not a fair election and he would not accept the outcome. Only recently has his name been entered on the list of those chosen by their fellow students for this signal honor. The man's name was Noel Thomas Dowling. He became a famous professor of constitutional law at Columbia University.

Regarding the most controversial dimension of an honor system:

Some students come to Vanderbilt without previous experience with an honor system. They may be unfamiliar with the principles and procedures of our system. This is one reason the Honor Council does so much to explain the system to new students. Once they understand it, some of our students may at first feel uncomfortable with the obligations of the system, especially the obligation to report, as well as to avoid, violations. At its roots all civilized society must be basically self-regulating. The self-controlled community is the best controlled community, just as the self-controlled person is the best-controlled person. Beyond this, we all learn from each other, and the approval or disapproval of one's peers is perhaps the most effective teacher of all.

There is another reason, however, why under our system we expect students to report dishonorable conduct that they see or suspect exists. When a student accepts the Honor Code and signs the pledge—as all Vanderbilt students do—he is subscribing to a twofold compact, one between himself and the University, and one between himself and his fellow students. The compact assumes that the University trusts its students and that they trust each other. When a student cheats under this system, he is not simply guilty of an isolated infraction of a rule, as an individual who has broken his word of honor. He is also guilty of an implied attack upon the honor of all. One who cheats, in a group where all have given their word not to cheat, is in reality attempting to use the character of the great body of honorable persons as a shield to hide his own transgression. An honorable student may reasonably resent a violation of the trust by a fellow-student as much as he would a false accusation against his own honor. It follows that the major responsibility for dealing with any breach of this trust must rest with students themselves.

... [T]he spirit of Vanderbilt and its honor system have across nine decades cultivated personal honor. We have not always been perfect, indeed we are imperfect this very day, but we have been better than we otherwise would have been.

At Vanderbilt, as I have said before and as you may hear me say again, our first concern is the human intellect but our ultimate concern is the human being. If we had to make a choice among human values, we would choose honor over learning, over skill, over understanding. Our concern for honor—for integrity (honesty, accuracy, logic)—extends beyond the classroom to all things all students do. This concern is traditional at Vanderbilt. I read with pride a comment about Vanderbilt athletics made a few weeks ago by Jimmy Burns, a sports columnist, in the Miami, Florida, *Herald,* at the time our football team went there to play the University of Miami. Jimmy Burns said, "The Commodores are rich in traditions and down through the years have adhered to the rules better than any college of my knowledge. . . ."

๑

In the talk I made to the Rotary Club my first month in Nashville, February of 1963, I spoke in part about a university's educational obligation to be hospitable to visiting speakers who expressed controversial viewpoints. When actually applied, the concept was uncongenial to many in Nashville, and also to some others farther away. It was clear to me that a university not only had an obligation to itself to respect the concept of open forum, but it would have difficulty doing so without a necessary level of understanding and support for the concept among its large off-campus constituencies.

When I was invited to speak to the Nashville Area Junior Chamber of Commerce on September 21, 1965, in the Hermitage Hotel, I thought the occasion a suitable one to speak about the essential importance of a free flow of information, ideas, and opinion in an institution that would be a true university. Tens of thousands of children and adults had benefited from the Chamber's physical therapy clinic in the Vanderbilt Hospital—a relationship for which the creative imagination and energy of Dr. Randolph Batson was importantly responsible. The proceeds of the annual Clinic Bowl games played in Vanderbilt Stadium had at that time totaled over $450,000.

The bulk of the remarks addressed free speech in a university, that is, at Vanderbilt.

In the United States we in higher education . . . are steadily concerned that there be sympathetic understanding of why universities conduct their affairs as they do. Universities need the confidence of the communities they serve. . . . For this reason I wish to say something . . . about visitors to American campuses, particularly the Vanderbilt campus, and about the freedom of speech accorded to them.

I know from my mailbox that with a few persons, at least, this is a matter of deep worry.

Two years ago . . . we obtained an acceptance by the President of the United States of an invitation to speak on our campus. . . . But not everyone was pleased. Came a letter from a Vanderbilt alumnus of 1945:

> I heartily disapprove of commemorating this anniversary of Vanderbilt's founding with a blatant political maneuver. Mr. Kennedy has no interest in Vanderbilt, and I am extremely disappointed that you would allow him to use this anniversary of ours as an opportunity to try to gain approval of the present administration in Washington. . . .

My correspondence about campus speakers comes from many points of the political compass. Last year, after it was announced that former President Eisenhower had accepted an invitation to appear on the campus as one of several speakers on the student-conducted program called Impact—a commitment I regret he was later required to cancel—I received a letter from an alumnus of 1925, again obviously sincere, protesting the appearance of partisans on the campus:

> I am quite surprised at the speakers listed. . . . [I]t would be difficult to find more biased Republican partisans than Mr. Eisenhower and Senator Thruston Morton. . . . I think that if this study is to be more than mere propaganda for certain philosophies the panel should include men of national reputation for unbiased opinions. . . .

With respect to another speaker on the Impact program—a program representing many points of view and presenting a carefully selected schedule of speakers—I had a protest from an alumnus who holds two degrees from Vanderbilt, the first awarded in 1932:

> I have decided that I cannot make a contribution this year [to the Living Endowment], on the basis of my disagreeing with the fact that Governor George Wallace has been invited to ap-

pear as a speaker. I can ascribe [*sic*] to the fact that students must hear every side of an issue, but in the case of Governor Wallace, on any campus, it must only make him feel that he has an audience to which he can stir up hate and intolerance.

We had other protests about speakers during the year. One of these, Carl Braden, a Communist, brought several letters. As I read the history of American higher education, it was ever thus. . . .

Professor Edwin Mims reported in his *History of Vanderbilt* an episode that I fully appreciate, because some of my people lived in Georgia on the line marched by General William Tecumseh Sherman from Atlanta to the sea. Chancellor Garland, Vanderbilt's first chancellor, created a turmoil when he announced that John Sherman, brother of General William Sherman, would address Vanderbilt students in chapel one afternoon. This was close to the War and daring indeed. Law students held a meeting of protest and others joined and trooped single file out of the building with student John Bell Keeble in the lead and two future members of the Board of Trust close behind, all playing "Dixie" on their mouth organs.

The anxieties that are felt by public-spirited individuals loyal to their alma mater seem to me to stem from three main sources.

One is the feeling that when a college or university allows a visitor to speak on its campus it is putting its arm around him, dignifying him, and endorsing what he has to say.

Second is the dislike of giving a partisan speaker—usually nowadays, but not always, an advocate of a political viewpoint—a forum in which he can propagandize and spread his doctrine.

Third, anxieties often stem, I suspect, from a lack of understanding of how universities must go about their business if they are to perform their classical functions of discovering, transmitting, and applying knowledge.

Let us look at the first of these three causes of concern. When a university acts formally through its chief executive officer to invite

A Placid Time, 1964–1965

a commencement speaker, or baccalaureate preacher, or visitor on some similar ceremonial occasion, it naturally seeks to select someone whose message it will consider appropriate in style and substance to the occasion. Such occasions often do "honor" the invited person, and the institution may in the public mind be credited with some responsibility for what he says, even though in actuality it cannot influence what he says.

There is no ambiguity, however, about the relationship of the institution to other speakers on its campus. It is the business of a university to maintain an open forum. In an open forum, if it is an effective one, conflicting points of view will inevitably be expressed. The institution does not endorse the statements of those who speak in its forum. What they say can in no sense be construed as the views of "the university" simply because they were expressed in a university forum. The forum is official, not the views expressed in it, just as on our campus *The Hustler* may be the official student newspaper, while the views of its editors are not the official campus opinion.

Last year 384 public appearances were made by visiting speakers to the Vanderbilt campus. Many obviously contradicted others and no single person in the university ... could possibly agree with all of them. ...

Think of the campus platform in the same terms as the library. No one to my knowledge has claimed that Vanderbilt dignifies and endorses the views expressed in the books it works so hard to acquire. We have books by every conceivable social protagonist, well written books and poorly written books, some impeccably sound and presumably some less perfect in their composition. We have books by Machiavelli and Thomas Aquinas, by Adam Smith and Karl Marx, by Winston Churchill and Adolf Hitler. These books are the materials with which faculty and students in a university work in studying the society of which they are a part, in teaching about that society, and applying knowledge for the benefit of society. So, and likewise, speakers who come to the campus are part of the university's traditional resources for study and evaluation.

The fear that misinformation, and ideas that a person considers undesirable, may be spread by visiting speakers is surely an understandable one. These are hazards of the educational process wherever it may be found, and especially these are hazards in an educational process dedicated to producing persons who will think independently and creatively. Partisan advocates do have a chance to spread their message. I might point out that there are many more partisan advocates of particular scholarly doctrines of little interest to the general public, but of great interest and controversy within a university, than there are political partisans who attract outside attention. Some speakers are invited, in fact, so that their message can be heard. But, as someone has said, there is no use trying to make ideas safe for students; you have to make the students safe for ideas. You have to develop within them their own powers of criticism and evaluation.

Young people, and especially young people in college, cannot be shielded from the winds of opinion in our world. There are books in every university library that carry views as daring as any visitor is likely to utter on our campus. As some of you know, Vanderbilt has received an award from the Freedoms Foundation at Valley Forge "for outstanding achievement in bringing about a better understanding of the American way of life." The award recognizes the effective work done by Vanderbilt's summer Institute on the Nature of Communism and Constitutional Democracy, a program that brings to the campus high school teachers from all over the country to learn about the nature of American democracy and Communism. . . . The students in this institute are required to read not only books that interpret the American system and examine Communism critically, and that oppose Communist doctrine, but they are also required also to read certain writings by Communist authors as part of the educational program.

A Placid Time, 1964–1965

You may have noticed last spring what happened when a visitor was prohibited from speaking on the Ohio State University campus. He was the Director of the American Institute for Marxist Studies in New York. He did not speak, but he stood silently on the stage while students read aloud from his books that they had checked out of the university library. . . .

Students eventually graduate and then they cannot be protected by their university from partisan debate. The university's obligation is not to protect students from ideas, but rather to expose them to ideas, and to help make them capable of handling, and hopefully having, ideas. . . .

The university . . . is the principal instrument through which our society examines itself. . . . Inevitably . . . tentative conclusions and firm conclusions will be reached . . . that criticize our society, as well as applaud it. The universities are one of the great sources of innovation in our society—social innovation as well as scientific and technological innovation. It is inescapable that controversial opinions as well as opinions that are broadly acceptable will emerge from this environment.

☙

On October 14, 1965, I spoke to the freshman assembly in Neely Auditorium under the title "On Joining the University." The remarks included words of welcome, of comfort, and of the obligation of those sufficiently favored by circumstance to become students, and graduates, of Vanderbilt. I said, as I often did, that universities are thought of as having three main functions: discovering, transmitting, and applying knowledge. A graduate might not carry from the university a responsibility to investigate or to teach in a narrow sense, although one could hope he or she would be an inquiring, innovative, stimulating person all through life. The graduate does have a responsibil-

63

ity, however, to try in all ways possible to help make a world hospitable to fair and sane living.

We have a Vanderbilt alumnus who in a few weeks will be ninety years old. He has spent his life trying to create a better world. His name is Willis Duke Weatherford, and with his three earned degrees from Vanderbilt he has worked unceasingly to better the lives of other people. For twenty years he was international student secretary of the YMCA. He was founder and for years president of the YMCA Graduate School in Nashville, conducted with the cooperation of Vanderbilt and housed in what is now Wesley Hall. He was founder of the Blue Ridge Assembly at Black Mountain, North Carolina, where I learned two nights ago several Vanderbilt students worked last summer. For ten years he was head of the department of religion and humanities at Fisk University. For half a century he has been a trustee of Berea College. He has written a dozen books on social and economic problems of the Southern section. He pioneered efforts to understand and meet the problems of the Appalachian Highlands. Long before the modern era, he labored courageously and effectively for racial tolerance and equal opportunity. He is a Vanderbilt man who has respected and responded to the obligation of service.

A university is a house of many missions, and service to the world can take many forms. There is no such thing as "the" Vanderbilt man or woman. I hope we will not have a "typical Vanderbilt product"—except as the qualities of gentleness and integrity may mark all our alumni. Vanderbilt men and women come from varied backgrounds and they go to varied futures. We are proud that one of our alumni is one of America's most respected bankers. But we are also proud that one of Vanderbilt's alumni was long the most constructive worker for agricultural reform in the Southern region. We cherish our corporation presidents and banking leaders, our lawyers and doctors of distinction, and these are legion, but we also cherish our winners of Pulitzer prizes, a star of the Metropolitan Opera, a notably successful theatrical director, the South's best-known newspaper editor, the nation's best-known sports writer, a speaker of the United States House of Representatives, senators, governors, congressmen over many decades, bishops, missionaries, engineers, military leaders, over all of the world, deans and professors, the father of the three most important women of modern China, inventors, foundation executives . . .

These people have all been productive in their individual ways. They have not been afraid to be themselves and to do what they could do and what they felt they had to do. They were, or are, independent and energetic individuals, infused with a sense of purpose. I like to think that all of our alumni, each in his own way, will, like Willis Duke Weatherford, contribute, quite simply, to making this a better world.

The drive for vocational success is pervasive in the United States. It affects the curricula in our colleges and the objectives of our students. I hope it will not obscure for you the values of a liberal education of the kind we pursue at Vanderbilt. Every now and then I sense that a student becomes impatient with the requirements that do not take him by the shortest route to the professional training he seeks. In a true university, however, there is a duty to become broadly educated. A liberal education contributes to enlightened social purpose, to wisdom in self-interest, to improved capacity for self-government.

I ask you to look at yourselves whole. I often say that at Vanderbilt our first concern is the human intellect, but our main concern is the human being. Hence you find the student religious centers, the institutions of student self-government, intramural and intercollegiate athletics, many varied social programs, carefully arranged cultural attractions, some other not so carefully arranged entertainments, varied and controversial campus speakers, a large and diversified library, and much more that can help the whole man to grow.

Speaking of the University

One special obligation of the liberal learning, of the whole man, I would emphasize, and would ask you to emphasize.

It is tolerance of opposing opinion.

The other day I read a passage from Harriette Arnow's book, *Seedtime on the Cumberland*, that described an incident that occurred near the end of the American Revolution. It went like this:

> A band of impoverished Tories came to the Cumberland settlements and asked permission to stay. Some were for driving them away, but [General James] Robertson [the founder of Nashville] objected: "This is a free country in which no man should suffer for an opinion. If they show themselves worthy I propose to let them stay. If their acts deserve it let them hang to the nearest tree."

General Robertson made a distinction between opinions and acts, a critically significant distinction for a liberally educated person to make. "No man should suffer for an opinion," said the founder of Nashville. This was true at the birth of the American Republic and it is true today. Those who join a university, an institution that cannot live without tolerance of divergent opinions, have a special responsibility to remember, interpret, and practice this axiom of a free society.

❧

Universities are made by people, and Harold Stirling Vanderbilt contributed significantly to the making of the modern Vanderbilt University. He was a great-grandson of Commodore Cornelius Vanderbilt, the founder of the University, and in 1950 was the first member of his family to become a Vanderbilt University trustee. He was president of the Board of Trust from 1955 to 1968, in which year he was elected honorary president of the Board, which he remained until his death in 1970.

A Placid Time, 1964–1965

Enlisting his significant and constructive interest in the development of the University was one of Chancellor Branscomb's major achievements.

Mr. Vanderbilt's fellow trustees commissioned Georg Lober, a leading American sculptor, to create a statue of him to be placed on the campus. But Mr. Lober died after he had begun, and the commission was transferred to Sidney Waugh, another leading American sculptor. Before he could complete the assignment, he too died, prompting an observation that no person who liked living should willingly become the third sculptor. But Joseph Kiselewski did, and the bronze larger-than-life figure, in academic robe, was unveiled in the center of the campus, in front of Buttrick Hall facing the library, on the morning of a beautiful day, November 5, 1965. I was among those who spoke on that happy day.

This bronze figure in its graceful placement at the center of our campus will be a joy forever. For Vanderbilt, the university, I thank all who have helped to bring it to us. And to Vanderbilt, the man, I say that the University has never had a prouder day.

For approaching a century, since these acres around us were farmland, men and women have been working to make this campus the home of a true university. Throughout the decades of effort, the reason and purpose have been our students. Daily, most of what we do, and ultimately, all of what we do, is directed to their growth—to greater learning about our world, to wider understanding of themselves, to deeper appreciation of beauty, to breadth of interests, to good sense, integrity, tenacity, courage, social conscience, temperate judgment, and if we are lucky, wisdom.

This statue stands for all these things and more. It stands here for a friend of extraordinary personal attainment, for one of the most versatile of Americans—a graduate of Harvard some months ahead of his class, a "capitalist" by his own designation in *Who's Who* who served on the board of many corporations and became chairman of the Board of the New York Central Railroad, the inventor of contract bridge, three times successful defender of the America's Cup that symbolizes world supremacy in yacht racing, and the living founder of Vanderbilt University. No better model could our students have.

Much continuity runs through the life of our university. Two years ago the student body included descendants of the first president of the Board of Trust, of the first chancellor, and of the Commodore himself. I like it that in this particular year the president of the Student Association descends from Bishop McTyeire (and also from a member of the Board of Trust who only lately left us). Perhaps we cherish most the fact that throughout the University's life members of the Vanderbilt family have repeatedly affirmed their belief in the purposes for which we strive.

Sixty-eight years ago a statue of our first founder was unveiled. The Chancellor on that occasion remarked, I think with a touch of pathos: "Far from his home, amid a land of strangers, on a spot where his eye never rested, this monument will stand. . . ." Today's monument stands, and Harold Vanderbilt stands with it, here at a place he can call his home, amid a land of affectionate and admiring friends, on a spot that he as much as any other person has helped to create. . . .

THREE

Conflicts Begin
1966–1967

D URING OUR FIRST FOUR YEARS AT Vanderbilt, Jean and I and the children enjoyed a more generous and hospitable welcome to the University and to Nashville than any family could reasonably expect. Vanderbilt, along with the rest of American higher education, however, went through a turbulent period from the mid-1960s until the 1970s, during which people of good will often disagreed. The period was one of "student unrest"—behavior that manifested itself vividly and violently on many campuses, and to some extent on all.

Several Vanderbilt institutional initiatives in the 1960s that were designed to stimulate student participation in extracurricular activities and to further engagement with issues of public policy had a beneficial effect when impulses of student activism became felt. The University had been promoting and defending the expression of diverse political and social views and encouraging attention, through student and other activities, to the country's social problems and political issues. In doing so it had prompted patches of controversy at the time of the first Impact program in 1964 and periodically thereafter.

The issue of a university's obligation to encourage an "open forum" came, however, to consume an enormous amount of administrative time. In early December 1966, we had what we called "a meeting of the University" in Underwood Auditorium. Some twenty-three University officers sat on the stage. Anybody could ask them questions about anything. The forum lasted from 7:00 P.M. to 10:30 P.M. and, after a fifteen-minute recess, resumed for another hour. It was at this meeting that a tall, appealing coed arose and asked about the dress code. Was it true that the coeds could not wear shorts on campus except to play tennis and then must cover them with a raincoat when going to and from the courts? Yes, replied the Dean of Women. Well, the coed asked, can I wear one of the new transparent raincoats? I said to a colleague sitting next to me, as gales of laughter engulfed Underwood, "There goes the dress code."

During and after the spring of 1967, some alumni and townspeople were outraged by the University's (they would say, the Chancellor's) willingness to permit properly constituted student and other groups to invite visitors of their own choice to speak on the campus. The whole nation was in a state of controversy over issues of civil rights and the war in Vietnam, with developments like the revolution in sexual behavior and a general challenge to constituted authority joining to stimulate contention, anxiety, and alarm.

Much has been written about the period of student unrest, both in the United States and abroad (where the triggering events were often different from those in the United States). For a while at Vanderbilt, the major focus of my attention and use of my time, especially during 1967, were directed at containing the threat to what I deemed to be an elementary university necessity—maintaining a free forum for debate on public questions. But I did not want to concede that the right to so fundamental an American educational and civic value as open expression of controversial thought could be seriously questioned at Vanderbilt; so I did as little as possible to fuel the public controversy—others were doing plenty of that—and proceeded with what I considered to be my, the University's, normal business. But in all the controversies that ensued, I had a firm resolve that I sometimes emphasized to colleagues: it is not enough for us to be right; we must also win.

In the mid-1960s, we sometimes had two meetings a year of the joint faculties, meeting in Underwood Auditorium. A special meeting was called for March 8, 1966. My report was long and detailed, addressing such matters as a new instrument of faculty government to go before the trustees later in the spring, the "profile" of information requested by the Ford Foundation to aid in assessing our request for a matching grant to serve as an incentive in a capital funds drive, the possibility that Vanderbilt would launch such a drive, planning for the expansion of the main student dining facility, Rand Hall, dormitory construction, and establishment of an honor dormitory for women in Kensington House. ("It imposes mature responsibilities on the occupants and so far the experiment has proved eminently successful.") I reported on a series of picnics and other entertainments held for students by the Heards, regular press conferences held for student publications, and many other matters that claimed the time and attention of my colleagues and me. ("Improvement in the diversity and richness of campus life—still with considerable distance to go—has, I think, been noticeable.")

I proclaimed the three-year successes of the varsity basketball team and explained my policy: "The Chancellor seeks to identify himself with such winning athletic teams as he can find, and when he cannot find them he defers respectfully to the prior claims of the chairman of the athletics committee, Vice-Chancellor Purdy." And then:

I have clutched the basketball team to my bosom. We have had the best three-year stretch in the long history of the sport at Vanderbilt. I must report to you, however, that even this policy has its pitfalls. Despite the record of sixty-five victories and fourteen losses in three years, twenty-two victories and four losses this season, I received after last Saturday's game the following telegram from an alert alumnus in Memphis:

> Former Army Coach Blaik once said he wanted his men to be sick when they lost. Your Coach Skinner sees nothing wrong in losing when expected to win. The winning attitude is an essential part in my opinion of the educational process a university should instill in its students. Our school appeared thrice and lost twice before regional television audiences. Your winning attitude is not too obvious. Lead onward.

I also spoke of the continuing efforts to improve the appearance of the campus, of my disappointment that no way had been found to relocate the electric substation behind Rand Hall, and of the effort to make the best of a bad deal by creating what "may be the first color-coded electric substation ... in the world." The major components of the substation were painted different colors and a large color chart was prominently placed identifying the function of each of the components—as someone said, by a code of many colors.

There were abundant other reports on detailed matters that I knew were of special interest to some, including: overseas programs; faculty appointments; the Computer Center; department chairmanships; new surgical suites; the emergence, on Vanderbilt's initiative, of the University Center in Nashville (Vanderbilt, Peabody, Scarritt, Fisk, and Meharry); comparable developments elsewhere in the United States; and initiatives to encourage year-round academic use of the campus. There was much more, but these illustrations convey at least some of the flavor of my effort to inform the faculties of events, achievements, plans, and hopes, and to solicit their reaction and to enlist their energies.

My father was graduated in electrical engineering from Lehigh University in 1893, and I spent my freshman year at Chapel Hill in chemical engineering. Thus, when an invitation came in 1966 to speak on April 15 at the spring initiation banquet of the Tennessee Beta Chapter of Tau Beta Pi, the national honor society in engineering, I accepted with pleasure. The dinner was held at the Biltmore Motel on Eighth Avenue in Nashville.

As an introductory sally, I urged the students being honored to take care of their health and quoted the six rules for keeping fit offered by the great medical authority, Satchel Paige:

1. Avoid fried meats which angry up the blood.
2. If your stomach disputes you, lie down and pacify it with cool thoughts.
3. Keep the juices flowing by jangling around gently as you move.
4. Go very light on the vices, such as carrying on in society— the social ramble ain't restful.
5. Avoid running at all times.
6. And don't look back. Something might be gaining on you.

Speaking of the University

I then cited the significance of education:

Everywhere on our planet, in well-developed and less well developed nations, education is the secular keystone of economic growth, of political development, of social progress. . . .

Everywhere we look, revolt against the established ways of our world thrives or threatens. . . . [T]he sweep of revolt is broad; the mood of revolt is persistent; the presence of revolt is normal. Broad and persistent, and normal, too, is the urgent need for all the informed intelligence, all the patient tolerance, all the disciplined energy that highly educated men and women can bring to bear on our common problems. . . .

I want to speak with you about the special responsibilities of highly educated persons in our part of the nation. . . . This South of ours, holding one-fourth or more of the country's citizens, has always been the nation's most distinctive section. . . . [W]hat educated persons within it do has long weighed heavily in the affairs of the Southern states, and also in the affairs of the United States. Wherever you or I call home in the future, within the South or elsewhere in our country or on the globe, this subject counts much in our personal destiny. . . .

What vision of the Southern future should we in this room tonight help fulfill? This question has deep meaning, despite the great varieties in our region that grow greater year by year. . . .

It is not enough for you or me simply to be educated. My father-in-law was president of a teacher-training institution in Alabama, and he used to ask that teachers be trained to do more than teach children how to read and write and do arithmetic. "*What* should children be taught to write? A pen can be used to forge a check as well as to write a poem. *What* mathematical problems should children be taught to solve? Addition, multiplication, and subtraction can be used to promote a swindle as readily as to operate a legitimate business." Teaching should be relevant to these public problems that need solution. By the same light, highly educated men and women must have public purpose in their lives.

Much has been said over the years about the South's liabilities and assets. Those of us who went to college in the 1930s recall that speakers on occasions like this often cited the region's deficiencies . . . as "the nation's number one economic problem."

In the years since, much progress has been made, and made in ways that make it clear that engineers played their part. [For example, the] South's per capita income rose in three decades from about one-half the per capita income of the nation as a whole to about three-fourths that of the nation as a whole. Many sources of strength have brightened the Southern picture. . . . [W]e have the greatest average rainfall in the country, are better fixed for water than any other region, have 40 percent of the nation's forest area, and now grow trees as crops where we used to grow cotton. And, we also show a gratifying increase in industrial and service enterprises, and in the highly important diversification of agriculture.

Despite the progress of many kinds, we in the South still trail. Other states and sections have moved ahead, too, some even faster. We still must educate three-tenths of the nation's children with two-tenths of the nation's school revenue. In recent years the South as a whole (like our Engineering School at Vanderbilt under Dean Rowe's energetic leadership) has taken giant strides in graduate education—that contemporary educational mission of soaring importance. Nonetheless, in the states of the old Confederacy, where one person in every four of the nation's population lives, only one in every nine of the nation's doctoral degrees has been awarded in recent years.

Let us accept the fact that we in our region have come far. Yet, despite the progress that has been made, we still have special challenges.

I think we need a vision to guide the Southern future. . . .

So I would say that our first obligation is to have a sense of obligation.

A second part of the Southern vision must, inescapably, concern Southern race relations. . . .

We must not look upon this condition as the heaviest of history's albatrosses about our neck. Let us view it as the South's mightiest chance for greatness. We, of whatever color, can so conduct ourselves that Southern progress in human relations in the last third of this century can be a stirring triumph of American self-government, a bright emblem of the democratic way, an envy of many lands. So I would say that our second obligation is to turn the continuing problems of race into opportunities, to make the weight of this heritage an important asset, to make the very depths of the problems that we handle with intelligence and success a source of pride and a credit to all.

Finally, a vision of the future South must embrace a vision of Southern education. . . .

In our society and in our time, economic prosperity, political development, the general welfare, and personal effectiveness are rooted in education. . . . In less developed nations, education is the main key to economic growth and political development. All around the world . . . education has gained an importance never before held by it in the affairs of men. . . . .

It is also clear that . . . the best investment a people can make is in their own education.

Our third obligation in the future South, therefore, is to give highest priority to the improvement of education.

All Southerners, especially highly educated Southerners, have much at stake—in a sense, everything at stake—in fulfillment of our Southern vision: in education, in human relations, and in the will to cross the . . . frontiers before us. All Americans also have an immense stake in the Southern future. . . . [A] concern for the social, economic, and political health of our state, section, and nation is a special obligation of highly educated men and women.

Conflicts Begin, 1966–1967

☙

Not long after coming to Vanderbilt, I became acquainted with Mrs. Preston Davie, a redoubtable New York Republican partisan of great energy and élan whose deceased husband was a kinsman of William Richardson Davie, who wrote and introduced into the North Carolina General Assembly in 1789 the legislation that created the University of North Carolina. In 1960 I had introduced Preston Davie when he spoke to the Friends of the Library in Chapel Hill. Chancellor Branscomb had known Mrs. Davie, and, in fact, while he was in office, she had made a handsome gift to Vanderbilt.

Mrs. Davie was a conservative Republican, very conservative. She knew thoroughly my reputation as a liberal Democrat, very liberal from her viewpoint. We immediately became fast friends. She had me sitting on the platform—way in the back, I insisted—in Madison Square Garden in New York City on October 26, 1964 (the then "new Garden" at Eighth Avenue and Fiftieth Street), when the Republican presidential candidate, Senator Barry Goldwater, made one of only three campaign appearances in that state laden with electoral votes. As a special guest I found myself in a waiting room seated with Mrs. Richard Nixon, admirably dressed and considerably less interested in being there than I. Mrs. Davie presided, Clare Booth Luce was one of the speakers, oratorical and effective, and Senator Goldwater spoke for fifty minutes.

May Davie was the chair of the Board of Trustees of the Robert A. Taft Institute of Government, headquartered in New York. Over many years it sponsored nonpartisan graduate level training seminars in American democracy for teachers. The institute was also concerned to increase mainstream political participation by minorities. I served as a trustee from 1973 to 1976. (As the "Taft Institute," the organization was still at work in 1994.) Very soon after I met her, Mrs. Davie enlisted Vanderbilt's help.

In 1965 Vanderbilt and Fisk universities joined, under Taft Institute sponsorship, in offering to high school social studies teachers of the Nashville Metropolitan Schools a series of eight Saturday seminars on practical politics. I was asked to speak about the program to the organizational meeting of the Metropolitan Council for Social Science of the Metropolitan Public Schools of Nashville-Davidson County, in the Hillsboro High School auditorium in Nashville, September 28, 1966.

Recalling earlier experience in other places, I reported that:

Repeated testimony from the teachers attending the seminars has consistently emphasized three things: first, many high school teachers of social studies consider themselves incompletely equipped to understand and interpret that complex and curious and uniquely important set of social phenomena that we call American politics; second, they are eager to become better equipped; and third, they can take effective advantage of opportunities afforded them to do so. . . .

Three broad aspects of social science seem to me to be extraordinarily important in the education of our students. Remember that we are developing minds and also are developing citizens. For either purpose, (1) students need to begin to understand the processes by which their society functions; (2) they need, also, to begin to understand the great social issues that confront their society; and (3), they ought to begin to become acquainted with at least some of the ways that these processes and issues can be systematically and effectively studied.

I related these conclusions to an experience of my own, thirty-five years before.

In 1931, when I was in the last year of junior high school in Savannah, Georgia, I had what I have since always recalled as a supremely significant educational experience. I had a "civics" course. It was taught by Miss Marie Bargeron. Miss Bargeron was a superb teacher, and we were all happy when toward the end of the course she married the physical education teacher and became Mrs. Logan.

I had always been an enthusiastic student of history, especially American history, as I still am. But this was the first course, and I believe the only course in my entire public school experience in that ancient time, that dealt explicitly with contemporary social events. I recall Miss Bargeron as being the most effective teacher of my junior and senior high school career in harnessing my enthusiasm, in stimulating intellectual curiosity, in developing a sense of personal identification with what was going on in the world, and in creating the sensation that I, individually, might have something to do with it.

I remember that we dealt at one point with public health problems in New York City, an unlikely topic for coastal Georgia, except that we had some too. I was impressed for the first time with the extended, constructive reach of public authority into the lives of citizens, beyond the highly visible realms of war, diplomacy, and the election of a president. . . .

This civics course stands out in my memory because it thrust us students face to face in an effective learning situation with a functioning society. . . .

Even this superlative course, however . . . lacked two of the three characteristics that I set forth as goals of social science study. I do not believe the course addressed itself self-consciously to the processes of politics, to mechanisms of social adjustment, to the devices by which the vast mesh of public and private interests in our country and in our world are brought together in friction and in harmony to become the daily life of the American people.... [T]he discussion was all of policy, not of process, all about what had been or should be done, not about the means by which government and society achieve, or might achieve, intelligent decisions effectively implemented.

Moreover, from this memorable civics course I do not believe I derived any sense of the means by which one could or should go about observing, analyzing, and understanding either the issues facing a society, or the procedures, organization, customs, values, and other qualities by which or through which a society functions. I would be embarrassed to tell you how old I was, how far my academic training had advanced, before I became explicitly familiar with the concept of methodology in social science study....

No one whom I can recall ever suggested that how one studied the decades preceding the War Between the States or the origins of the Depression or the tensions then tight between Japan and China might have something to do with how much one could learn and, therefore, understand and, therefore, eventually do.

I then drew contrasts between the physical and biological sciences and mathematics, on the one hand, and the social sciences and humanities, on the other, emphasizing that fundamental economic, political, and social issues of our society cannot be escaped, that they are every person's concern, that all students in our schools have citizen obligations and opportunities, and that "social studies are concerned with these general obligations and opportunities of citizens everywhere, as well as with specific social issues or processes themselves."

Conflicts Begin, 1966–1967

After all, all of us are faced by the current dilemmas of our society, whether we be chemists or poets or sociologists. How can we remove the causes and alleviate the suffering of mental illness? How can we bring the world's growing population into balance with the world's resources and political capacities? How can we make our increasingly specialized science and technology politically responsible? How can we satisfy the aspirations for democratic government in many parts of the world where the conditions inherently necessary for that kind of government are undeveloped? How can we reconcile the dynamic momentum of nation-states with the manifest necessities of a peaceful world community? How can we overcome appalling poverty for some in this land of incredible plenty for most? How can we provide personal opportunity and reward for individuals long denied them, without discriminating against other individuals who have already attained them? All about us, everywhere, in crime rates and accident tolls and social deprivation and public disorder and disrespect for the law, lie relentless, besetting problems of our civilization.

Within a few years—looking back it will seem like a few months—our students will be asked to deal with questions of this kind. They will have no choice. We have no choice but to do our best to prepare them to do so.

The curriculum revolution has only begun in the social sciences. The achievements in mathematics, modern languages, and the natural sciences have made us aware of what is possible in curriculum improvement, in the reorganization of subject matter, in new insights into effective teaching procedures. Now, attention is turning to social studies. If I understand what I read, several dozen development projects of national significance now under way promise to alter radically our teaching about man and society.

While acknowledging that colleges and universities have responsibilities in these matters, I emphasized that success can come earliest and most effectively from the efforts of those who are on the line in social science teaching in the schools, those who were represented in Nashville that day in the new Metropolitan Council for Social Science.

❧

In the 1960s New York City had both a Tennessee Society and a Southern Society. It fell my lot to speak to each at a dinner meeting, the Tennessee Society in 1966 and the Dixie Dinner of the Southern Society on February 24, 1967. In my experience in New York, long before joining Vanderbilt, I had never found Southerners defensive about their origins. They had succeeded as much in the worlds of finance, business, the law, and education as able persons from elsewhere, including the city itself. But there remained a regional pride and spirit that many of their number observed sympathetically the natives of other places lacked.

The Southern Society dinner was thus for some a social event of some acclaim, a formal dinner dance in the Terrace Room of the Plaza Hotel, beginning at 7:30 P.M., the hour affording time for successive preparatory gatherings, to two of which I was invited, and where I, knowing what lay ahead, was abstemious and where others, doubtless for the same reason, were less so. It was through the courtesy of Vanderbilt alumna Margaret Mahoney, then associated with the Carnegie Corporation and later president of the Commonwealth Fund, that I and others of Vanderbilt were invited to one of these festivities. At dinner, I was seated with the speaker's lectern on my left and an attractive college-age student on my right who turned out to be the daughter of General William C. Westmoreland, then commander of American troops in Vietnam. At 11:15 I was introduced to give the speech of the evening.

I had been told by a friend about a previous Dixie Dinner that he had attended. The speaker was introduced with fanfare at midnight sharp to give "his address." He arose, gave his house number and street name in Princeton, New Jersey, and sat down. I planned to meet the challenge, first, by speaking no more than fifteen minutes, and, second, by devoting thirteen of the fifteen minutes to my best attempts at humor.

I explained, "I feel like the television commercial that interrupts the program—unavoidable, and the shorter the better, especially when you can't change channels."

Then I borrowed a story from the repertoire of Vanderbilt trustee Madison S. Wigginton, who was present, the point of which was not lost on the audience:

When I find myself bestowing words on an occasion like this, preceded by joyous preprandial indulgences and with even greater joys impatiently awaited ahead, I think of the prayer of Brother Maxwell in Mississippi. . . .

This particular Wednesday fell about the middle of August, when torrential rains were playing havoc with the cotton crop. Cotton was even more important to the life blood of Mississippi then than it is today. The faithful had gathered and the pastor called on Brother Maxwell to pray in conclusion. In true Presbyterian fashion, he thanked the Lord for all of His manifold blessings which are new every morning. Finally, he spoke his innermost thoughts by concluding, "And now, O Lord, we thank Thee for all this rain, although God knows we don't need it."

I urged the eminent New York Southerners present to campaign to get our national government to provide their native

South with Reconstruction reparations comparable to the aid the Marshall Plan provided for the reconstruction of Europe after World War II. I also argued that "the South is due a usage fee for the profitable privilege the North has enjoyed in using [the] genius and energy and talent over the years" of those sitting in the Terrace Room that night. There was more of this, but only about ten minutes more. I invoked, among other ploys, my discovery that in fund-raising

> there is a real difference between trying and succeeding. I saw a clipping from a New Orleans newspaper of 1849 that makes the distinction rather clear. The legislators of Louisiana meeting in Baton Rouge were acting on a bill to punish seduction. The clerk read a section which said, "If any man by making false promises shall seduce any chaste female," he shall be punished. A legislator immediately rose to say, "Mr. Speaker, I move to amend this section by inserting the words, 'an cotched,' after the word 'chased' because it stands to reason that a fellow may chase a female all day, and if he don't cotch her, there's no harm done."

There were serious strains that ran in and out, and toward the end I asked the Southern Society members to remember

> that long before modern economists proclaimed the prime dependence of a society's welfare on education, Benjamin Franklin truly said in the eighteenth Century, "An investment in knowledge always pays the best interest."

On April 5, 1967, I gave the James Schouler Lecture at the Johns Hopkins University in Baltimore—in the then new classroom building on the Homewood campus—on "The South's Future in Higher Education." It was the first in a series of three, the second to be given a week later by Governor Win-throp Rockefeller of Arkansas (a Vanderbilt trustee) on the economic prospects for the South, and the third, a week after that, by black leader Charles Evers on the political future of the South, of whom I said, "Speaking as he does from the heart of the present, what he will say must assuredly have meaning for the heart of the future."

The year 1967 was a demanding one for the nation. The war in Vietnam was increasingly a source of controversy and civil anguish. And the nation was in the throes of radical changes in social practices, especially some in race relations that were long overdue and that produced deeply rooted tensions in many persons and places, and violence in some.

My thesis this afternoon carries three messages: first, that the greatest leverage for Southern progress can be found in the improvement of Southern higher education; second, that while to improve Southern higher education requires generally the same measures as to improve higher education in the nation as a whole, four of these measures have special significance in the South; and third ... that these four measures confirm that matters of race continue to have a peculiar historic significance in Southern affairs. ...

First, we have special need to remember the individuality of education. All education occurs within an individual. The processes of educating may require several students to sit in a classroom, but if anything significant occurs in or out of the classroom it is a highly personal and individual matter.

It is important to remember this about higher education in our time, and especially in our South. Larger and larger proportions of young people will attend colleges and universities in the future. The college and university campus will consequently become an increasingly important place of contact—sometimes a place of linkage, sometimes a place of confrontation—between the people who are young and the qualities that are old in our society. The campus affords a physical location and an educational process where each student seeks to find, hopes to find, ought to find, a view of the world and his place in it that gives satisfaction and makes sense to him.

Colleges and universities have always helped their students toward these objectives. I believe, however, that in our land now affluent in personal alternatives for young people, the task is more difficult to perform than ever before. American higher education finds itself with an enormous obligation to direct sensitive attention to the subjective problems and individual dilemmas of young men and women. This function of higher education is of special significance under the changing conditions of race relations in the South—although it is of pervasive importance everywhere in the United States.

This is saying more, I think, than that we need to focus attention on undergraduate education as opposed to graduate education, or on teaching as opposed to research, or that we should have smaller classes or more honors sections, or that somehow the contemporary pressures for academic attainment should be ameliorated.

Many students in Southern colleges and universities are themselves Southerners; many students who come to those institutions from elsewhere in the country will become Southerners. Those students who are white and those who are Negro will live in an increasingly desegregated society that will require of them personal resources of intelligence, integrity, imagination, patience, energy, and fortitude—and sometimes in proportions that have seldom, if ever, been required of Americans before.

The conventional posture of the American college and university has in a very special way been passive in the attitude it has adopted toward its students. The institution was there; the student could profit if he wished.

Contemporary pressures require, it seems to me, that to do its job properly the institution must now seek affirmatively to perceive, analyze, and understand the qualities of thought, feeling, ambition, and perplexity that define the individual student. In the South, the departure of segregation imposes new and often unfamiliar expectations on people, especially on the young people who will be living in the increasingly integrated society of the future. The strain inside the individual can be severe. The college and university need to help him fashion an outlook adequate for himself and his times.

Having said this, I turn to a second matter, again one of crucial importance to higher education generally in our country, but again one of special significance in the South.

A college or university campus, but especially a university campus, must establish within itself processes that conduce to the dual objectives of adaptation and stability. A society that would be productive, peaceful, and just must have the means to examine itself, to question itself, to change itself. It must also make secure the due processes by which this self-scrutiny and deliberation on the results of self-scrutiny occur. But adaptation and stability, change and permanence, energy and order are not always compatible. . . .

Full academic freedom is apparently not yet secure for all types of Southern colleges and universities. It needs to be if academic institutions are to be of greatest value. To be meaningful, academic freedom depends on adherence to certain values, and on the effectiveness of certain processes. Threats to those values and processes can be as damaging to academic freedom as the more familiar constraints imposed on individuals by higher authorities, or imposed by individuals on themselves.

We face a special circumstance in our time. The varied tactics of the civil rights movement have brought tangible results; advocates of other, different causes now sometimes seek to employ these same tactics. In historical perspective, however, the moral imperatives activating the civil rights movement seem to me to be unique, just as the moral imperatives that motivated the abolitionist movement before Emancipation were unique. Routine transfer of the tactics of civil disobedience . . . from the civil rights struggle to other arenas of social action can destroy values toward which the civil rights struggle itself has been struggling and which make its successes most meaningful. The concept of civil rights has no meaning without the rule of law.

A university . . . has a function of investigation and questioning. Ultimately, anything can be examined and questioned, including even our best accepted assumptions and values. This educational process of inquiry itself rests, however, on basic conditions that must prevail if the university and college are to function and survive.

These assertions mean to me that institutions of higher education must interpret, make understandable, and within themselves enforce the mutual dependence of, on the one hand, inquiry, free debate, and effective modes of social action, with, on the other, integrity, order, and due process.

We must ask colleges and universities to pursue as educational goals, and in governing their own affairs, the ironical twin tasks of insuring certain effective mechanisms of change and insuring certain values of stability in society. These twin tasks have special significance for the student on the campus, and I think especially on the Southern campus. A self-governing society, a political democracy, the rule of law, all depend ultimately on the understanding, support, self-restraint, self-discipline of individual people. The campus is a crucially important place where these qualities are re-enforced and developed. . . .

Now, a third requirement for the South's future in higher education:

Universities and colleges are doing more things, and doing them better, than formerly. For these reasons, along with general inflation and improved faculty-staff compensation, costs have risen. The condition in general across the land has prompted and been made possible by larger and larger state appropriations, larger and larger federal appropriations, larger and larger private giving.

The pinch on state-supported institutions is tighter in some states than in others. Although it is difficult for an administrator in a private university to understand it fully, President [Milton] Eisenhower and I hear from our colleagues in the state institutions of the severe financial handicaps under which they labor. This is unquestionably true in some locations, but I suspect it is not equally true in others.

In privately financed higher education, however, a crisis of the first magnitude is building. Costs are rising at a faster rate than income from endowment and income from tuition. In prospect is a permanent gap between needs and the revenues that can reasonably be anticipated from these two sources. I can tell you that at Vanderbilt the percentage of our operating income coming from endowment and tuition fell from 86 percent in 1935 to 83 in 1950 to 57 in 1958, to 45 in 1966. Generous private giving has grown, with the consequence that donations are increasingly depended upon to help pay the cost of annual operations as well as of capital expenditures. But I doubt that private universities—and I include the strongest of them—can expect to derive sufficient regular income from private giving campaigns to sustain them indefinitely. This does not mean that these institutions will not continue to gain in strength and usefulness. It simply means they will go broke at a higher level.

In this national context, the South has even greater relative needs if it is to bootstrap itself to improved quality and quantity in higher education.

The general situation across the country, the crisis in the private institutions, and the special needs of the South make it clear that increased educational income is needed. State and local governments must continue to increase their investments in higher education. I hope that support of higher education from individuals, corporations, foundations, and other private sources will rise. Perhaps, as has been recently suggested by the president of the Ford Foundation, the institutions themselves can improve the management of their own investment funds. There is genuine doubt, however, that all of these measures together will prove sufficient. . . .

General institutional support is needed, and it seems to me necessary and inevitable that the President and the Congress will address themselves to the most effective ways to confer this support for the maximum educational yield to the country. . . .

Finally, higher education for culturally and financially disadvantaged Southerners requires special action. Increased opportunity for Negroes, especially, is the unsung frontier of American higher education.

The South has an enormous economic stake, to say nothing of its human stake, in improved higher education for all Southerners. The stake is especially large among those Southerners who have been inadequately schooled for advanced education. These include many Negroes who ... have labored under many generations of handicap. How to provide best for the higher education of Negroes is a question highly important to the future of the South. I do not believe we have yet answered that question.

Approximately one-half of the Negroes in the United States now in colleges and universities are found in the predominantly Negro institutions of the South. These institutions are acknowledged by all observers to be uneven in their quality and in their capacity for development. Because of poor preparation and other factors of previous unequal opportunity, certain students find it possible to attend only the less demanding of these institutions. Under existing conditions this situation will continue. Although some white students attend some of the predominantly Negro institutions, they are relatively few, and the institutions remain with few exceptions predominantly Negro. While the numbers of Negro students attending predominantly white institutions has been growing, in most instances it is still low. The net result is a continued high degree of separation by race in Southern higher education.

Enormous national attention is being directed to segregation patterns in elementary and secondary education. Wherever Negroes live in large numbers, local school boards and national policy are concerned with the conditions under which de facto segregation can be and should be modified for educational reasons. Professor James Coleman of this university, working with my colleague Professor Ernest Campbell at Vanderbilt, has been notably identified with research that assesses the effects of differing patterns of segregation in elementary and secondary schools on motivation and achievement.

We in the South must inquire whether some of the same issues are to be found in higher education. If it is true that for subtle psychological reasons or for tangible material reasons students in a predominantly Negro college or university suffer significant handicaps, then that fact must be recognized as the South plans to develop to the fullest the personal resources of its citizens.

More nearly adequate higher education for Negroes in the South will clearly involve many measures. The program of the Council of Southern Universities to strengthen the faculties of institutions presently attended predominantly by Negroes, as well as your own institute's Experienced Teacher Fellowship Program, will help. The voluntary enrollment of more Negroes in certain predominantly white institutions and of more whites in certain predominantly Negro institutions would contribute to this objective. A hard-headed analysis of the predominantly Negro institutions and selective concentration of resources on those most capable of development should be attempted. (Predominantly white institutions in the region, I must say, require enormous improvement, too.) I suspect that only after sharp improvement in the quality of the best predominantly Negro institutions will more racially balanced student bodies within them develop on a voluntary basis.

Efforts must be made to break down the intellectual isolation that characterizes the conditions under which faculty members work in some predominantly Negro institutions. Interinstitutional working relationships can contribute stoutly to this end.

Through all of this, the ambition should be to raise the level of aspiration of Negroes for higher education, and to raise the sights and capacities of predominantly Negro, as well as of predominantly white, institutions. All these things require money in large sums. They also, however, require clarity of objectives, and I do not believe we yet have consensus on what those objectives should be.

The needs of our future Southern higher education are formidable. We must respond to the new, special needs of individual students in our time. We must preserve order through change. We must have extraordinary amounts of money to attain the needed quality and quantity of higher education. We must attend especially to the higher educational needs of the culturally and financially disadvantaged. To meet those needs will require all the ingenuity that we can muster.

❦

The most overt friction that I encountered as chancellor surfaced in the spring of 1967 around issues of "the open forum" mentioned at the start of this chapter. The students' Impact program presented a spate of controversial speakers on April 7 and 8, including, among others, Martin Luther King, Jr., Senator Strom Thurmond, poet Allen Ginsburg, and civil rights activist Stokely Carmichael. Sharp adverse reaction both before and after the program was evident in remarks heard and mail received, and in sundry other ways. Somebody organized a campaign that brought an avalanche of disapproving postcards to my mailbox. Most conspicuously critical were the policies of the *Nashville Banner*, wholly owned by Vanderbilt's (and my) senior trustee, James G. Stahlman. Mr. Stahlman vigorously voiced in print and otherwise his disapproval—nay outrage—that Vanderbilt's Chancellor would permit Carmichael to appear on the campus. The *Banner* sustained its attack, mostly on page 1, well into July of 1967. Mr. Stahlman and I had been authentically cordial friends from my first arrival at Vanderbilt, and became so again after this episode. He subsequently made very generous financial contributions to the University.

I did not respond publicly to the many criticisms voiced in 1967, and in answering those who wrote, whether they approved or disapproved the University's policy, did not argue the merits of the issue. It was necessary, however, to address our trustees on the subject in their spring meeting, which I did on May 5, 1967. I spoke from notes, essentially as follows:

At the request of two trustees and because of the general interest in the matter, the subject of the recent Impact program was put on the agenda. In discussing the matter I would like to follow this procedure: I will make a statement, then listen to comments from any wishing to make them, and then I will make a closing remark.

I accept full responsibility for whatever goes on on the campus, and particularly for the Impact program and similar activities. I do not propose to respond, however, to certain allegations in the press, but that does not mean that I accept all the assumptions and conclusions of the press. Rather, I want to explore the matter as one of general University policy that is of concern to us all.

I have received three types of proposal for action today: that I ask for a vote of confidence, that restrictive measures of some kind be imposed on the campus forum, and that a committee be appointed to study Vanderbilt's policies and procedures regarding this matter. I believe it would be undesirable to take any one of these actions, and therefore I propose that on completion of our discussion this afternoon we proceed to the next item on the agenda.

I now want to explain why I recommend this course of action. We should remember that we are talking about a general campus matter, not just one special organization. There are some eighty chartered campus organizations.

I then described the origins of Impact in 1963, alluded to programs at Randolph-Macon, Princeton, and elsewhere that Vanderbilt representatives had studied before launching Impact, listed a number of other Vanderbilt organizations that had sponsored speakers of their own choice during the academic year 1966–67, and reminded the trustees that at the luncheon they had just attended that day twenty-three of the twenty-eight student guests were Impact leaders. I described the membership of that organization's advisory and executive committees and told of my relationship to the organization— which, essentially, was to help when invited to do so but otherwise to keep hands off. I listed some of the highly diversified speakers of the past and mentioned some of the eighty-eight who had been invited to speak at the 1967 Impact. I gave my opinion that the 1967 program had been a highly successful, widely applauded, and educationally useful enterprise. I then stated why, though I would be grateful,

I oppose a vote of endorsement or confidence. In my view, I have simply conducted myself and the University's affairs in a normal way for a true university, and I do not feel the need for a vote, and believe the University's position is weakened if the impression is given that either you or I do feel the need. My views and convictions on the subject have been explicit, deeply held, long-standing, public, and exposed to this Board.

Conflicts Begin, 1966–1967

I then cited my remarks at the installation ceremony October 4, 1963, the speech I gave to the Junior Chamber of Commerce in September 1965, and a relevant discussion in the Board of Trust meeting of May 14–15, 1965. I also referred to my experience, or record, in inviting diverse speakers as chairman of the Carolina Political Union in 1937 and 1938 when a student at the University of North Carolina. I said that I felt that since there had been no change in my attitude or policy since coming to Vanderbilt, I saw no need for Board endorsement.

In discussing why I believe restrictive actions to be unwise, I ignore legal and constitutional aspects of the matter, except to call your attention to the fact that they exist. I oppose restrictive action on three grounds: the educational usefulness of an open platform, the practical difficulties of closing or controlling it, the undesirable consequences for the University of attempts at restrictive action.

It hardly seems necessary to burden you with a defense of the free exchange of ideas, or of the freedom to hear and the freedom to read for our students, or of the educational value of these freedoms: rather, let me speak to the fear that we will contaminate young minds. I would like to read remarks I made to the Nashville Junior Chamber of Commerce September 21, 1965.

I then quoted from that speech, excerpts from which appear in chapter 2 above, and emphasized that even if one accepts the principle of a restricted platform, the practical difficulties of agreeing on who should be kept away and who should not were immense. I pointed to the difficulty, even if an institution throws down the gauntlet of restriction, of protecting students from unpopular ideas, citing opportunities students had to read offending views in publications easily accessible to them (including newspapers) and to hear them in meetings off campus, and alluding to experiences on some other campuses.

I reported, for those interested, that we had not been able to discern any adverse impact on undergraduate admissions. We had received at least one letter from a prospective faculty member expressing anxiety over any repressive step that Vanderbilt might take. I gave an analysis of mail I had received and acknowledged that there can always be gifts or other support that an institution can lose unknowingly when maintaining an open forum, but—if one must consider such things—far more important would be the adverse effects on the University of the perception given to government and foundation screening committees to which universities look with hope for grants and other support should an open forum not be maintained.

I then addressed the mistaken belief that somehow we exalt a speaker by having him on the campus and drew on the argument in my 1965 Junior Chamber of Commerce speech that an invitation to speak does not constitute an endorsement of what is said. I then cited leading American private universities that supported an open forum, told some other places where Ginsburg and Carmichael had spoken, and cited by name prominent trustees of those institutions who surely had to be deemed sensible and trustworthy. There was more. I ended by saying that we at Vanderbilt cannot "claim the satisfaction and rewards of a university and not fulfill the conditions and run the risks of being a university."

Mr. Stahlman then spoke at some length, highly critical of my position—which I chose to call the University's position—following which comments were offered by several trustees. In the weeks before the board met I had consulted in person or by phone almost all the members and felt secure that a strong majority understood and would uphold my position if a vote were necessary. None was necessary and eventually a trustee proposed moving to the next item on the agenda, which was done.

❧

On May 10, 1967, I spoke to the Executives' Club of Chicago in the Great Hall of the Pick Congress Hotel, largely under the aegis of Vanderbilt alumnus Wyatt Jacobs, class of 1929, who was first vice-president and presided at the meeting. It was a large gathering and everybody seemed to be a board chairman, president, vice-president, partner, judge, commissioner, or otherwise significant. After I spoke about the general state of higher education at some length, an extended question period followed.

Here are my comments about the importance of higher education and its condition in the South:

Under these circumstances, the social analyst—a political scientist or a journalist, for example—or the social activist—such as a politician or a reform group leader—oversimplifies if he asks merely: What is the decisive factor in the social situation? Or, what is the controlling element? It may be a proper question, however, to inquire where energy for change and improvement can most effectively be applied. To ask this question does not imply that there is only one point of significant leverage. It simply asks which is the most important one. I have concluded that higher education is the most important one in the United States, and I will offer you three quick observations to support this conclusion.

First. In a modern scientific, technological, industrial society it seems clear that in purely economic terms, in purely monetary terms, the best investment a community can make is an investment in education. Perhaps this is true of all kinds of society, ancient or modern. One of America's leading economists, Professor Theodore

W. Schultz of the University of Chicago, has done work leading to "the view that the principal cause of American productivity in the past lies in the large and continuous rate of investment in what? In education." I have also read the conclusion of two other economists, Frederick Harbison and Charles A. Myers, who found all around the world a high correlation between investments in education and a country's per capita gross national product.

Second. The quality of all education stems from the quality of higher education. The scope, character, and effectiveness of the elementary and secondary schools in the United States are derived directly from higher education. Not only are the teachers trained in the colleges and universities. Their techniques, standards, aspirations, and self-understanding are fashioned there more than anywhere else.

Third. As you in Chicago, especially, know well, the connections between colleges and universities and the daily life of the communities where they live are ever mounting. They are symbolized of course in the inexorable trend toward universal higher education. But they involve much more. Business, government, the arts, the professions, communities of all dimensions that seek to improve the lives of their citizens look more and more to the colleges and universities. They look to higher education for trained and productive personnel, for ideas, for new knowledge, for ways to apply old and new knowledge, for help in a million other forms. In America, we simply cannot arm for war, plan for peace, keep a prosperous economy, enhance esthetic appreciation, or go to the moon, without the sustained and carefully articulated efforts of the college and the university system.

We in the Southern states are especially sensitive to these facts because, viewing our region broadly, higher education across the South still lags in the quantity and in the quality of its development behind higher education in certain other sections of the nation, notably the Northeast, your Midwest, and the Far West.

Conflicts Begin, 1966–1967

We have been improving measurably, but we still have far to go. . . . In an area with about one-third the national population, embracing some sixteen states, the universities in those Southern states in 1950 produced not one-third of the Ph.D.'s in the nation but only about 9 percent of the nation's Ph.D.'s. By 1961, this percentage had risen to 14 and now in 1967 it is 17. But look how far we are behind.

Such statistics are quite useful in my part of the world as a spur to our efforts, and as a reminder that we require extraordinary jumps upward in higher education. They make us very sensitive to the fact, too, that higher education everywhere is in many ways a self-fulfilling process. While the natural factors at work often mean that educational effectiveness leads to further effectiveness, as strong institutions grow stronger, these factors also mean that where higher education labors under handicaps, in any place in the nation, those handicaps tend to persist and to nag tenaciously.

Wisdom, courage, and many kinds of commitment are needed to do what is needed for our colleges and universities in that section where I live and work. I say that in order to say also that wisdom, courage, and many kinds of commitment are needed everywhere in our country if we are to benefit in some full measure from the extraordinary national resources, and the extraordinary potential national resources, that these institutions constitute.

❧

The Faculty Assembly customarily met in Underwood Auditorium of the Law School. My fall presentation to it on September 14, 1967, addressed a wide array of matters including the implementation of the recommendation for a new University Senate, the receipt of $4,053,000 from the National Science Foundation for science development in the College of Arts and Science, one of $2,503,000 from the United States Public Health Service for science development in the Medical School, plans for the renovation of the former chemistry building, Furman Hall, the report of the important special committee on the University's several athletic programs—including intercollegiate football—chaired by Professor Ewing Shahan, processes and issues of student self-government, and much more, including issues of continuing importance.

Among the many matters on which I reported, however, was a new one. Since the arrival of our first black undergraduates in the fall of 1964, colleagues and I had attended closely their experiences. In the early years, when the numbers were small, I often held sessions in my office to which all black undergraduates were invited. In the spring of 1967 I had reluctantly concluded that assimilation into undergraduate campus life was proving more difficult for most black students than normal for most other students. The consequence of the lack of previous association on a basis of equality among black and white contemporaries hampered the assimilation of black students into the full range of educational and extracurricular activities. This led me to a decision that I reported to this meeting of the Faculty Assembly.

Last spring a number of our Negro undergraduates requested consultations in which they could express concerns. We held these consultations, in some of which I personally participated, and we have agreed on a procedure by which further discussions and actions can take place this fall.

I mention this to be sure you know that we are addressing ourselves explicitly to the needs of our Negro students. It seems to me that the principle on which we have been operating—that all Vanderbilt students shall be treated alike by Vanderbilt without regard to race or color—may have proved insufficient. We may be in the ironic position of needing to treat our Negro students differently in order to treat them equally—that is, in order to afford them a reasonable opportunity to gain a personal and educational experience equivalent in its general value to that we believe we afford to most other students.

I mention this subject also to remind you of the enormous importance that attaches to your own personal and pedagogical relationships with these students. From my own detailed discussions with certain of them, it is clear that you and I can by our own attitudes and conduct influence enormously the attitudes and conduct of these students in their highly special and difficult circumstances. I urge your careful and sympathetic consideration of their sensitivities and of their needs.

☙

University administrators are sometimes given a chance to speak about pedagogical substance. Such occurred at an occasion observing West Virginia University's hundredth Anniversary in Morgantown, on November 28, 1967. I spoke in Mountain Lair, the new student center, saying in part:

I would like to assert that six types of instruction should be sought through, and in addition to, the instruction intended to equip the student with the mathematical, verbal, and factual tools of a liberal education. These six types of instruction contribute, it seems to me, to developing in the student the qualities of mind that I have described as desirable.

(1) Comparative analysis over time is essential. History that seems to the student to be dead is poorly taught. Continuities of problems through changing forms, and changes in the substance of problems under different circumstances, can be etched clearly by comparative historical analysis.

(2) Comparative analysis across cultures, contemporary and historical, can do likewise. The comparative study of religion illumi-

nates vividly the richness and variety of human experience. It also reveals the limiting lens of a single cultural perspective in seeking to discern form and content and to keep fact separate from bias. . . .

(3) The study of logic—formal logic and scientific method— offers the impetuous personality a neutral, impersonal, corrective standard. It can enable the liberally educated individual to do more with what he has, to reduce unnecessary error derived from faulty inference.

(4) When differences in modes of thought are delineated, as may be achieved in philosophy, a powerful contribution to liberal education results. The fact that men have viewed themselves and their world, and the relationships among them, in radically differing ways can force on the student self-awareness, a self-consciousness about his own processes of problem-solving, hardly attainable otherwise.

(5) The liberally educated person needs to understand the contemporary, pragmatic social rationale for honor, honesty, accuracy, along with their origins as ethical standards.

(6) Experience in dialogue and intellectual confrontation, and recognition of their necessity in problem-solving, are essential to a liberal education. The capacity for confrontation and recognition of its role are necessary for optimum democratic decision-making in a group. They are also essential for optimum personal decision-making.

One of the early deans of the Harvard Business School, Wallace Donham, said:

> Businessmen do not undertake the hard intellectual job of securing a general grasp of these complex problems through prolonged exchange of varied viewpoints. Most men think their duty done when they listen to and discuss one-sided presentations of narrow controversial topics. The hard study of relations is not undertaken. Under such conditions it is no cause for wonder that leadership fails.

Conflicts Begin, 1966–1967

Another side of this capacity for intellectual confrontation was commented upon last June by Hedley Donovan, editor-in-chief of Time-Life publications. Addressing the New York University graduating class, Mr. Donovan spoke of the "ability to be wrong," and suggested that contemporary university graduates might well teach Americans how to be wrong. "All it takes is courage, honesty, self-respect, grace—and sometimes a sense of humor can help."

He spoke of the inevitability that some of us in our country will be shown by events to have been wrong about Vietnam. We shall all need each other again, he was saying, and when this conflict subsides, as surely it will, we will need to be able to take up again together our common work for our common country.

Mr. Donovan then went on to say that how to be right is something of an art, too, an art that makes it easier to turn to a new agenda, and observed that the ability to do these things is enhanced through liberal education.

❧

I have sometimes said that during the half dozen or so years from 1967 to 1973 I never relaxed once. Not technically true, of course, but I was constantly on the alert for local and national matters that someone might make relevant to Vanderbilt's welfare.

At some point during those years I met with a group of students—as I often did—this time about their desire to stimulate controversial awareness on the campus about a heated issue, the precise nature of which I have mercifully forgotten. What I remember clearly, however, is the chief spokesman, an intense graduate student with what I called liquid eyes, behind glasses with octagonal frames. From the dialogue, it was clear he would have been called "a Communist" by many persons in the circles I frequented. He kept wanting to know whether he and his friends could do various things, "without getting you fired." They did not want, he made clear, to get me fired, explicitly because they worried someone worse might replace me. I suppose I was grateful for his sentiment, but I said he should let me worry about that, by which I meant I would not be worrying about it. The poor fellow was killed that summer in a motor accident in the Soviet Union.

FOUR

Conflicts Mount
1968–1969

IN 1968, AS USUAL, FATE TOOK ME BEFORE diverse groups. On February 29 the event was a Lenten dinner at Christ Church, Nashville, sponsored by the Episcopal Development Corporation. Having grown up in another Christ Church, in Savannah, Georgia, where my parents and grandparents had been married, and where Jean's and my four children had been christened, I took the liberty of saying something early.

I have never thought that all educated people were the products of formal education. And I certainly have never thought that all individuals who survive the processes of formal education emerge as "educated" in any broad and meaningful sense of the term. These confessions of an educator perhaps give me license to say, in a similar vein, that I think it hazardous to assume that all truly practicing Christians are associated with organized churches, or to assume that everyone actively involved in an organized church is correspondingly loyal to the substantive precepts of his faith. . . .

Every now and then I hear someone urge a minister, or a prominent church layman, to "stick to religion" and not mix in other matters. Somewhat more often, I hear someone urge a faculty member or a student, or even a university administrator, to "stick to education" and not mix in other matters.

Speaking of the University

I suspect that a fair number of churchmen and educators would be pleased to stick to anything that would make their lives simpler. But I do not see how the teachings of Jesus, or teaching in the academy, can have significant meaning if disconnected from the world around. In a limited sense, of course, there are types of religious and educational activity that need not extend beyond the study. Understanding the liturgy of the church or the rules of grammar, for example, are largely private undertakings, but man cannot apply his precepts or his knowledge except to the world around him. . . .

In my judgment we have tonight in Nashville and elsewhere across the nation an overwhelmingly and transcendently significant community condition. This condition embraces the greatest danger and the greatest hope of any domestic situation in a century. This condition is the relations between white Americans and Negro Americans. It is not in my view a question of whether a church or a university chooses to be involved in this matter. All of us, willingly or not, all of us white and Negro, are inescapably involved. My voice to you says that the church and the academy ought to be involved—deliberately, consciously, imaginatively.

As I view the matter personally, there are four aspects of our crisis.

First, concepts of human dignity, concepts of human equality before God and the law, concepts of democratic government and self-determination are commonplaces of our time. Concepts of equal economic opportunity, of equal educational opportunity, of equal opportunity to advance and make one's own way are other commonplaces of our time. Nothing is more powerful than an idea, and nothing travels more quickly than a thrilling idea.

Moreover, as I read the history of peoples in older times, and observe what has occurred in our country and around the world in our time, I reach the conclusion that aspirations to personal freedom, to personal self-fulfillment in material and spiritual and psychological ways, are innate in the human breast.

Conflicts Mount, 1968–1969

A simple fact of the matter is that *so many persons of color have for so long been thwarted in these aspirations because of their color that an enormous steamhead of frustration has built up.*

That seems to me to be one aspect of the present condition.

A second aspect is more subtle and more important. I remember the reaction of one of my close friends after he entered the Army during World War II. He was a man of great diligence, very conscientious, and of great potential usefulness to the armed forces. He was embittered in his early days. "Why?" I asked him. Because of his treatment by the sergeant who ran roughshod over his feelings, his dignity, his personality. "I am an individual," my friend said to me. "I am a person." I am me, this white Californian was saying, a vital unit in the order of things and, the way we in this room look at the world, the essential unit in the order of things: the individual person.

As I look at race relations in the United States today, it seems clear to me that *a critical component of our present crisis is an ethical and psychological one. So much depends on attitude. So much depends on willingness to treat others as really equal.* So much depends on according to others the dignity that we expect for ourselves. So much depends on looking past the trappings of life and seeing the soul of the individual. So much depends on how things are done as well as on what is done.

The third aspect of our crisis concerns the fundamental structure of order in our society. *The rule of law is challenged. It is imperiled by those who offer brute force as a substitute. It is also imperiled by those who would ask the law to do more than the law can do.* No matter how dedicated and fair and efficient he may be in law enforcement, the policeman cannot remove the original causes of the riots he is sent to quell. When the rule of law is threatened, orderly government is threatened, safety of the person is threatened, freedom of thought and belief are threatened, all the material and spiritual values for which men of all colors have striven in America are threatened.

Finally, to me *the most frightening aspect of our critical condition is our failure to recognize it.* I sense among persons of good conscience and great influence a failure really to understand.

With the most sophisticated medical care in the world, the United States, I hear the Secretary of Health, Education and Welfare say, ranks thirteenth among nations in its infant mortality rate. Why? The enormous number of deaths of children under one year of age among the Negro poor is the chief reason.

One of our most constructive, temperate, and perceptive Negro leaders cites conditions of unemployment and restricted educational opportunity to help define the crisis. One-third of non-white young people between the ages of sixteen and nineteen in twenty of our metropolitan cities are unemployed. Only 11 percent of such white youths are unemployed.

The average Negro family income in the United States has been running at 55 percent of the average national family income in the United States. Low family income inevitably means limited educational opportunities for children in the family. Negroes constitute 11 percent of the American total population and 3 percent of the American college population.

In my view, the crisis of our current condition is so acute that no state and no community can with good sense practice a policy of business as usual. The national stress is as great as during the Great Depression or World War II. In historic periods of national crisis, the church and the academy have mobilized themselves to serve the needs of the country. I would make bold to say that the churches and universities, and perhaps especially in our community the Episcopal Church and Vanderbilt University, have special obligations to do so again today.

You may ask what needs to be done. We in America and in Nashville need to try with all our will to provide the full opportunities and rewards of our remarkable society to persons of color, to enhance the human dignity of all, and to create conditions that secure the rule of law. We need to pursue these goals relentlessly, with imagination, with innovation, with every means that offers hope. We need to act in a spirit that appreciates and affirms the dignity of all human beings—in a Christian spirit, if you will. This means that we must all commit ourselves to this problem, as we have in the past to many other community affairs, and, because it is our most urgent problem, it has the highest claim on our attention, our time, and our talents.

❧

Pepperdine College—now University—in Los Angeles in 1968 had a number of alumni of Vanderbilt's Divinity School on its faculty and staff, including its president, Norvel Young. I spoke at its commencement exercises on Pepperdine's Culver City campus on April 14. It was Easter Sunday, which I interpreted as a Christian assurance to mankind of God's love and mankind's hope. After reciting a long and lugubrious litany of the nation's woes, I continued:

Let no one feel fatigued.

It is as true as it is old to say that the test in life is not the problems but how we meet them. The ultimate joy and the greatest glory and the final meaning of the human experience are struggle and achievement—for most, struggle and achievement, in a noble common striving to which men can commit their faith, their honor, their learning, their courage, their strength, and if need be all the rest of the days of their lives.

And let no one feel dismayed.

Our country is revealing enormously vital reservoirs of civic ambition and social energy. In these present years I myself find among multitudes of our countrymen enhanced idealism, enlarged allegiance to objectives beyond one's self, intensified scrutiny of the assumptions and biases of our lives—in brief, an enlivened and serious and widespread preoccupation with the general welfare of the United States and its people. Forces are working among the old and the young, pouring forth into the lifestream of the nation, refreshing its temper and renewing its fervor.

And let no one feel frightened, either.

Thirty years from now, looking back, you will conclude that the 1960s were a great formative stage in American history. The permanent American Revolution has quickened in the last fifteen years, especially in the last five years. All of us have been part of it, and you who are being graduated today will have the good fortune to become more a part of it.

Revolutions, even including permanent revolutions that, like the American Revolution, are generally continuing and relatively bloodless, are ragged, dangerous affairs. The phase of the American Revolution through which we are now going is no exception. Ignorance, arrogance, prejudice, impetuousness, shortsightedness, stupidity, violence, and much more, among those who would advance the Revolution as among those who would obstruct it, threaten the Revolution, as indeed they have always threatened man's progress. But these human perversities are in some degrees inescapable in all our affairs. As we seek to control and diminish them, let them not blind our view. If we move to the fulfillment of America's promise of justice, opportunity, and a meaningful life for all, we need have no fear. We can welcome each dawn serenely with courage and hope.

Now, men and women of training and dedication and good will—as I call you graduates of Pepperdine College—cannot do the impossible. You know that and I know that. No sure destiny makes it inevitable that our nation will succeed, or even endure. I draw my sanguine judgments from the facts of the nation, from characteristics of the nation with which you will live and work. Four of these characteristics especially define America's possibilities.

The material productivity of the United States, let us note first, is exceptional. It is just because our productivity is indeed enormous, that the dissension over its distribution is intense. The fact of dissension, however, should not blur another fact. The inventiveness, flexibility, dynamism, and large scientific base of American competitive business and agriculture add to a national strength so great that many of us in our time have mistakenly come to take it for granted.

The adaptability and the capacity of our political system, let us note second, are formidable. I mean the procedures and institutions of our governments—of our formal and informal, of our visible and invisible governments. The resourcefulness displayed by those arrangements of power, in accommodating to the social and economic needs of Americans, has wrought, in the grand contours of the record, a remarkable American history. Our political system has failed us on occasion, or perhaps we could say we have failed it on occasion. But its continuity and frequency of effectiveness are unmatched in the history of self-government.

Let me ask you in passing not to underestimate the difficulty of governing the United States of America: over three and one-half million square miles occupied by over 200 million people. These people are joined together in hundreds of thousands of organizations and associations—public and private, formal and informal, large and small, legal and illegal, that demand of government and society more by way of opportunity and privilege and reward than ever sought before in the story of the earth. We expect our political system to accommodate, even to encourage, wide ranges of individual diversity, and simultaneously to assure basic community unity. We expect it to guarantee freedom of expression in most of its forms, and to uphold freedom of action in many of its forms, and at the same time to promote community consensus broad and deep enough to support tough decisions and delicately balanced compromises about infinitely complex and diverse matters of intimate concern to powerful segments of citizenry. We expect the system to insure primacy for majority opinion along with primacy for minority rights. We ask it both to maintain order and to enforce many precise restraints on those whose task it is to do so. In its aspiration to satisfy simultaneously so many human values, the American system of government is the most ambitious undertaking in social organization in the world's history. It is, so far, also the most successful.

The American dream, moreover, I remind you as a third fact of our nation, is largely intact. It is ironical, but the bitter struggles of these years through which we are now living give testimony to this fact of our nation. Striving to fulfill the American dream is what has caused the bitterest frictions in our society, in our history. The successes of the permanent American Revolution accelerate expectations. Expectations, in turn, breed frustrations which the Revolution seeks to overcome. Seldom ever will the timing be in perfect phase. The animating ideas of the Declaration of Independence and the American Constitution and the Gettysburg Address are deeply woven into the fabric of our aspirations. Pragmatism, the capacity to achieve consensus, and the ability to give as well as to take are also intimate parts of the system of values that make it possible for a government of people to be democratic and effective and enduring. One cannot create this matrix of popular government overnight; some have never been able to create it at all.

I am sanguine this afternoon, however, most of all because of a fourth fact of our nation, and that fact is you. I do not know you personally, but I do know many Vanderbilt students, and recent students, and some others elsewhere, and I will sum them up and sum you up by saying you are worthy of your nation's heritage and of your nation's hopes.

The test of the future will not be how long or how short one's hair is cut, but how well we solve our common problems working together. How well we solve our common problems working together will depend in crucial measure on how educated persons behave and especially on the qualities they bring to their civic concerns.

We who are gathered here this afternoon, and others like us across the land, have much to do together to make America's dreams come true. The majesty of the challenge inspires the spirit. No generation ever embarked on a more exhilarating adventure than we have ahead, nor with more precious prizes at stake. The demands on each of us are formidable in this great crusade—for crusade it must be—if we would bring work and schooling and homes and health and justice and peace and hope to all who lack them in our land.

※

Vanderbilt's Board of Trust meetings were long held in private, but beginning in the 1960s, as social tensions and student and faculty activism increased, the trustees made adjustments toward two goals: improving their own understanding of the evolving environment and removing the mystery about the conduct of trustee business. That mystery was thought to create suspicion and therefore lack of confidence in the University's governance. Among the steps taken, faculty and student observers were invited to sit in Board meetings, representatives of both groups were invited to make presentations, a category of young alumnus trustee was created (one member of the graduating class elected each year, after an advisory student poll, to serve a four-year term), and press briefings (to which campus journalists were welcomed) following board meetings were regularly scheduled. Discussions of personnel matters were held in executive session.

On May 17, 1968, in the Rand Room of Rand Hall, I pointed out to the Board that universities had always been affected internally by external national events—the Civil War, the flu epidemic during the Great War, the Great Depression, World War II, and the G. I. Bill of Rights, among many examples. I said I felt it necessary to address the Board on the impact of the changing national environment on American universities, including "private" universities. In the light of the intensified social activism throughout American society, sometimes resulting in violence, I felt I should speak to our trustees about its effects on Vanderbilt, and on how Vanderbilt should conduct itself under the changed conditions.

It may have been in this meeting that I also emphasized to our trustees the changing mores in which young people were growing up. I had not found much time in those years to go to movies popular among our students or to listen to the Rolling Stones and other entertainment favorites. I therefore had embarked on a personal program of self-education, looking and listening, and recommended the process as a useful avenue to a better understanding of the young for antiques like myself. I then spoke about one crucial dimension of the contemporary environment.

The present crisis in human relations involves (1) the obstructions to a racially harmonious society, (2) the aspirations of nonwhite citizens for full partnership in the society, (3) and the menace of disorder posed by the clash of obstructions and aspirations.

The sharp point of the crisis is the fact of deprivation, or the sense of deprivation, on the part of many Negro Americans.

I want to tell you how I feel the present national environment will affect Vanderbilt and what I feel we should do in the light of the condition. The present national environment includes many influences on our institutions of higher education. Issues deriving from the fighting in Vietnam, from the unfavorable balance of payments, from federal budgetary stringencies all have their effects. The crisis of the biracial society, however, is the pervasive and critical and more lasting one.

We live in a nation in which the aspirations of Negroes are increasingly expressed and supported. And we at Vanderbilt live in a metropolitan area whose population is 20 percent black.

I believe the only viable course for Vanderbilt is to be emphatically, officially, and visibly a contributor to the solutions of the nation's and the community's difficulties.

Let me illustrate the kind of thing I mean by citing some on-campus actions that Vanderbilt has already taken.

Most important of all, in May of 1962 the Board of Trust completed the process of opening all schools of the University to applicants without regard to race or color.

Sometime after that action, the Vanderbilt Admissions Office began recruiting in predominantly Negro high schools as well as in predominantly white high schools. We now have approximately forty undergraduate and thirty-five graduate students who are Negroes.

Special scholarship funds for financially disadvantaged graduates of Southern high schools were subsequently obtained, approximately 70 percent of the recipients being Negroes. . . .

Vanderbilt Hospital has been totally desegregated.

Vanderbilt employment practices are no longer racially discriminatory. Negro applicants for positions have been actively sought. . . . In policy, all categories of employment within the University have been desegregated. For example, last year Vanderbilt employed twenty-six Negro clerical personnel; this year forty-six are employed. Last year we had 188 Negro technicians and this year 212. Our Personnel Office has a grant from the United States Department of Labor which will enable us to upgrade twenty present, semiliterate employees to eighth-grade reading, writing, and computation skills. In practice, Negroes have been increasingly placed in supervisory and other positions previously closed to them. Vanderbilt has one of the highest proportions of employees who are Negro of any major employer in Nashville. Present employees include one or more key-punch operators, laboratory technicians, stenographers, clerk-typists, cafeteria cashiers, housekeeping supervisors, and registered nurses, including one head nurse. We are an "Equal Opportunity Employer," and I shall recommend to the Executive Committee of the Board of Trust next month that we subscribe to Project Equality. And be it said that we have kept hourly wages ahead of the minimum-wage escalator.

The first Negro faculty member was appointed July 1, 1964. We presently have four Negroes on the faculty. . . .

Dr. James Carter, assistant professor of biochemistry and a specialist in pediatric malnutrition, has just been given a Milbank Award valued at $40,000 to be spent over a five-year period. We believe he is the first Negro so recognized.

Careful and deliberate instructional programs have been carried out with numerous categories of University employees, including the security force, to inform them of the special problems that can arise involving racial attitudes.

Much similar counselling has been done by the Dean of Men and the Dean of Women and their staffs with individual students and with student groups.

A Human Relations Council consisting of five faculty members and seven administrative officers, on which I myself sit, was organized last fall and has been meeting with representatives of the Afro-American Club. We seek to know all the concerns of these students, and to let none of them go ignored. We contemplate two meetings during the coming summer and regularly scheduled monthly meetings during the coming academic year.

The faculty of the College of Arts and Science has formed a Race Relations Committee of five members to receive requests and advice from Negro undergraduates in the college concerning college academic matters.

Conflicts Mount, 1968–1969

We try to show an understanding attitude. At the time of the death of Martin Luther King, Vanderbilt followed the lead of Metropolitan Nashville and, as requested by a number of white students, lowered the American flag to half-mast for a period of time. I myself attended a memorial service for Dr. King led by members of the Afro-American Club on the terrace of Rand Hall and also attended a community-wide ecumenical memorial service at St. Mary's Catholic Church on Fifth Avenue, downtown. In response to student and faculty requests, classes were dismissed for two hours the day of the funeral.

In due course, the faculty of the Divinity School will be asking that certain funds it and Divinity School students have collected be contributed to the $55 Million Campaign and used to finance a scholarship in the Divinity School in memory of Dr. King. When such a request comes, I will commend it to the Executive Committee of the Board of Trust.

By listing these illustrations, I do not mean to suggest that these are all the on-campus actions taken by Vanderbilt relevant to the present national environment. Individual faculty members, students, and others have done much in addition in a similar mood.

In the larger community of Nashville and nearby, Vanderbilt has a long history of participation in community enterprises. Our role in the current cultural affairs interest of the Chamber of Commerce and in the Nashville Plus program, and our determination to initiate a Graduate School of Business to meet clear local and regional needs, illustrate this involvement. Vanderbilt has in recent years also engaged in a number of undertakings related to the subject we have been discussing. Here are some examples.

Four years ago we joined with Peabody, Fisk and the public school system to establish the Nashville Education Improvement Project. This was a forerunner project—financed in Nashville by a grant from the Ford Foundation of more than $3 million extending over five years. It was followed by five other similar Education Improvement Projects subsequently developed in Durham, Atlanta,

Huntsville, New Orleans, and Houston. This project is designed to develop and test teaching materials, techniques, and equipment for instruction of culturally deprived children from pre-school instruction through grade six. Special alphabets, language laboratories, teacher training programs, and other aspects of the effort have been warmly received by public school personnel and will have a clear, lasting impact within the Nashville school system.

The Vanderbilt-Meharry Cooperative Medical Program formalizes and encourages working cooperative relationships between the two medical schools of long standing.

Fisk and Vanderbilt have joined for three years in sponsoring seminars in practical politics for high school teachers of social science, under the sponsorship and financing of the Robert A. Taft Institute of Government.

A faculty member in sociology has held a joint appointment at Vanderbilt and Fisk during the past year, and in recent years other such appointments have been made.

The Vanderbilt Engineering School is engaged in giving broad program assistance to the Engineering School at Tennessee State University in faculty development and curriculum development, with special attention to the improvement of the graduate program. This work is being done under grants from the American Society of Engineering Education and from the United States Office of Education, under Title III of the Higher Education Act.

Next year two appointments in biomedical engineering will be made in cooperation with Meharry.

Under the leadership of Leonard Beach, dean for institutional relations, conversations have been held by Vanderbilt with a number of institutions, some of them predominantly Negro, looking toward increased interchange of faculty and students among the institutions of Nashville, and more effective sharing of library and other resources.

The Vanderbilt chapters of Phi Beta Kappa and Mortar Board

have helped Fisk work toward establishment of corresponding chapters on its campus.

Vanderbilt has a contractual relationship with Alabama Agricultural and Mechanical College in Huntsville to assist it in general institutional development. Delegations of administrators, faculty members, and students from that college to our campus, and vice versa, have made visits during the past year. . . .

Vanderbilt has a grant of $200,000 from the Danforth Foundation to enable it to find and accept and give special training to Negro applicants to its Graduate School. . . .

Vanderbilt was a charter participant in Project Opportunity, under the aegis of the Southern Association of Colleges and Schools, by which special academic encouragement is given to promising junior and senior high school students in predominantly Negro schools.

Vanderbilt was a leading participant in the Council of Southern Universities in its efforts to establish through the Southern Fellowships Fund programs to improve the quality of staff and faculty in institutions presently attended predominantly by Negro students. I myself negotiated the $5 million grant from the Danforth Foundation to fund the initial phase of the effort.

In these and other activities, Vanderbilt has taken a part in community efforts to help solve at the local level the kinds of problems that add up to the national crisis.

The character of the national environment, of the intense national crisis that surrounds Vanderbilt, requires us, however, to do more than we have been doing. I have in mind four types of things.

First, on the campus, we need to give even more attention to the fact that we are preparing white and black students to live in a quite different society in the decades ahead from that which we in this room grew up to know. The black students require great attention. In recruitment, in special arrangements made for them on campus, in willingness to understand their problems, in assisting white students to accept them as equals, in providing the time-consuming communication and consultation required, and in many other ways that recognize the unique condition of these students, we must seek to make Vanderbilt an educationally effective place for them and for our white students.

In our employment practices at all levels—administrative officers, faculty, technical and clerical positions, and elsewhere—Vanderbilt will need to give equal opportunity on all occasions and special opportunity on some occasions to Negroes.

Second, in the community of higher education in Nashville, in central Tennessee, in the South, in the nation, Vanderbilt will need to make special efforts in its relationships with predominantly Negro institutions. These are extremely difficult times—and in my judgment more difficult times are ahead—for cooperation between predominantly white and predominantly Negro institutions. Many elements on predominantly Negro campuses view with great skepticism associations with white individuals and white institutions. Nonetheless, we must, in my judgment, do all we can to strengthen the important educational resources represented by these institutions.

Third, Vanderbilt will need to take part in many community activities directed at curing the social and economic ills of Nashville's Negro population. We are joined with the Chamber of Commerce in the Nashville Plus program—incidentally under the general chairmanship of David Steine, a professor in our Department of Economics and Business Administration as well as a businessman—and in other activities designed to improve the total life of Nashville. There will be other activities in which mature and concerned Negro citizens will need all the support they can muster for legitimate community objectives. These legitimate community objectives will not always be familiar to us, but I am convinced that where the university can help—in education, in health, in social adjustment, in economic development, and otherwise—it must.

Finally, Vanderbilt, most of all, must by its general stance and public appearance stand for the open society. I myself—who am more often thought of as your chancellor than as a private citizen—must continue to express my conviction that the crisis we face is a crisis for us all. Vanderbilt must accept the opportunity that lies before it to help solve the most important set of problems facing the nation. We must dedicate time, talent, imagination, and energy to these problems on and off the campus. If we and enough others do likewise, we may live through the present storm and have a great university, and life can be richer for us all.

❧

Beginning in the late 1960s, some Vanderbilt students sometimes displayed behavior that disquieted, or outraged, persons off the campus, and some on. On balance, they were not as disruptive or violent as some who engaged in highly publicized obstructions and occupations of buildings at other colleges and universities, although some Nashvillians seemed to think so. Most people, including university people, like for their institution and themselves to be liked—especially when recruiting students, faculty, and donations. As much as possible, I avoided fanning the flames of controversy. I did not rush daily into print, and publicly and privately I explained that periodic controversy is inherent in the life of a vital university. But on some occasions I felt it necessary to speak out. Such an occasion was the Annual Alumni Luncheon in Rand Hall on June 8, 1968.

Disruptive occurrences on some campuses across the United States have spurred thoughts among alumni of all institutions about how their own colleges and universities are governed. I sense a growing apprehension among former students that the difficulties of one could become the difficulties of all.

Speaking of the University

I therefore want to say something to you, brief though it must be, about the governance of your university. In recent years my colleagues and I have spent much time on this subject, and I want to give you something of our general philosophy, and a few of its concrete implications.

If you read Professor Edwin Mims's *History of Vanderbilt University,* you will find that the internal governance of Vanderbilt has been a matter of continuing attention from the beginning. You cannot read that history, especially chapter 8 of Part I, "Student Life in the Early Years," or chapter 6 of Part II, "College Life in the Nineties and Beyond," without concluding that our students of today display extraordinarily good manners and good behavior, and that the campus of 1968 enjoys a calmness and equanimity often lacking in years before.

Every now and then someone says that our present-day students are too assertive, are not sufficiently respectful of authority. I cannot help recalling that fraternities, dormitories, certain student publications, and other features of our campus life that we now accept as normal were in the early years adamantly prohibited by the University and its stern Victorian governors. In each instance, aggressive student pressures, including highly critical vocal demands and often explicit violation of regulations that had been proclaimed by faculty, trustees, and chancellor, brought the changes in the rules.

Nor was decorum always model. One year student violence on the campus required Dean Tillett, then the vice-chancellor, to telegraph Chancellor Kirkland that the University was in a state of rebellion and to come home at once. Students rioted after an intercollegiate football game in 1896 and the trustees very nearly abolished the sport. I will refrain from reciting others of Professor Mims's illustrations. Doubtless some of you could ornament the record with recollections of your own.

The main point is simply that from its beginning Vanderbilt has been altering and adjusting its ways of doing things, including its system of internal governance, in order to create a harmonious and productive educational community.

The word community is important here. A university is not a government bureau, nor a military regiment, nor a bank, nor a corporation, nor any kind of authoritarian pyramid in which the peak rules the base. The best universities never have been. A university is a society that is in many crucial aspects self-governing. Ultimate, formal, legal authority may rest in a board of trustees, but that board through custom and affirmative action disperses effective governing power to many places throughout the institution. That is the way universities are run, and run best.

I want to mention four matters that are in my view of decisive importance in maintaining and enhancing a harmonious and productive educational community at Vanderbilt.

Effective participation by members of the university community in university decision-making—accompanied by adequate internal communications—is a first requisite. In a university, as is true more broadly in a democratic society, if those with a stake in the decisions have an appropriate part in making the decisions, the decisions will be better, and better respected.

The most important continuing component of a university is the faculty. A university is lost without faculties that are themselves main sources of initiative, innovation, and energy.

This past year we put in motion a new system of faculty government at Vanderbilt. During a period of two years, it was formulated by the faculty and approved by the trustees. Its details are not important for our present purposes, but the fact that it provides new and improved ways for faculty to know authoritatively about the University's affairs, to contribute to important policy, and to take part in making certain precisely defined kinds of decisions, is enormously important to the strength of our internal community and to the spirit of mutual confidence that we hope will pervade it.

We seek to enjoy a spirit of mutual confidence with our students, too. Let me mention three particular things, among others, we try to do.

We do all we can to keep the lines of communications open. I spread the word that any student can come to see me at any time— and some do—and that I will receive him at the earliest possible moment—and I do. I accept all invitations to gatherings in fraternities, sororities, dormitories, and other student places except where a physical conflict prevents. My colleagues do much more of this than I. We believe students should have access to anyone they wish upon the campus.

We believe, also, in student self-government. Student self-government has many assets to commend it, including its capacity to help develop independence and self-reliance in the student himself. A separate major asset of student self-government, however, lies in the fact that many problems can best be solved, or only be solved, by students themselves.

The record shows that in 1911 moral conditions on the campus had become lax to an unusual degree. Professor Mims declares in his history that Chancellor Kirkland and the faculty appeared helpless to control the situation. A committee of students was appointed—appointed, incidentally, by a student who later became and still remains a member of our Board of Trust—"to investigate moral conditions in the University and devise some plan for a wholesome student control of the same." The committee of students created a system of student self-government that is still the basis for our system today.

No student complaint is too trivial (or too abruptly put) for serious treatment. And I always try to ask the student to propose a remedy to defects he perceives.

We also invite student participation in certain formal councils of the University. We have been doing more of this of late and will do more of it in the future. Students now sit on the Student Affairs Committee, along with staff, deans, and faculty members. They sit on the new Athletic Committee, along with faculty, alumni, and trustees. Student representatives have formal ways of meeting with committees of the faculty about curriculum and other academic matters. Within several departments, and within all the schools, opportunities are open to students to make suggestions or to help make the rules.

We try to be a community working together, not for any reason except that this is the best way for this particular kind of community to work.

Now a *second* matter, closely related. *Procedures and policies governing student behavior have been undergoing change almost everywhere these last few years.* The rules of conduct at Vanderbilt are reviewed (and usually changed) at least once annually. During recent months an extensive reexamination of the regulation of student conduct has been under way with students themselves taking vigorous part. When the new regulations are proclaimed they will be a product of extensive and appropriate student participation as well as of participation by faculty and administrative officers.

When I speak to student groups—and this seems to me, and perhaps to some of them, to be often—I emphasize the obligations and necessities of educated people in their own self-government. In welcoming new students in September, at the convocation during Parents Weekend, in addressing the women of the University, and on similar occasions, I do all I can to encourage integrity, self-reliance, concern for consequences, and mature recognition that it takes a lot of thought and work and wit to make the world run right.

The successful governance of institutions, of any kind of institution including universities, requires more than rules and regulations and procedures for the type of participation in its affairs appropriate to its members.

Sense of purpose and sense of satisfaction with the common enterprise, are as important to the government of a university as to the government of a nation. Corporate managers long ago found them to be important to the efficiency and profit of their business organizations. This is the *third* matter I want to speak about.

My colleagues and I have concentrated much attention on developing a stimulating campus intellectual life. Nothing so summarizes for faculty or students the vigor and quality of a university as the tone and adventure of campus intellectual life. If thoughts come fast and ideas excite and the air is charged with challenge—in a climate of free and tolerant debate—then we of the inner campus community feel the University is doing much of what it should be doing. We, therefore, at Vanderbilt have tried to satisfy the hunger felt by young and old for an interesting and invigorating intellectual and cultural climate.

The Faculty Lecture Series, the Vanderbilt Forum, the student Arts Alliance, the Impact program, Parents Weekend, the chamber music series sponsored by the College of Arts and Science, ad hoc events like the Mock National Convention held in 1964, the literary magazine *Spectrum,* vigorous student publications, student participation in off-campus civic activities, student visitations in faculty homes, encouragement and recognition in several explicit ways of effective undergraduate teaching, and many other undertakings on student, faculty, and staff initiative have been pointed toward encouraging a stimulating and satisfying campus atmosphere.

A *fourth* matter in these years in which we now live is crucial to the goal of a productive educational climate. . . . *All universities live in a very special contemporary national environment that affects directly and immediately the sense of purpose and satisfaction of students and faculty.* This very special contemporary national environment also affects directly and immediately the university's obligations to the society that in the largest sense it is sustained to serve. . . .

American colleges and universities have usually wanted to keep themselves apart from the rest of the community. . . . Nonetheless, many occasions in our history have reminded colleges and universities that they are very much affected by what goes on in the society around them. . . .

I then emphasized again, and at some length, as I had in earlier speeches to other groups, that the conditions we faced embraced obstructions to a racially harmonious society, that, nonetheless, the aspirations of black citizens for full partnership in that society persisted, and that the resulting dangers of frustration and disorder posed by the clash of obstructions and aspirations placed before Vanderbilt significant opportunities as well as obligations.

&

On December 6, 1968, I gave the ninth Daniel Coit Gilman Lecture at the dedication of the Thomas R. Turner Auditorium Building of the Johns Hopkins University School of Medicine in Baltimore. In addition to an important historical relationship between the Hopkins and Vanderbilt medical schools, Dr. David E. Rogers had recently moved from the chairmanship of the Department of Medicine at Vanderbilt to become at Hopkins dean of the medical faculty and medical director of the Johns Hopkins Hospital. Another Vanderbilt colleague, Dr. Robert Heyssel, had also recently moved to Hopkins. (He would later become president and chief executive officer of the Johns Hopkins Hospital and Health Systems.) I spoke under the title "The Modern Paradoxes of the University," saying in part:

I propose to examine certain selected paradoxes that characterize four major aspects of contemporary universities: their missions, their support, their governance, their students. If paradoxes can be eliminated, more effective and efficient institutions become possible. If they cannot be eliminated, but are explicitly identified, some existing frustrations and frictions can be spared.

The missions of a university. One thing is sure. Institutions of higher education are engaged in a lot more than higher education.

The modern university is at once both the creature and creator of the society that supports it. That is its basic inner contradiction, or the root of its glory, or both, depending on your point of view. Life would be simpler if the university were merely a service facility, registering society's needs and responding to them, like a manufacturer who makes the products, and only the products, he is able to sell. Life would be simpler, also, if those who make up the university were literally independent, pursuing their own interests, and to the extent that they influenced the external world at all, doing so incidentally, or at least by their own choice. . . .

A central paradox of most higher education is that it is concerned with many things other than higher education. Let us look at one of them.

Teaching, research, and the application of knowledge are the three traditional university functions, eternally cited on occasions like this one. The fact of the matter, of course, is that for many decades almost all universities have performed another function of enormous internal and external importance: public entertainment.

Universities entertain the public in various ways, but their overwhelmingly important contribution to the entertainment of the nation is intercollegiate spectator sports. (I introduce this topic at Hopkins knowing full well that you have not met this particular university responsibility as enthusiastically as you have some others.)

About twenty years ago the Alabama legislature by formal action requested that the University of Alabama and the Alabama Polytechnic Institute (now Auburn University) resume the traditional athletic rivalry that they had by institutional decision suspended some years previously. The resolution said that in the opinion of the majority of the members of the Alabama legislature it was to the best interest of the two schools and of the people of Alabama that such athletic relations be resumed. The request took the form of a House Joint Resolution and fixed a deadline for compliance. I was living in Alabama at the time and the notion was about that institutional appropriations depended on a proper response. Similar commands to competition, though perhaps less formally and less visibly expressed, pervade the governance of virtually every public university and most private universities across the country.

The nature of the paradox is often obscured by those who feel compelled to reconcile the demand for spectator sports with other university objectives. I prefer the booster club president who just says he wants to win, to the faculty member who tries somehow to make a good gridiron show part of the educational mission of the institution.

The effectively enforced demand for public entertainment is only one facet of a deep conflict in the expectations of American universities. Mr. Robert Hutchins has in recent years heavily emphasized the contrast between the intellectual, inquiring, thought-provoking, objective, criticizing functions of the academy, and the "service station" activities undertaken by most universities, presumably especially the state institutions, presumably not excluding the medical schools. The roles of objective investigator, of detached critic, of speculative thinker, of teacher who develops those intellectual capacities in students, are one thing. The roles of subsidized industrial consultant, of problem-oriented researcher, of teacher equipping students with attitudes and skills to make them effective in a highly structured profession like law, social work, or medicine, may be another. The roles may not always be incompatible, but they are different, and they often are in competition and sometimes are in conflict.

Urban universities like Hopkins and Vanderbilt and Columbia have poignant knowledge of the lack of coincidence between Mr.

Hutchins's ideal functions of the academy and the functions imposed by the pragmatic world that surrounds urban universities. The "obligations" an urban university comes to feel toward its "neighborhood" result from the facts of urban life, and not from the original purposes of the institution. The obligations of universities have always been subject to shift. . . .

The support of universities. The multiplicity of divergent activities of the contemporary university assures it of divergent, and frequently antithetical, constituents. No collection of activities functionally so diverse and financially so expensive can prosper in our society without deeply rooted and widespread external popular support.

The university's inherent need for autonomy, for independence of the sources of support on which it is dependent, creates the paradox of its support. It must make all its constituents feel they belong to the university without also making them feel they own it. It must get them to give to the university what the university wants to get, and in return give to them only what the university wants to give. A university must extract financial support from a wide variety of constituencies that hold competitive or contradictory ambitions.

The context in which this support must be found has certain inconvenient features.

First, some university constituents like to vote with their money just as do some contributors to political parties and candidates. A certain proportion is always threatening to withdraw its financial support if "the university" does not do or stop doing something or another. Others vote with their money by earmarking donations for specific purposes they favor. The university can easily become a means to someone else's ends.

A strong and alert institution will be willing with impunity to bite the hand that would feed it, to turn aside support for ends that it cannot properly claim or make its own.

Also, attitudes among a university's external constituencies are curiously ambivalent. On the one hand, the institution is revered, its degrees prized, and the talents of its faculties are sought, and bought, by outsiders. Its scientific research and resulting technological innovations are applauded. Simultaneously, the conditions of freedom required for the university's greatest effectiveness are assaulted, sometimes by the very interests that benefit most from its well working. Freedom for scientific inquiry and thought—the greatest source of revolution in society—almost everywhere goes unquestioned from without; freedom for social inquiry and thought, to help society in evolutionary ways accommodate to the revolutionary consequences of the laboratory, almost everywhere is challenged from without. . . .

It is no wonder that faculties, deans, directors of development, presidents, and trustees must be on guard to remember that they raise money in order to run the university, not run the university in order to raise money.

University governance. The central paradoxes of university governance are that the trustees who have the legal authority don't have actual control, the president who has formal control doesn't have commensurate power, and the faculties (and sometimes students) who have most of the power leave things undone. Given the size, complexity, cost and national importance of universities, the resulting inadequacies will not be ignored.

These structural characteristics of the university are accompanied by anomalies of university leadership readily apparent to deans and presidents and which, for that reason, I may be excused for mentioning on this occasion.

Presidents, and especially deans, are witness to a curious organizational phenomenon embodied in the behavior of their faculties. Faculties are expert at working change in their own scholarly disciplines; many display extraordinary originality and flexibility in their own professional work. Taken together, faculties are the greatest authors of change in our highly dynamic society—directly through their own innovations and through the skills and spirit of innovation they generate in others. In the face of this, faculties become mystifyingly lethargic when it comes to changing their own institutions, the universities. They are the ones largely responsible for making universities, in many of their internal operations, the least innovative institutions (unless the monasteries are included) in our society.

University and school chief executive officers enjoy the paradoxical experience of periodic changes in their own job descriptions, through no cause of their own or of those who engaged them for the great adventure. I do not jest when I ask how many university presidents now in office were chosen for their aptitude for collective bargaining, for their tactical skills in adversary social action, for their experience with the theory and practice of urban guerrilla warfare. The job has changed and perhaps it is no wonder that many who have held it also have changed.

Presidents are alternately amused and dismayed to be held fully accountable for everything taking place in their institutions, knowing the real range of their actual control. They accept the honor of the thing, however, and diligently take recourse to persuasion, friendship, skill, showmanship, and other resources of improvisation, to become "interpreters" of other people's actions, in defense of their own record, which was often not of their own making in the first place.

What this third set of paradoxes means, following the first two, is that we have an institution of contradictory and unsteady purposes, dependent on multiple and fickle sources of support, governed by a system in which authority and responsibility often do not meet.

The students. Students are a very mixed bag, and anything said of one may not be true of another. The more audible student attitudes and more visible student behavior of recent years, however, are deeply penetrated with paradoxes. And through the paradoxes runs a deeper contradiction of root importance to the university and to the country. Some samples, first, of surface anomalies.

Conflicts Mount, 1968–1969

In urgent tones, a student ridicules the concept of *in loco parentis*, on the notion that university regulation of the girls' dormitories stunts personality development and unjustifiably hampers personal freedom. "Our personal lives are not your concern." The student, perhaps the same one, then pleads that the university has an obligation, in the name of intellectual freedom as one of them said to me, to protect students against the requirements of the Selective Service system.

A student clamors for admission to the university and then turns up styling himself enslaved by the university's rules.

Students condemn as authoritarian an institution that affords them the most extraordinary freedom of action and belief and that refrains voluntarily, out of allegiance to its own values, from bringing its powerful and undoubted sanctions to bear against them.

None of these anomalies, nor others that might be cited, make wise the blind and unbending reaction that sometimes has come from critics of recent campus conduct. There is, in fact, a great irony in the outcry on some campuses against student influence in the affairs of the university. Many an accepted feature of many a modern campus came into being, in years now past, as a direct result of student initiative or protest, including such respectable campus fixtures as fraternities, student publications, dormitories, dining halls, athletics, and most interestingly of all, central college libraries. There is, nonetheless, a basic paradox in one strain of contemporary student activism that merits grave attention.

Some recent campus behavior has been deeply sincere as well as highly energized, characterized by laudable social concern for one's fellow men, a remarkable decline of bias, and mature practical idealism.

At the same time, some recent campus behavior has been deeply anti-intellectual, even to the extent of becoming neo-Fascist. Anti-intellectuals have interfered with the rights of students to hear— the Secretary of State, for example—and to talk to employment representatives of American government and industry, for example.

They have frequently disregarded fact, perspective, logic, and consequences, in favor of ignorance, self-righteousness, fantasy, and force.

The paradox is especially appalling inside an institution dedicated to developing man's unique and priceless tool, the human mind.

The qualities of university life I have mentioned do not tell all there is to tell about universities. You will be comforted to know that I do not plan to tell all this afternoon. The characteristics exposed do suggest that we have much to do inside our universities.

We need to admit our functions, recognizing without apology that universities have always been inescapably and pragmatically responsive to the surrounding society. American universities have been brought to their present eminence by a society that cherishes their utility. If we do not organize ourselves to do what clearly we have to do, others will organize our universities for us.

During 1968 and 1969—and before and later—many persons were deeply perplexed by protests and demands advanced, often petulantly, by young people, usually students. The question, at bottom, was Why are they doing these outrageous things? The 1969 Convention of the Tennessee Congress of Parents and Teachers met in Nashville, holding sessions in the Mediterranean Room of the Sheraton Motor Inn. The theme of the meeting read: "Now is the time to give vitality to the moral and ethical values of American democracy." Asked to speak on April 23, I said in part:

The program for this convention reveals your concern for this theme. You are pondering among others the problems of children in trouble before the courts, children emotionally disturbed, comprehensive health care, schooling in low income areas, the choice of national goals, the choice of national means. All these concerns reflect our system of values.

We who work with young people and their education have had a new kind of concern these past few years. News of disturbances on American campuses jars us daily. I even saw the other day that students in a sixth grade were protesting the change in status of a teacher.

Inevitably one wonders what is happening to the young. I find it useful—as well as fashionable and comfortable—to remind ourselves that the young have often perplexed the old. I remember one summer day forty years ago overhearing a lengthy conversation among ancient relatives deploring the evils into which youth had fallen—bootleg booze, cigarettes, fast cars, rumble seats, lipstick, and dresses cut low in the back. My father produced a newspaper editorial reflecting very much the mood expressed in that conversation. It had been written exactly one hundred years before.

Remember the famous quotation: "What is happening to our young people? They disrespect their elders, they disobey their parents. They ignore the laws. They riot in the streets inflamed with wild notions. Their morals are decaying. What is to become of them?" Thus wrote Plato twenty-three hundred years ago.

Remember, then, that a conflict of generations is not unique to the United States, nor to the 1960s. Lewis Feuer, a professor of sociology at the University of Toronto, has recently written on the conflict of generations, demonstrating that massive student protest is a recurrent phenomenon of modern times. He points out that "social revolutions in Russia, China, and Burma sprang from student movements, while governments in Korea, Japan, and the Sudan have fallen in recent years largely because of massive student protest." In a detailed analysis he concludes that the conflict of generations is a universal theme in history, and that generational consciousness has become especially pronounced since early in the last century after the political reaction following the French Revolution.

Speaking of the University

I invite your attention to four of the common characteristics displayed by youthful protest movements in different countries in different decades.

First, said Professor Feuer, "the conflict of generations derives from deep, unconscious sources, and the outlook and philosophy of student movements are rarely materialistic." Rather, they are "moved by an emotional rebellion in which there is always present a disillusionment with and rejection of the values of the older generation." "Adolescence," another writer has said, "is the true day for revolt, the day when obscure forces, as mysterious as growth, push us, trembling, out of our narrow lives into the wide throbbing life beyond self." In other words, do not make your acceptance of the reality of youthful protest wait for your rational understanding of its origins, of the reasons it has come about.

Second, the psychological origins of student movements assure those movements of an inescapable degree of irrationality. Their sources in feeling and emotion have guaranteed in one youth movement after another over the past century and a half that the urge for psychological gratification often prevails over the rational course of seeking proclaimed objectives by the swiftest and most pragmatic route possible. Creating a fuss is often more exciting than achieving a goal.

Third, a student movement will normally not arise unless there is a sense among the young that the older generation has discredited itself and lost its moral standing. Immediate social objectives, program goals, do not inspire the spirit of revolt; rather, particular causes are sought out as avenues of expression. Last week I was speaking with a colleague from the United Kingdom, the chief administrative officer of one of Britain's most important universities. He described bitter disturbances on British campuses. Knowing that the issues were obviously not the ROTC or Afro-American studies or our war in Vietnam, I asked what the controversies were about. He was not absolutely sure in each case. It was always some local question, plus a general wish to run the place. The common characteristic is the spirit of revolt, not any particular features of society revolted against.

Fourth, a recurring characteristic of protesting youth is a sense of dissociation from the guiding elements of the society, a psychological feeling of lack of participation in shaping events, and consequently a lack of feeling of responsibility for them.

I mention these things because they bear on that feature of the contemporary educational scene most on the minds of people like you and me, and because they relate directly to the vitality of the moral and ethical values of our democracy. If we wish to ease frustration, preserve the common peace, and see the idealistic energies of youth flow into effective channels of public purpose, we will do our best to shape our institutions in accord with the moral and ethical values we prize.

❦

During the years of campus unrest it was especially important to create as much understanding of student attitudes and behavior as possible among alumni. I spoke again on June 7, 1969, in Rand Hall, as I had in the year before, to Vanderbilt's Annual Alumni Luncheon about contemporary campus life. I spoke over the years to off-campus Vanderbilt groups with some regularity, the Vanderbilt Woman's Club in Nashville perhaps being the best illustration, usually giving a general report on institutional matters. But to the especially important annual reunion luncheon I observed ruefully in 1969 that university presidents were becoming as famous as football coaches, albeit for different reasons, and I pointed out, also alas, that as their job description changed many occupants of the position whom I knew had also changed. From comments and questions that came to me I knew that many persons off campus were curious about how a fellow who held such a position viewed his fate.

On some of this I had spoken before: e.g., on the increased interdependence of universities and the larger society with consequent impact on university financing and institutional autonomy. I said that "the increasing interconnection between the world of action and the world of the campus leads in our present day to a second anxiety ... the dangerous anti-intellectualism" apparent on some campuses. I commented, also, that if "I read the moods of our time rightly ... respect for the university's capacities for self-government has never been lower among the people of our country."

Reaction is setting in all around, against those who destroy the processes as well as the places of learning, and against the concepts as well as the institutions of freedom that seem to tolerate them. We of the universities cannot preserve the university's freedom and autonomy unless we can make the university's life make sense in the eyes of the larger community in which we live.

These are three great anxieties I feel as I contemplate American higher education. Institutional autonomy declines. University freedom is threatened from within. University independence is threatened from without. You may properly ask me, as I ask myself, what do we do about it all?

The first thing that we try to do at Vanderbilt—and have been seeking to do long before the current features of campus behavior appeared across America—is to operate our institution with full respect for a fundamental university quality. A university is a community in which different categories of people pursue together, in different but related ways, the larger purposes of the institution. The intellectual enterprise of learning and learning how to learn, of discovering and learning how to discover, of applying what is known and learning how to do that is not like any other human endeavor.

It is for this reason, I recently wrote in the *Alumnus*, that he who views a faculty member as simply an employee of a university, and the university as simply his employer, inadequately understands the function of the faculty member and the nature of the university. Similarly, it is too narrow to view a student as simply a customer who pays his money and takes his choice. And, correspondingly, it is inadequate to consider an administrator or trustee, be he an assistant dean, chancellor, or chairman of the board, as an authoritarian link in a hierarchical organization of direction and control. There is an inherent give-and-take relationship in study and learning, in developing the mind, in creating something new, that requires different kinds of relationships among people who make up a university community. They are all parts of the community, each essential to the other while performing a different function. The university's task is to make itself function most effectively as a teaching and learning and discovering instrument of society.

To be sure, no community, including a university community, lives by everybody vaguely and generally milling about. Any community, including a university community, must have rules of the road, structure, duties, obligations. These rules of the road and the structure and duties and obligations necessary must in a university community, as in other kinds of communities, be defined so that the purposes of the university can be pursued most successfully.

For this reason I do not use the concept of "faculty rights" or "student rights" or "administrative rights" in determining the proper roles of these groups in the functioning of a university. Every now and then someone says, "It is the right of the faculty to do so-and-so." And someone else says, "What right has the faculty to do that?" My reaction invariably is that the question is not one of right, but of how the university can best be run.

Speaking of the University

I take the same position with regard to the much discussed contemporary matter of student rights. I am willing to say for myself that the chancellor of Vanderbilt has no inherent rights, no natural rights inherently and immutably vested in the office. I have views as to what the chancellor of Vanderbilt should be permitted to do without interference from others, and what he should not be permitted to do without interference from others, if the University is to be run best. I hold the same philosophy with regard to the part students should play in running, governing the institution. Do not be put off by intemperate assertions from students or others as to the part they want to play in running the university. The only question is how to make the university function best.

We have sought at Vanderbilt, with some success, to maintain unity as a university community, and to function through orderly processes of institutional self-government. This is partly a matter of machinery, but more importantly a matter of spirit and confidence and widely shared assumptions.

❧

FIVE

A National Condition
1970–1971

THE INTENSITY OF CAMPUS ACTIVISM and civic unrest in much of the nation reached a crisis during 1970. The killings at Kent State University in Ohio and Jackson State College in Mississippi occurred later in the spring, but already in March civic disquiet was widespread. I knew that university officers could not fail to attend the deeply rooted developing events, both outside and within their institutions. Yet, even in the maelstrom, school had to keep.

On March 9, 1970, in the University Club on the campus, the Nashville Vanderbilt Club celebrated the twenty-fifth anniversary of its founding, and I was invited to speak. Composed of faithful alumni, it had rendered many services to the University, including sponsoring parties following the first home football game each year, serving as host for the annual Homecoming Luncheon, seeing to a "Black and Gold" party in May, and providing judges for the annual Homecoming Decorations Contest. Also, from my first year, it had created the annual award of the Chancellor's Cup, given by the chancellor to a faculty member in recognition of constructive student-faculty relations outside the classroom.

I acknowledged that it was impossible to address the entire Vanderbilt alumni community of several thousand living in Nashville in one setting, but welcomed this chance to speak to at least a segment of them. I told them that I suspected that the main questions on their minds in these times were two: "Why do the young behave the way they do? Why does Vanderbilt behave toward them the way it does?" Acknowledging that those questions could never be answered completely, I offered some observations, speaking from notes, about the young.

First: In a very real and important way, it was ever thus. It is not evasive, but very relevant, to remember the fact, though not to be blinded by the fact, that anxieties among the older among us over the younger among us is a recurring human phenomenon.

Then came Plato, the quotation I often used in those years to show that youthful disrespect of their elders and of constituted authority was nothing new, nor was the decline of their morals. I suggested that an historical perspective is helpful in these times, and reported that in trying to keep these matters in focus for our trustees I recited frictions and incidents from Vanderbilt's past like those mentioned in my talk of June 8, 1968, to Vanderbilt's Annual Alumni Luncheon, reported in the last chapter.

The very serious point, first, is that we must not let our shortness of memory, or egotism, obscure our efforts to understand our present times.

Second: The kinds of problems our nation, our society, our young people face are in at least two significant ways different from those we ourselves faced when most of us attended college. We are beset by new common problems that in reality make every nation—

certainly the United States—a "developing" nation. The first difference is that not only do we have the classic common challenges of national defense—and of keeping fed, clothed, and covered—that is, maintaining an adequate prosperity adequately shared—but, also, we have the new contemporary urgencies of pollution, crime, inflation, mental health, drugs, erosion of resources of many kinds, and race, and on and on.

"Making a living"—preparing oneself to earn a living—is simply not the necessity and challenge for some of our young people that once it was. They assume the livelihood. The community problems are the ones, rather than the individual ones, that are seen by many young people—but not all young people—as requiring their attention.

Another difference is the incredible complexity of these and other problems—in fact, and as perceived—making uncertain a man's, or mankind's, ability to solve them. Consequently, we find two things happening: some young people make strident demands for solution, and assert themselves in their attempts at solution, in ways that are unfamiliarly vigorous; or, some young people try to flee from society and its problems, and their problems, and take refuge in the caves—the caves of the Aegean, the caves of drugs, the caves of anger.

Third: There is a world-wide trend toward assertion of individual personality against organized institutions. I will not attempt to assess its origins, but it is here and it is an important part of a syndrome of youth attitudes manifest all over the world—in the United Kingdom; in Addis Ababa, Ethiopia; in Katmandu, Nepal; in Hyderabad, India; in Bogotá, Columbia; and elsewhere.

This mood that asserts the claims of the individual personality against organized institutions includes, at the least, demands for, or desires for:

(1) a decentralization of control in human affairs, for example, within the structure of the U.S. federal system, or the Scottish inde-

pendence movement, or the demand for neighborhood control of public programs, including schools;

(2) weighing of individual participation as a value in human affairs greater than some other human values—such as the value of technical efficiency;

(3) an emphasis on the interdependence of human affairs—a decline of the concept "that is none of your business" (except, of course, as one may say the words, on his own behalf), a decline in acceptance of the established assumption that there are institutional compartments that may appropriately be considered sacrosanct, insulated from penetration by unauthorized individuals, protected in their privacy by law or custom.

This assertion of the individual personality against organized institutions is often iconoclastic, sometimes courageous, often egocentric, sometimes generous, often puritanical and moralistic. It may be constructive or destructive and it is frequently maddening—but it is there. It has had a profound effect on the organization, functioning, and governance of the Roman Catholic Church, of labor unions, of colonial empires, of public libraries, even of grammar schools, and certainly of colleges and universities.

This world-wide mood is a phenomenon of the world community of the intellect, not of parochial concerns, and a tribute to our rapid communications systems; and it is one of the impulses underlying the expectation of students that they should have greater autonomy in all of their collegiate affairs, from designing their academic programs to all other aspects of their college experience.

Fourth: Let me say, finally, something that is as conspicuous as it is true, and yet is sometimes forgotten: Standards of taste and behavior have changed in the United States.

They have changed later and more slowly on the college campuses than in the society generally—but they have also, now, changed on the campuses. After all, the parents had the students for seventeen years or so before they reached the campuses.

A National Condition, 1970–1971

I then invoked a partial list of cultural changes since "our day" that had influenced the young of 1970: the disappearance of Hays Office restraints on the movies, the changes in language and behavior in books and magazines, the manifest impact of television on style and conduct, the introduction of drugs into secondary schools and their availability in ordinary home towns. The point: "Colleges and universities are creatures as well as creators of the society that supports them and that they serve."

So, I have said four things: the young have perplexed the old before; we are beset by new kinds of problems of new urgency and complexity that have their effect on youth; we live in a world that sees assertions of individuality antagonistic to traditional, organized systems; and we have a world characterized by sharply changed criteria of tastes, attitudes, and behavior. All these facts of our time help to shape our students and our institutions. The institutions are not passive or idle, but now, as in the time of Chancellor Garland and of Chancellor Kirkland and of Chancellor Carmichael, the kind of university we have is a product of the relationships among students, parents, faculty, trustees, alumni, and all others who make up the whole university.

❧

Events on and off American campuses in the spring of 1970 greatly deepened divisions in attitude that were already rending the United States. The Cambodian "incursion," as it was called, by American and South Vietnamese troops on May 1 triggered fierce reactions across the nation, seriously exacerbated by the killing of four student demonstrators by inexperienced National Guardsmen at Kent State University in Ohio on May 4 and by a similar tragedy at Jackson State College in

Mississippi on the night of May 14–15. The country was swept by waves of anguish, outrage, and protest.

In May I was asked by President Nixon to come to the White House as an adviser on campus tensions. The invitation was a result of circumstances that I described to a campus convocation in Neely Auditorium on May 8.

The past week has been one of deep grief for our nation. I have felt it as I have watched my own children, and the men and women who are students at Vanderbilt, living their lives of study and work and feeling and thought and hope. . . . I have felt it as members of various college and university communities across our land abandoned the practices of freedom and reason on which universities rest. I have felt it as our colleges and universities drifted further and further apart from the rest of the nation around them. And I have felt it as we have pursued national policies overseas, whatever their origins, that deeply divide us and help to erode the foundations of our common faith and mutual trust.

No one of conscience or insight or wisdom can escape the feeling of grief; and all persons of all kinds must share the blame.

During this past week many of you here have been laboring in ways of your own choice to show your grief, to help create the conditions that will remedy the errors of the past, and mend our nation of the future. Not everyone describes our present crises in the same way; not everyone offers the same solutions. What all Americans can agree upon is that we have a crisis, a crisis of confidence in ourselves. And all Americans will agree that we must work our way out of this crisis of confidence in ourselves, and out of all the dilemmas and disasters that create it.

Twice in the last two weeks I have been in a group of eight university presidents who met with the president of the United States to discuss the conditions of higher education in our country and the relationship of the federal government to them. Yesterday, at President Nixon's request, these eight university presidents from across the nation again met with him. For approximately one hour and thirty minutes we discussed the distress, frustration, and anger found this week among large numbers of students and faculty and others. . . .

Our language was forceful and explicit and made, among other points, the following ones:

That disaffection and disillusionment in educational communities across our country are so deep and widespread that we have a true national emergency, a national crisis;

That this crisis extends even in some quarters to a loss of confidence in our political processes;

That this condition is produced in part by the conflict in Southeast Asia and the Cambodian decision;

That it is heightened by the tragic events that have occurred on several campuses, especially at Kent State University;

That feelings of distrust and alienation on the campuses have been increased by hostile comments by members of the administration, especially about individual institutions and persons;

That the feelings of concern and resentment extend to large numbers of persons of moderate and conservative political viewpoints;

And, that there is a widespread belief among members of the educational community that the President and his advisers have not been adequately sensitive to feelings and convictions of large numbers of peaceable men and women of good will and deep patriotism on the campuses of the nation.

Our group proposed to the President that the quality of public decisions affecting higher education in the present crisis can be improved if students, faculty members, trustees, administrative officers and others who make up higher education had a direct way to express to him and others in the White House their anxieties, their judgments, and their recommendations. We urged that a position be created close to the President, occupied by a representative of the educational community, through whom the President could hear from students, faculty, trustees, and the other constituencies of higher education in the country. We know that communication must be a two-way street, but we proposed that this individual be the representative of the campuses to him, not his representative to the campuses. Our group nominated to the President for the position two persons not of our own number, stating the assets we thought each would bring to the task.

The President listened attentively. He clearly appreciated the emphasis with which we spoke. He emphasized his desire to understand.

Following the meeting the President sent word that he would adopt the proposal, that he preferred to have one of the group of eight who had called on him, and that he wished me to undertake the assignment. If the crisis is as grave as we represented it to him to be, and if the need to increase communications from the campuses to him is as great as we stated, and if that need could be filled at least in part by the creation of the position we recommended, he thought one of our own number ought to be willing to try.

I spoke with William S. Vaughn, president of the Vanderbilt Board of Trust, who conferred with other trustees. He authorized me to accept the assignment for the period between now and June 30, 1970, with the understanding that I would be available for important University obligations between now and then, the principal one of these being the commencement exercises on May 31. To emphasize the independence of the position, as representative of the campuses, Mr. Vaughn proposed that I decline compensation from the United States government and remain during the period of the assignment as chancellor of Vanderbilt. President Nixon gladly accepted this last provision of independence. He stated that it is in the spirit that motivated him to create the position.

What good can come of it? I have worked on assignments from other presidents, and over the years have worked for departments of government and committees of the Congress. For some time I have been chairman of the Council on Federal Relations of the Association of American Universities, seeking to represent the interests of Vanderbilt's type of university in matters of national educational policy and financial support in the administrative and legislative councils of our government. I have no illusions about myself, or about how much I can do, or about how easily anything can be done, by any one person.

I do know that nothing worthwhile can be done unless all of us apply effectively all the competence and energy and conviction we possess to the solution of the very practical, complex problems that beset us.

Many of you have been working, peacefully, for peace. You have been seeking with determination and within the rules of this university to advance the causes of peace and of happiness for the United States and for the world. And you of many varied viewpoints have done this in rational ways that increase the power of your message.

The President demonstrated to me yesterday his willingness to listen. I will do my best to help him hear. You can do your best by continuing to work with all your heart and mind for your goals of education at Vanderbilt and peace in the world.

❧

My duties at the White House did not end until after mid-July. But meantime, other important institutional responsibilities had to be met. Harold Vanderbilt died in Newport, Rhode

Island, on July 4, 1970. Chancellor Branscomb and I spoke at a memorial service in Trinity Episcopal Church in Newport on July 7. I said:

In every part of Harold Vanderbilt's extraordinarily versatile life, this good friend of all of us displayed prodigious natural talent hinged to an implacable will to excel. Joined with his humor and modesty, and the fact that he was a gentleman, these qualities made him one of the remarkable men of personal achievement in our century.

Four years ago we unveiled a handsome statue of Harold on the Vanderbilt campus. Speakers proclaimed his virtues accurately, and therefore at length. When his time came, he said simply, "Makes me feel like quite a fellow."

"Mike" Vanderbilt was, indeed, quite a fellow: at St. Mark's School, where he won the Founder's Medal for scholarship; at Harvard College, where he graduated months before his class; and here in Newport, where from *Osprey* to *Vim*, in *Enterprise*, in *Rainbow*, in *Ranger*, he became the world's ranking yachtsman.

He was always quite a fellow whenever he could go faster, on the sea, in the air, and—no one who ever drove with him in a motor car will ever forget—on the highway.

He was quite a fellow at the New York Central; at the helm of *SP 56* in the First World War; in Virginia where championships are given for raising corn; at the bridge table where he won his own Vanderbilt Cup; and at Vanderbilt University where he was our living founder and the institution's most sustained source of strength.

He once said, "It is better to lead than to be forced to follow."

He led with his originality, the originality that produced a "blueprint roll of innovations in yacht design, rigging, sails and tactics," the originality that transformed the international rules of racing and auction bridge, that created the Club Convention, that produced half a dozen important books, that made two university chancellors think twice about everything, and three times about most things, they submitted to him for consideration.

He led because he looked to the future. He had instinctive wisdom in choosing goals and in designing ways to reach them.

He led, too, with tenacity—with patience, with capacious memory, with care for precise detail, with powers of unbreakable concentration, with infinite capacity for taking pains, with relentless determination to succeed—to win without quarter and without rancor against competitors and against circumstances.

He was able to lead because he was decent, unselfish with his world's resources, held faith in human capacity, and had ability to harness disparate talents to a common purpose.

Harold had a sense of his heritage. It was a source of standard and of strength. He leaves his own heritage, which we shall hear across the years just as his "quarterdeck voice" once was heard across the waters round about us here, where he has now been laid to rest.

❧

The institutional disquiet of 1970 took many forms and was reflected in a general skepticism of constituted authority throughout society and in inquisitiveness about many matters not normally the targets of inquiry. Universities especially, including Vanderbilt, were subject to didactic probing, aggressive query, and, from some sources, heated skepticism.

I felt I understood the origins of the attitudes being manifested. Even when they were trying and exhausting to deal with, I felt that Vanderbilt's and my best response was to take them seriously—as surely those who held them did. The chancellor or president of a complex, authentic university has many constituencies, but the most important single constituency to the institution's welfare in the long run is the faculty. Consequently I tried in the semiannual meetings of the combined faculties, especially during these tense years, to respond as fully as possible to as wide a range of their expressed concerns as feasible. We had four meetings of the Faculty Assembly in 1970 and 1971, in the fall and spring of each year, and my prepared notes and text for each average around forty pages, with time allowed for questions and discussion when desired.

In the meeting of the Faculty Assembly in Underwood Auditorium on September 10, 1970, there were standard matters on which reports were made, such as a reminder of the monthly meetings of the Faculty Senate, in Room 123 of the Law School, to which all Faculty Assembly members would be welcome, reports that the Consultative Committee of the Senate had met nine times during the past year, with me usually present, and the Senate Executive Committee had met fifteen times, twice with me present. The provost introduced new faculty members, I reminded all present of the importance of the Vanderbilt Honor System, about which I had spoken the previous afternoon to entering students, and much more of a recurring nature was handled.

I confessed to the faculty that I was "perplexed—as on occasion I have said before—by the proper balance between informing and burdening you with the endless series of matters outside the classroom and laboratory and library and hospital that a modern university must deal with." I mentioned as illustrations, among others, long-standing pollution-reduction efforts with our smokestacks, the urban renewal program on land adjacent to Vanderbilt, planning for more satisfactory faculty, student, and visitor parking, and developments in the operations and attitudes within the Board of Trust. Also, I stated my belief that the question hour at Faculty Assembly meetings was not adequate for the "discussion" that I felt many faculty members desired. I noted that I had asked both the Executive Committee and the Consultative Committee of the Senate about the desirability of initiating "a general faculty question hour and other means by which faculty members can keep informed and my administrative colleagues and I can have the benefits of knowing directly of their interests." In the same vein I mentioned the activation of a Senate Ad Hoc Committee on Constitutional Revision under the chairmanship of Professor Harold G. Maier and the work of the Commission on University Governance chaired by Professor Charles F. Delzell.

These illustrations should make clear that a determined effort was made to give the faculty who were interested a sense of participation, a feeling of inclusion in the life of the University beyond their primary responsibilities for teaching, research, and professional service. There had been a flap about the adequacy of the hours that the McGugin Center was open to faculty and to students other than intercollegiate athletes. There had been skeptical grumbling about the artificial turf recently laid in the stadium. About the latter, I explained that "in the eyes of some it was the greatest University advance since the stadium itself was built in 1922." Knowing, however, that it was no joking matter for many, I explained that the cost would be amortized by the Athletic Department through lower maintenance requirements and from additional income from rentals to high schools and others that the durable turf would make possible. Also, I reported that I was told that the number of practice fields needed by Vanderbilt itself would be fewer, thereby freeing up some land.

The long agenda of other matters on which I reported included reports on the 1969–70 Living Endowment fund-

raising campaign among alumni, successful completion of the
$55 million fund drive (1966–1970), the number of black stu-
dents, the bequests of Harold Vanderbilt, student enrollment,
the financial condition of the University, the appointment and
functions of George Kaludis, who had become vice-chancellor
for Operations and Fiscal Planning, the organization and functions of a "newly formalized Budget Committee composed of
senior administrative officers," and much else.

At this meeting, five months after the eruption of demonstrations on campuses across the country occasioned by the invasion of Cambodia and other events, I said to the Senate:

Across the nation we are unquestionably in for a year of uncertainty and anxiety. It seems to me that durable changes in colleges
and universities are in process, not all of which we understand, and
not all of which we have in some places in higher education been
able to cope with. One thing is nonetheless clear—at least to me: a
university has the necessity and the obligation to maintain the educational freedoms necessary for it to be a university: (1) the open
forum in all its forms; (2) freedom of access and movement; (3) and
a climate of civility and poise within which education can take place.

Last May, in the reactions to Cambodia and Kent State and Jackson State, you helped essentially to produce one of Vanderbilt's
finest hours—an hour when in all the heat and emotion and tension
the University stayed true to its fundamental value: intellectual freedom. We had many outbursts of deep feeling and protest, but all
with respect for the right of others to express their views, and all
within the rules.

From the bottom of my heart, I thank you. In the final analysis,
faculty have the primary responsibility and primary opportunity in
a university's effort to maintain a community of common values and
aspirations, and in its duty to maintain its basic educational freedoms. We have been fortunate at Vanderbilt. We have also been

hard-working. Your successes have reaped their greatest reward—a better university than we otherwise would have had. The loyalty of the University and its students to university values is also noticed outside.

❧

My assignment at the White House led to an invitation to address the National Press Club, which I did in its building in Washington on September 11, 1970. During the previous summer while working in Washington, I had spoken on a number of occasions to groups within the government about attitudes and actions among the young, to convey my interpretation of causes and consequences, and to solicit reactions. These audiences included a group in the Department of Agriculture, another group in the Department of Health, Education, and Welfare, the President's "sub-cabinet" assembled in the State Department auditorium, and on June 24, for sixty-five minutes, the president's cabinet in the White House. All the presentations were made from notes, all of which are concise and some of which at this distance in time are cryptic.

My remarks to the National Press Club, however, were formally prepared. They do not replicate in detail what was said on each of these other occasions, but they do convey many of the themes and stances of the earlier remarks. A lengthy formal report that I made on completion of the assignment was introduced into the *Congressional Record* of August 5, 1970, by Representative John Brademus.

Here are excerpts from the remarks to the National Press Club:

What I want to do today, with you who inform the nation, is to discuss in some detail the nature of the national crisis in higher education. There will be no headlines in what I want to say. There may be no news, in your workaday sense, in it either. But there may be some thoughts and analysis that will be useful to you as you observe and report on higher education.

Why, in 1970, do I say that the conditions faced by higher education constitute a national crisis? After all, campus discontent is not new. Dissent and disruption marked many a nineteenth century campus in America. The issues were public as well as educational. Police on campus and weapons on campus were live issues in some places. Students have confounded their elders at least as far back as the time of Plato. . . .

Nor is student questioning of accepted national doctrine an innovation of the 1960s. A 1936 Roper poll among undergraduates conducted for *Fortune* magazine found 68 percent of those interviewed favored a "revision of our attitude about property rights." Six percent of them chose *communism* and 24 percent chose *socialism* as terms that suggested ideas toward which they felt sympathetic.

Nor is anti-war sentiment on and off the campuses novel. At the height of World War II, in February 1944, a Gallup poll found 14 percent of a nationwide sample saying it was a mistake for the United States to have entered that war. In April 1952 Gallup found a majority believing our entry into the Korean conflict to be a mistake. Polls among students also revealed substantial antagonism to the Korean conflict.

What, then, makes the present situation critical?

First, the scope and depth of anxiety among sincere, patriotic, rule-obeying students are the greatest in our history. College students now constitute a larger proportion of the country's total population than previously and are drawn from more diverse backgrounds. It seems clear that the student protest movement last May and June was the largest we have known. Forty-eight percent of a sample of students on four-year campuses of all types—large and small, prominent and obscure, public and private, north, south, east, and west, in all fields of study—said they took part in some kind of anti-war protest activities in May. And if you talked to many of these students, you know something of the deep intensity of their feelings.

The anxieties of these young persons extend beyond the conflict in Southeast Asia to many other concerns inside and outside the nation, on and off the campuses. Whatever the causes, there is in our country a segment of white and black young people who are baffled, disillusioned, angered.

And that leads to the second reason the situation is serious. Many talented individuals of great potential social influence are at an important psychological and intellectual stage in their development, a stage when lasting personal attitudes and convictions are shaped. If their disaffection remains deep and colors their continuing outlook, we all will feel the consequences.

Third, the unrest in our society is not confined to students. Attitudes and behavior on campuses—in all of their variety—stem in significant measure, although obviously not wholly, from the public issues of the day. There is a relationship between the state of the nation and the state of the campus.

The style and substance of American life have altered—to the joy of some and the dismay of others—in speech, manners, dress, theater, magazines, books, newspapers, music, motion pictures, radio, television, the arts in all their forms. The accepted ways of doing things in race relations, in rearing children, in churches, in labor unions, in corporations, in elementary and secondary schools, in government bureaucracies, in elected legislatures, in many other institutions of our society, including the family itself, have been questioned or defied. We find ourselves at odds not only over vital public policies, but over the customary ways of dealing with them. Violence has grown generally throughout the society, and justice is everywhere delayed.

Fourth, on a limited number of campuses a virulent intellectual intolerance has developed that constitutes a real and present danger to the basic educational freedoms necessary for a college or university to function properly. Educational institutions are accustomed to threats to their freedom from without. Blind, self-righteous intolerance among a small minority of students and faculty on a campus—intolerance that obstructs the open forum, limits freedom of movement, and substitutes force for reason—is as grave a threat as ever came from without. This intolerance is sometimes linked with efforts to make the college or university into an engine of partisan politics.

Finally, fifth, the reactions among men and women of good will across our land to these developments in higher education are themselves another reason higher education, and the nation, face a crisis. State legislators, members of Congress, parents, alumni, taxpayers, citizens generally are divided among themselves in their understanding and reactions to what has gone on. Many are angry and hostile. In the United States, in the long run, higher education will never flourish or serve the nation best while there is aggressive distrust of it in any major sector, among old or young, on or off the campuses. A degree of tension has always characterized relationships between colleges and the places they are located and between intellectuals generally and others in society. Hostility of new intensity, however, is now evident on the part of persons who don't understand what they see, or when they do, don't like what they understand.

The causes of all this are much debated. What is meant by "all this" also provokes dispute. I discover, when I discuss campus unrest with others, that one person equates the subject almost exclusively to the latest bombing, another to unkempt appearance and marijuana, another to the impeccable, highly motivated conduct of a son at home or the girl next door.

In all events, the campus conditions that preoccupy us these days embrace two important elements: on the one hand, an awareness of social responsibility and determination toward civic improvement, constitutionally encouraged, traditionally applauded, educationally appropriate, involving dissent and free expression and voluntary citizen action of many kinds; and, on the other hand, violation by some of the basic necessary rules of our society, including the civil liberties of other human beings.

Student unrest in a particular nation, or on a particular campus, at a particular time, will stem from the particular circumstances of that nation or that campus. Peaceable student dissent and violent student disruptions have occurred in nations where the contemporary issues are quite different from those in the United States.

Two years ago I discussed with officials in Ethiopia and Kenya the origins of student protest in those countries, and more recently I did the same in Nepal and India. Developing countries in many parts of the globe, highly industrialized nations like Japan, West Germany, France, and the United Kingdom, and nations on both sides of the Iron Curtain have experienced student movements in recent years. These movements are related to other social developments and their origins are difficult to sort out. We clearly have, nonetheless, a global phenomenon.

Basic tides are running that shake the static aspects of society in all world cultures. The traditional stabilizing influences of religion, family, social custom, historical teachings, political and economic conventions, and education have weakened, creating greater susceptibility to challenge and change in all kinds of institutions.

The immediate circumstances in the United States that underlie student unrest include unresolved public issues—Southeast Asia and the destiny of black Americans being, in my view, of foremost present importance. But they embrace other circumstances on and off the campuses as well.

The delay of entry into adult life is probably a basic factor. It has produced difficulties on campus not because colleges and universities have changed from the olden, golden days, but because the students coming to them have changed. Students are physically more mature and educationally better prepared than they used to be. And their families have reared most of them in greater economic abundance and with fewer self-restraints than used to be normal. The increasing diversity of students in their origins, preparation, and goals calls for greater flexibility in requirements, a richer curriculum, greater independence in course selection, more useful student contributions to the governance of institutions, and more varied living conditions than previously permitted by most colleges and universities across the country. Subtle psychological stimulants, doubtless seldom understood by students themselves (or the rest of us), can affect what they advocate or protest about on or off the campus at a given time. Nonetheless, campus protest usually involves substantive issues, and these vary from one institution to another, just as they vary from one nation to another, just as they will vary from one time to another.

I believe that most of us in the United States feel that colleges and universities are essential to our welfare. We look to them not only for education and training but also as a source of leadership and of ideas. As a nation we have invested huge sums of money in them, and as individuals some of us have invested much of our lives in them. And these are, after all, our children who go to them and our children who express their concern about the quality of their lives and our lives. The young man or woman who comes to the campus as a student brings most of his basic equipment with him—ethical values, standards of taste, personal habits, even many of his intellectual concepts. We all had a part in making him what he is, and we all have a stake in his future.

Persons young and old who have lost confidence in our ways of government—local, state, and federal—can recapture it, with help. That hope lies in the further hope that we can, through government, attack with success the problems that face us. When we have a policy in Southeast Asia that can be understood more clearly, there will be less vehement dissent. When we attack more effectively the problems of our black citizens, which are equally the problems of our white citizens, there will be less vehement dissent. When we move more effectively to meet other pressing needs in our society, there will be less disappointment and unrest.

I do not think that in the long run our leaders can lose, and I am sure our country cannot, by displaying compassion, seeking understanding, and encouraging tolerance.

I believe that at all governmental levels concerned citizens—including young people and blacks and anyone else who feels disaffected—should, along with everyone else, be welcomed into the political processes. Many who have expressed their concerns in the past through traditionally approved methods need the proof that the system is truly open to them and truly does work. Those who have deserted reason and law need the demonstration even more. Nothing is more important than the reasonableness of our laws and the quality and equality of their enforcement.

☙

On August 25, 1971, the day before the arrival of new undergraduate students, I was asked to speak at a dinner in Rand Hall that honored the Women's Advisory Committee, VU-CEPT, and other student orientation leaders. The theme they had adopted for that year's orientation program was "Get It While You Can." I said in part:

I wrestle each year, on this day, with how I can say tomorrow night, in ways that will be effective in the cozy climate of Memorial Gymnasium, before two or three thousand students and families, that same thing: "Get It While You Can." I have to say what I have to say, but it occurs to me that in the greater informality and intimacy of your association with new students that you will have during the coming week, you may be able to get some of the messages across better than I. Let me separate out five matters that are, in my view, especially important for our new students to understand, and, consequently, that might be on your mind as you seek to help them become oriented to Vanderbilt.

After all, let me say first, the main purpose in being here is formal education. That is not the only goal nor the only reward, but it is their reason, and your reason, and my reason, for being at Vanderbilt. To appreciate the values of formal educational opportunities, talk to those who have been denied them—or read what Malcolm X or Eldridge Cleaver has written about the way they devoured books once they learned, in a real way, to read them. The personal and public problems of this world simply will not be solved by good intentions and good will alone. Anyone who really wants to play a constructive part will have to master skills, information, and the processes of thought, and for most of us capturing those must begin with formal education.

Drugs are a second matter. "Where It's At" seems to me to say some very useful things in ways that seem to me will probably communicate effectively to those most in need of hearing them. Hard drug addiction may well become, and therefore may well now be, the most acute problem faced by our nation, and other nations as well. Nothing you can do that points to dangers and solutions—to sensible self-interest in confronting drugs, to available channels of help—can be too great.

The importance of self-government is greater at Vanderbilt than in most universities and probably all high schools. That is a third matter to emphasize. The freedom and discretion and authority that go with the various components of student government at Vanderbilt carry with them heavy obligations. This is newly and crucially true with respect, especially, to the degree of dormitory autonomy we have created in the last year and in the operations of Interhall. It will be no surprise to you that many people—students and non-students, parents and non-parents, on and off the campus—consider changes we have made in dormitory government, and consequently in dormitory regulations, to be unwise and a shirking of Vanderbilt's institutional responsibility. Abuse of freedom endangers freedom, and I would hope that our new students understand that as campus citizens they have inescapable responsibilities to the rest of us on the campus in the ways they self-govern themselves.

Now, fourth, the health of the University and the happiness of its students rest importantly on our sense of oneness, of community, on each of us feeling a degree of ease, of feeling at home on the campus. Our white students and our black students must do all possible to enable our new black students to be comfortable. Most of all that means every one of us here now, and every one of those joining us tomorrow, must carry in his heart, in his feelings, unbiased respect for every other human being—regardless of his color. That is Vanderbilt's, our nation's, and the world's greatest need.

Finally, as part of the effort to make our new colleagues feel at home, I hope you will do what you can to emphasize the reality of ease of communications on the campus—with other students, with faculty, with administrative officers—"Where It's At" gets in some blows on this point—and, if you will, with me personally. I always say in welcoming remarks, and I will again tomorrow night, that my door is open to any student who wants to walk through it. Last year, six days after I said it, Robert Slocum, a freshman from Macon, Georgia, walked in, wholly on his own initiative for a talk—to my delight. But not many do, which is perhaps to be interpreted as a good sign—and, of course, there is a physical limit to how many could be accommodated. But I am dismayed occasionally at the senior reception we have each commencement afternoon to have a departing graduate say, "well, I'm glad I had a chance to shake your hand at least once." I am dismayed, because I would have liked to have shaken his hand sooner, especially if he really cared, but also because somehow his tone sometimes suggests he would like me to think that he thinks our sparsity of contact was my fault and not his!

Last fall, with the cooperation of the Student Association, I held a series of breakfasts for students, five in number from the end of September to the end of November. For the latter ones, we announced in the press that if someone wanted to come, all he had to do was call up and show up, and some did. On the suggestion of Student Association leaders, we did not offer the breakfasts in the spring semester. I have offered to do the same thing, or some variation, again this year.

My wife and I are honored to accept invitations extended by individual students—we have had a number of enjoyable evenings in Oxford House—or from organizations. I recall last year we attended an open discussion session at the Phi Kappa Sigma House to which many students not belonging to the chapter came, and a supper at the KA House. And I recall rap sessions last semester in Kissam, Carmichael East, McGill, and the ZBT House. (The ZBT's field a softball team every spring for a game against the "Administration All Stars." Sometimes we, the All Stars, win.) We have picnics and Parents Weekends, fireside sessions at the chancellor's residence, and seek out other occasions of many kinds to meet and be with students. My point is that accessibility is a two-sided equation, and I would hope you would do what you can to convey the spirit of genuine hospitality that I think almost all of us on the campus feel toward new students—both when they are new and all the rest of the time they are here, too. All they have to do is avail themselves of it.

I have dwelt on this point because every now and then I realize how hard it is to maintain the spirit of open communication that we foster and in which I take great pride at Vanderbilt. I received a letter last year from a coed who, in effect, deplored the fact that I had not been accessible to her and other students. So I looked at the calendar and found that I had spent an average of one and one-half hours per day for the previous ten weeks in meetings of one kind or another with students—and that making no allowance for time away with our former students, and with other individuals and organizations whose donations help pay the costs of our students' education.

You can get across gently the spirit of what I am saying—and it applies to other administrative officers and faculty, too—far better than I: to feel at home with each other takes initiative on all sides. Thank you for all you are doing, and good luck in the months ahead.

🥀

In the fall of 1971, the Vanderbilt Graduate School initiated a weekly seminar on "The Nature of the American University." That such a seminar was created itself flags one of the intense preoccupations of that period of intense social unrest in the society, a period accompanied by political agitation on virtually all campuses and by physical violence on many of them. Faculty and students were trying to understand better the political and intellectual period they were living and teaching in. I was asked to help initiate the series in 114 Furman Hall on October 18, and said, in part:

Among the paradoxical dichotomies that run through university life—and that form the matrix of dilemmas in which every university functions—are four of special significance to this task—understanding the nature of the American university—and to the interaction between society and university that gives rise to this task.

The first is the inherent conflict between the function of transmitting existing information or values or skills, on the one hand, and the processes of evaluation, criticism, and creativity that question whatever is existing, on the other. Education generally has served much-remarked stabilizing functions of socialization and acculturation for our society. Taxpayers, parents, satisfied citizens, and hosts of others with a belief in the ongoing way expect it to do so.

At the same time, especially in our time, the enormously expanded investigative, research dimension of universities is busily spawning and spreading new information, insights, and speculation that build to new technological systems, new social conditions, and new philosophical critiques, all of which add up to a formidable challenge to the existing qualities of society being transmitted.

A second pair of contradictory qualities lies in the need for a university to be at once utilitarian and independent. It must in its most fundamental achievements serve the society that supports it; otherwise it will not be supported. The greatest social utility of the university is as critic and inventor—to achieve which it must maintain fundamental intellectual independence from its sources of support. The practical benefits of crop research are evident to the most demanding utilitarian citizen. The value of social ethics is probably less evident to him; yet in fact social ethics may require not only support but support for which the university is not held accountable in any but the largest sense.

Tension between campus and street flows from both these conflicts. From the outside the university may appear to be changing more than preserving the way of life. And it appears to appeal for the protection and nurture of society while resisting anybody's effort to direct its work.

A third dichotomy separates the university as institution from the actions of the people—hopefully intellectually free people—who make it up. . . .

In the contemporary American model, a faculty member may choose his own objects of research, may choose whether and what professional services he wishes to render outside the university, and often what and how he will teach. He has the privilege of doing these things, however, only because he is of the university. And the university has no life without him. So observers without and within assign responsibility to the university for what he does—urban analysis or military research, for example. . . .

Fourth, and finally, the educational freedom necessary for this strange institution, the modern American university, to be effective must be sustained by consensus in the society outside. And this when the university is the sponsor of curiosity, skepticism, criticism, creativity, change—all of which can challenge and erode established social consensus.

The consensus needed on and off campus to support campus intellectual freedom requires basically the same kinds of social values, political principles, and degree of cultural homogeneity that a free, democratic political system requires. That means, in turn, that when such a larger political system is endangered, the free university is likewise imperiled.

That is one reason extreme stress in the American social system threatens the university. If our institutions of government prove incapable of handling the nation's problems in accordance with democratic procedural values, the campus will feel directly the impact of whatever authoritarian, anarchistic, or other alternatives in government emerge.

Extreme social stress poses dangers for the university for another reason also. The revolutionary who seeks to derail the existing order assaults the university, not alone because its vulnerability makes it an inviting target for disruption, reason enough, but also because it is the central secular institution in our society outside of government itself. To maim the university is ultimately to damage the society.

In these complex circumstances, a university's obligation (to itself) to maintain conditions of educational freedom essential for its own work includes, but also extends beyond, the traditional basic insistence on an open forum for all and on unfettered inquiry within its own precincts. Their price, as always, is eternal vigilance against attack from any quarter, near or far.

Speaking of the University

The social values of open forum and free inquiry cannot be realized without the political neutrality of the university as an institution, except where the university itself is the issue.

And it is important to add that a university's obligation to intellectual freedom must embrace a subtle and pervasive commitment to the canons of reason in all it does, an obligation that extends to all members of the community of scholarship, in classroom and out, an obligation that is not invariably fulfilled.

With freedom in the university dependent ultimately on freedom in the society, and with freedom in the society dependent ultimately on the effectiveness of social, political, and economic institutions, a university's self-interest in intellectual freedom impels it—meaning all those who compose it—to do all it can through its own processes to help make the society succeed, to help make it open, just, safe, prosperous, peaceful.

Higher education in America is now entering a significant period of transition and reshaping, probably as profound as that it went through in the nineteenth century. The purposes and ways of work of universities will be basic parts of the agenda. The enhancement of intellectual freedom will require universities to deepen their paradoxical roles of serving the national needs on which that freedom ultimately depends, without losing their independence, or the distinction between themselves as institutions and their members; of fortifying the consensus of values that undergird intellectual freedom, without becoming enslaved to a static order; of helping to maintain the continuity and stability of the larger community, without foregoing the obligations of critic and creator.

Neat tricks, if we can turn them.

❧

During 1970 and 1971, as in all years, I spoke on a large number of formal occasions—at least ninety-two, about half from a prepared text, the rest from notes. Omitted from the eight selections offered in this chapter are several presentations to the Faculty Assembly, to entering students, to Vanderbilt Clubs in eighteen cities, formal presentations to the Duval County (Florida) Medical Society, at the Society of the New York Hospital Two-Hundredth Anniversary Celebration, to the American Philosophical Society in Philadelphia, along with two lengthy presentations to staff meetings of nonacademic Vanderbilt employees, and commencement exercises at Converse College in Spartanburg, South Carolina, at Indiana State University in Terre Haute, and at the Johns Hopkins University in Baltimore. It was always thus, although the mix evolved somewhat with the temper of the times.

I include here in closing this chapter some of my understanding of "The Seamless Web of Health and Polity" conveyed in the Alan Gregg Memorial Lecture of the Association of American Medical Colleges, in annual meeting in the Washington Hilton Hotel in Washington, D.C., on October 29, 1971.

Six years ago you were good enough to invite me to speak to you on the relationship of the educational program of a medical school to its university. . . .

Relating the activities of medical colleges to the nation's health, and the nation's health to the rest of the nation's concerns, is more nearly my topic today. . . .

The World Health Organization's 1946 definition has become famous: "Health is a state of complete physical, mental and social well-being and not merely the absence of disease or infirmity." That ambitious and adventurous concept is reflected in many definitions of purpose advanced by laymen and health professionals alike. Just to assure the absence of disease and infirmity is a formidable undertaking by itself.... To add positive responsibilities for complete physical and mental well-being clearly inspires the spirit, but doing so adds gigantic burdens to those accepting the responsibilities. When the definition of health is expanded, moreover, to embrace complete social well-being, most of the limitations on the jurisdiction of health professionals begin to disappear.

An expansive concept of the responsibilities that fall under the heading of "health" is evident in many of our contemporary undertakings. I was intrigued recently to read a statement of goals of our Vanderbilt Center for Health Services—an important coalition of faculty, students, and staff from several schools within Vanderbilt University that has been working in Appalachia and in the inner urban area of Nashville, Tennessee. Here is the statement of the "Goal and Role of the Center":

> The purpose of the Center is to encourage and to pursue improvements in the delivery of health care by means of university interdisciplinary and intercommunity cooperation. For the Center's purposes "health" means not only freedom from disease, but also the general well-being of an individual— social, political, economic, environmental, educational, and psychological.

That concept of health embraces a large segment of human experience and human aspirations. In addition to broad definitions of the concerns that properly fall to health personnel, there is another factor that extends the jurisdiction.

Modern concepts of the origins of disease and infirmity erase what boundaries remain. Reflect on the many sources of disease and infirmity ascribed by diagnosticians of mental illness, by epidemiologists, by advocates of comprehensive health care, by students of psychosomatic medicine, and in fact by sensitive and artful family physicians. Modern concepts of the origins of disease and infirmity extend the potential concern of medical students, of your students, quite literally to everything in the world—to every single phenomenon, natural and otherwise, in the world. To accept the World Health Organization's definition of health does not, of course, compel every health professional to take on an inchoate, limitless responsibility for achieving the ultimate goals inherent in the definition. It is quite clear, nonetheless, that the corporate scope of health concerns is increasingly proclaimed as increasingly all embracing.

Concepts of human development extend to cultural, social, and psychological as well as biological aspects of growth. Environmental influences are cited along with basic genetic characteristics as crucially influencing the development of biological organisms. Here are two recent public assertions: "Probably the single most important factor affecting in a negative way the health of our youth is poverty in about one-quarter of the nation's children." "Mental health is not exclusively a psychiatric problem, or a psychological problem, or a taxpayer's problem, or a legislative problem. It is all of these, and more. It is a problem of the whole social fabric."

Health is immediately affected by air and water pollution, consequences of the physical and social sprawl of contemporary industrial civilization. Also by housing, transportation, and education. Also by cultural and psychological variants that determine an individual's sense of identity. Also by diet, and the agricultural and advertising practices that affect it. All of these matters that affect health hint at the limitless scope of health concerns.

The broad concepts of health that have become commonplace since the Second World War are of more than merely abstract interest, as you in medical education, most of all, know. These broad concepts of responsibilities and causal connections carry significant operational consequences. The discussions marking the two-hundredth anniversary of the New York Hospital last May—among persons from many parts of the world—exposed, as those who were present will recall, extraordinarily complicated dilemmas—financial, organizational, administrative, ethical, political, and medical dilemmas—faced by modern university-based medical centers. The implications for medical education of the new conditions require our attention. . . .

These broad concepts of health obviously have important consequences for the health goals we choose to seek in our country, and therefore inevitably for medical education in our country.

One conspicuous consequence is so obvious that perhaps, for that very reason, it requires special mention. We simply must have continuing self-appraisal, reappraisal, continuing analysis and re-evaluation of health goals and of the practices used to reach them. Like many a call to virtue, that injunction is easy to hear, difficult to keep in mind, harder still to follow.

But beyond this, four clear needs emerge.

First, if the drive for increased consumption is endemic in the American ethos, increased labor and financial efficiency is a necessity. Health expenditures have been growing faster than the gross national product at an accelerating rate. Somebody has said that health expenditures may approach ten percent of GNP by the end of the 1970s. As with higher education generally, the proportion of national effort reflected in health expenditures creates a new environment. The public interest stake in the way of doing things assumes an order of importance significantly greater than before.

Concepts of "efficiency" and "economy" cannot be narrow. There have been significant savings in manpower and money in recent decades from the reduction in the incidence of infectious disease. Most of us in this room grew up in the threatening shadow of infantile paralysis. I have never seen a tally, but the money savings from medical advances, even narrowly defined, must have been enormous during the past twenty-five years.

Money spent for health research broadly conceived may well be the cheapest dollars one can spend for improved health. In passing,

A National Condition, 1970–1971

let me say that I myself have never comprehended the notion of a competition between medical research, on one hand, and the delivery of health services, on another, phrased sometimes as though the two were antithetical to each other.

Dramatic changes, revolutionary advances in the management and administration of all phases of the health establishment, are essential if we are to pursue the ambitious goals of health implicit in the World Health Organization's concept. . . .

Now a second consideration. Heightened division of labor within health-care systems, and between health professionals and other segments of society, is inevitable. You will understand why I labor the point. It carries an implication of grave consequence for you and your medical colleges. The role of the physician as the uniquely central, dominant figure in health care will change. It has changed already. It will change more, as comprehensive definitions of health are more widely accepted and applied, and as multiple causes of illness are more widely understood and attacked.

Now to the third matter warranting mention. . . .

Our social and political processes need to breed a rationalizing of expectations. All know and many say that social choices must be made, public priorities must be set. David Rockefeller, speaking on the economic aspects of environmental improvement, has emphasized that there is no such thing as a cost-free benefit. Addressing a graduation class last June, he noted the reality that we can improve our environment if we increase productivity. But we can do it then only if we use the proceeds that flow from increased productivity to restore the environment, rather than to purchase additional amenities of life. That is the type of choice to be made.

Finally, it strikes me that the goals we expect from a health system require searching, ethically oriented scrutiny. Differing concepts of life, and of health, and of death, and differing values attached to each, are exposed not only in the works of cultural anthropologists, but also in private arguments and public debates in our country over birth control, abortion, and the mercy of medically prolonging the hopeless life of the living dead.

In an earlier and simpler day, most could agree that a person was ill and that he should be made well. In more sophisticated and complex times, it is less easy to agree on who is "really" ill, or whether the condition, however called, warrants treatment, and if so, how long and how much. "Complete physical, mental and social well-being" is not itself an operational definition. The society and its health professionals need more closely defined and limited objectives in the competition for social priorities and the resources to reach them. All these considerations require that "health consumers"—a term growing in prominence—do more than simply accept broad notions of what their physical and mental well-being require. They must also accept, or develop for themselves, new understandings of the expectations they can most sensibly and feasibly hold.

The central meaning of these things for you of the Association of American Medical Colleges seems to me manifest: All health is now public health.

The interconnections between health and the rest of society, the costs in money and manpower, the expectations of health consumers, the competition for resources among the many goals of our lives—all work to make public health policies and private health practices matters of central concern to the political systems of the nation, of the states, of the communities of America. Neither public nor private hospitals, nor medical schools, nor their universities, nor combinations of institutions, can address the intricate problems they face except through and with the aid of government, including government at local, state, regional, and national levels. One inescapable consequence of that condition is that the health of citizens depends on the health of our democratic governmental institutions.

Government, after all, is the vehicle for comprehensive common action in our country. Government cannot perform its essential functions without improved governmental institutions of many kinds. Improved governmental organization and procedures, sufficient money from somewhere, better articulation among the several levels of government, better technical personnel, better political leadership—all are necessary if our society is to choose wisely its objectives, in the fields of health care and elsewhere, and if it is to achieve them.

The assessments that have come my way of the political situation in some metropolitan areas have been something less than heartening. Nonetheless, the future of hospitals, of community health systems, of medical schools, of university-based medical centers, of health care generally, very directly depends on the quality of the governments of our country, in all their forms and operations.

This is true because of the financial and related requirements of a rational health system. It is true, also, because many of the impediments to good health in the country can be addressed only through governmental action. It is government that can regulate drugs, cigarette manufacture, highway safety, the food industry, as well as make appropriations for health activities in preference to other claims for the public dollars. Processes of education, and political, cultural, economic, and other values—the true culture of the community— are at stake. . . .

We have seen, moreover, a new political dimension grow during the past decade, one of grave importance to health-care systems and medical education. Direct citizen participation has become increasingly influential in many governmental decisions, including some in jurisdictions smaller than a city's government. Citizen participation often appears to be especially important in governmental activities affecting health. . . .

In recent years in the United States citizens have been asked, or have been asking, to engage in a new kind of political behavior. The poor, welfare recipients, neighborhood residents, the old, and those expecting health services, among others, participate in various forms of local decision-making or advising, in realms where they never before took part. We know from the urban press that these new participatory procedures have often been awkward, and sometimes raucous. We have had little community experience in developing habits and skills of political life that make this form of participation effective in the new circumstances.

I was more than a little interested to read recently a discussion of "organizational procedures" adopted by a community group having on it physicians and others concerned with the delivery of health services.

One rule said that meetings should be held from time to time in several areas and other locations "for convenience to community representative members."

The next rule said: "Roberts Parliamentary Rules of Procedure need not be strictly adhered to. Discussion should be free and open and should proceed to consensus agreement."

We do not have vast experience in our culture in making institutional decisions in that way.

The characteristics of contemporary United States government are crucial to good health because the extensive health goals our society seeks require massive governmental intervention. The interests of health—of health personnel, hospitals, medical centers, medical colleges, and all the rest—must have representation, in fact inevitably will be represented one way or another, by default or otherwise, in the Congress of the United States, in state legislatures, in city councils.

One must not think of a monolithic health community that should, or will, represent itself in councils of government. Differing interests and values are found within single segments of the health establishment, including "private practices" and medical education, and they have and will find public expression. The point is that all health professionals, all practitioners, will find that what they do and want to do are matters of public policy. Among all of the implications of our changing world for the practice of medicine, delivery of health care, and the character of medical education, this fact strikes me as uniquely important. . . .

The full health education of physicians and other types of health personnel will not be complete in the future without attention to the social and political context within which they must function—even in their most highly specialized and technical capacities. They are participants in the political process, desiring to be so or not. Their effective participation will be greatly influenced by their breadth of viewpoint, by their understanding of the full society within which they function, and by their understanding of the processes of decision-making that will ultimately determine what they and their institutions are asked to do, are permitted to do, are forced to do.

SIX

The End of a Century
1972–1973

THE DESIRE—OFTEN IT SEEMED A clamor—for attention during the late 1960s and early 1970s by the wide variety of persons who made up the University is only faintly suggested by the small number of excerpts that can be included in a book of this size. When speaking to the local chapters of the American Association of University Professors in Memphis on January 7, 1972, I reported that I had recently been visiting classes of my own choosing at Vanderbilt, sometimes as often as once a week. I said I did not think the practice would necessarily improve the quality of the University's instruction, but I thought it rather buoyant of one Vanderbilt faculty member to begin his chemistry lecture the day after my visit by saying, "Today we can go faster. The Chancellor is not here."

A slice of the mood of the early 1970s was evident in comments I made when opening a special meeting of the Faculty Assembly that I called on March 7, 1972.

One of the explicit purposes for which the Faculty Assembly may be convened is to permit members to direct questions to the chancellor or other officers of administration, or to the chairman of the Faculty Senate. Although in the past formal opportunity has

been afforded to those present to ask questions, the previous business has usually taken sufficient time to discourage the exercise of
that prerogative. I thought that today we might experiment by setting up conditions that would encourage members who wish to do
so to put questions or to discuss issues of interest to themselves.

"Communication" has been the watchword for several years
throughout all reaches of our society, not least on university campuses. Difficulties are explained as a consequence of inadequate
communications; successes are explained as a consequence of successes in communication. Much the same can be said for the blood
brother of communication, consultation. An enormous amount of
faculty and executive time goes into keeping our university knit together with a sense of community. Our community is one in which
all constituencies wish to feel informed, consulted, and influential—including trustees, parents, professional and non-professional
staff, donors, students, former students, and others, as well as us
in this room. I am myself on the telephone, on the platform, on
the road much of the time seeking to send, and hoping to receive,
communications.

There is an interesting dynamic in the process. The more one
seeks to increase the volume and significance of communication and
consultation with his several constituencies, the more the anxiety
created in any given one of them—out of fear, I suppose, that the
others are getting a disproportionate share of attention.

A current case in point is reported to me by our solicitors in the
Nashville Living Endowment Campaign this spring. They tell me
that a major theme of reaction among our local alumni is that the
Chancellor and the University will not listen to them, does not
communicate with them, does not care what they think. They even
say that our trustees are unresponsive, and of course they gave up
on the faculty long ago. The contrapuntal fact is that during the last
three years I have repeatedly received questions from student
groups, and sometimes from faculty members, revealing a deep-

seated anxiety that university policies are inordinately and unwisely shaped by concern for alumni opinion.

Whenever one of us, you or I, seeks to relate successfully to a particular constituency, there is frequently a reaction from others. Members of the faculty have at times expressed in our forums the view that some of their faculty colleagues, or I, or other administrative officers, have devoted entirely too much attention in recent years to student affairs. And then I read a confidential comment by a Vanderbilt trustee that Heard is really a good fellow, except that he is a blind captive of the faculty. And, of course, on our own campus, he who looks often in the direction of one school may find himself thought to be unfaithful to the others.

I have proposed a number of times in the past to officers of the Faculty Senate that we hold for faculty members a "meeting of the University"—the kind of open, question session that worked, in my view at least, with great success for students over a period of recent years. For one reason or another this suggestion has never been taken up. If after today we want to repeat this kind of meeting we can do so.

❧

The Alumni Luncheon in Rand Hall on June 3, 1972, was my tenth in office at Vanderbilt, the tenth of what turned out to be twenty. My remarks at the luncheon constituted a report on Vanderbilt at work and illustrated the responsibility I felt to keep alumni and other University constituencies informed about the multifaceted state of the University. For some examples, the following information was imparted to the faithful:

At last week's commencement, 1538 students were graduated from Vanderbilt, receiving fifteen different kinds of degrees, awarded for work in the eight schools of the University. . . .

The End of a Century, 1972–1973

The report on the University is good [except that] its financial deprivations are serious; its needs are great. . . .

Next March 17 will mark the hundredth anniversary of the founding of Vanderbilt. Our centennial celebration will extend from that date until the fall of 1975, one hundred years after the doors of the first building—now we know it as Kirkland Hall—were opened. . . .

Earlier University anniversaries brought together on the campus great convocations of academic personages from about the land to commemorate the past and contemplate the future. In the new circumstances of our lives, such gatherings no longer serve the old purposes. We therefore plan to mark the anniversary in other ways that will celebrate the event and simultaneously encourage our self-appraisal and planning and the selective strengthening of our resources.

We look toward a series of separate Centennial Lectures by eminent persons under the sponsorship of schools and departments.

A number of important educational organizations will hold their regular meetings on the campus: the annual meeting of the Association of American Universities will meet here in April 1973, the triennial meeting of the United Chapters of Phi Beta Kappa will convene here in August 1973, the annual meeting of the Council of Southern Universities in the spring of 1974. . . .

A Centennial Medallion has been approved by the Board of Trust. . . .

It will all begin next March 17 in an event to which our trustee William H. Vanderbilt has invited all other descendants of the Commodore and their families.

Our ninety-ninth year was made a signal one by the award of the Nobel Prize in Physiology or Medicine to Professor Earl Sutherland of the Medical School, the first Nobel Prize awarded for scientific investigation by a faculty member in any institution in any state of the Old South.

This notable distinction did not, however, stand alone. Two other members of the faculty were elected to the National Academy of Sciences—bringing our total to four (we had none ten years ago)—and literally dozens of our faculty received regional, national, and international distinctions. . . .

In the course of the past year 541 faculty members have published professional writings, including over half a hundred books of their own, with others edited, and more than eight hundred articles.

Last December, the Andrew W. Mellon Foundation chose Vanderbilt for a special award—one million dollars—as one of only eight universities in the nation, and the only one in the South so honored, an award made to "leading private universities which have exercised special responsibility over the years for setting and maintaining high academic standards." . . .

I also reported on the retirement and replacement of four important administrative officers, the completion of the Eldon Stevenson Center for the Natural Sciences (named for trustee and benefactor Eldon Stevenson, Jr.), the completion of a Lucite sculpture by Nancy duPont Reynolds (wife of one alumnus and mother of another) for placement in the center, the completion of the Joe and Howard Werthan Building (an addition to the Medical School), the construction underway of the new Olin Hall of Engineering, and the prospective ground breaking for the Madison Sarratt Student Center.

The first class had been graduated from the new Graduate School of Management. Enrollment applications were strong, especially, as always, in the Medical School, conspicuously so in recent years in the Law School, always in the College of Arts and Science, and in the early 1970s in the Nursing School. The Board of Trust had authorized admission of women to the College of Arts and Science to equal the admission of men.

The End of a Century, 1972–1973

(Admission of women had previously been limited to one-third of the entering class.)

I also reported on other phases of Vanderbilt's life, including the new undergraduate programs in Regensburg, Germany, and Madrid, Spain, and negotiations underway to open a comparable program in Great Britain.

All of this is to say to you that your university is at work, that it is fulfilling the purposes for which it was created, for which you came here, for which our present students come, and to which we dedicate our best talents, year in and year out.

❧

During the years 1972 and 1973 I spoke formally away from Nashville on something over thirty occasions in the United States. These included appearances in, among other places, Syracuse, St. Louis, Orlando, Philadelphia, Memphis, Evanston, Baton Rouge, Seattle, Boston, San Antonio, Atlanta (more than once), and New York City (several times). There is a temptation to over indulge in illustrating the subjects on which a university officer can spend time.

But the most important work was always at home, and in my concept the most important constituency—if a constituency can be so designated among several essential constituencies—was the faculty. Consequently, I have several times drawn excerpts from remarks to Vanderbilt's Faculty Assembly. Here are some from the manuscript for my meeting with it August 31, 1972.

The progress we have made and are now making in solving our extraordinarily difficult—though far from unique—financial problems is a direct credit to the deans of the schools, chairmen of the departments, and others who carry budget-making responsibilities. They are strong advocates of the interests of the colleagues whom they represent, but they are also realistic and tough-minded and patient and cooperative. I thank them. We all stand in their debt.

I spare you a recitation of the numerous elements that make up our financial posture.

I do want to say, however, that responsibility for basic budget policies rests with me. I must persuade our trustees to do what I deem wisest for the University—or in case of disagreement I must implement the policies they adopt—but the first and main responsibility for our financial policies rests with the chancellor. I am aided by an advisory committee known as the Administrative Budget Committee, on which sit the provost and several other senior officers of the University. The deans of the schools do not sit on this committee—although they participate in intensive budget discussions with the provost and other administrative officers. Most of the individuals on the Administrative Budget Committee have faculty rank (and extensive faculty experience) along with their current administrative roles. Adapting a suggestion from the deans of the schools, I am inviting, beginning this semester, the dean of the Graduate School and the chairman-elect and secretary-elect of the Faculty Senate to join the Administrative Budget Committee, to participate on the same basis as other members of the committee. The chief feature of that participation is that each member of the committee represents the University—the institution as a whole—not a particular constituency.

This invitation may not bring undiluted joy to those persons receiving it, but it seems to me they can make a useful contribution if they are able to take part. I remind you that this is an advisory group. We do not take votes. On occasion the group finds itself in the position of Mr. Lincoln's Cabinet—opinion is divided eight or nine to one, but the one constitutes the majority.

The End of a Century, 1972–1973

I make no attempt in our meetings of the Faculty Assembly to announce or acknowledge significant new honors or grants that have come to the University, but I do take note today of the recent award by the Ford Foundation of what is called a "Venture Fund Grant" of $250,000 to Vanderbilt to support educational innovation in the College of Arts and Science. It recognizes what the Foundation's officers consider to be constructive, imaginative, educational advance through changes in the College in the recent past. It seeks to encourage more in the future. In another capacity, I saw a Foundation document about this grant—after the grant was made—which made two things clear. Foundation representatives were much impressed by various college faculty members whom they visited on our campus, and they went away with a very high opinion of the educational statesmanship of Dean Holladay and Provost Hobbs. They were meticulous in pointing out—rather more conscientiously than I for one [as a member of the Foundation's board] thought absolutely necessary—that their decision in the matter was not influenced by any such notions about the Chancellor. I commend the college faculty and wish it well in further progress during the coming year. . . .

Equal employment opportunity, regardless of race, creed, color or sex continues to be a high University priority. Vanderbilt has operated under a plan approved by the U.S. Department of Health, Education, and Welfare since 1969, designed to end discrimination on the basis of race and sex in all job categories of the University. The University's Affirmative Action Plan seeks to increase the number of women and minorities in areas where they have not been represented in proportion to their availability and to ensure fairness and equity in our personnel procedures. All areas of operations are considered, including hiring, classification and recruitment procedures, participation of women and minorities on advisory committees, equity in compensation, and future personnel needs. Vanderbilt obtains a written statement from each business concern that provides services for the University, outlining that concern's efforts to comply with federal specifications ensuring fairness in employment. Our Opportunity Development Office, headed by Mr. Walter R. Murray, Jr., is located in Room 330, Kirkland Hall.

I want to note progress in reaching our objectives as an equal opportunity employer. During the 1971–72 academic year, nine of twenty-two faculty appointments in the College of Arts and Science were women and there was one minority appointment. For the year now beginning, 1972–73, so far women have been named to six full-time faculty appointments, not including appointments in the School of Nursing. Our goal is eight female appointments. In recruitment of minorities we have substantially exceeded the stated goals. Seven full-time and six part-time additional black faculty members are joining us this academic year.

In the non-academic areas of the University, there has been similar progress. We have adjusted our goals to comply with Revised Order #4 of the Department of Health, Education, and Welfare, which specifies guidelines to end sex discrimination. Even though the employment force as a whole has decreased in size, we have substantially increased employment of minorities in all targeted categories, and women in professional, managerial, and official categories. One recent appointment deserves special notice. Mrs. Mary Young was a supervisor in the Rand Hall dining room. She is now our first black Food Services manager and will direct the Divinity School Refectory. I have known Mrs. Young for ten years and I cordially applaud the appointment.

There was more to be said about establishing equal employment opportunity.

I will announce soon the membership for a Commission on the Status of Women at Vanderbilt. Its charge will be to examine the current status of women—among students, staff, and faculty—and to recommend to the chancellor any changes it considers desirable. There will be sixteen members, including ten women and six men. Seven will be faculty, five students, and four staff. The students include undergraduate, graduate, and professional students; the faculty include tenured and non-tenured. Each of the schools is represented by a faculty member or student or both. The commission will be co-chaired by Drs. Macalyne Freeman and Mayer Zald. I am grateful for intensive work by Executive Vice-Chancellor Surface on this matter.

We are not yet perfect in equal employment opportunity. There are two necessary pleas for your help that I must make.

We have one especially important recurring problem.

Staff recruiting simply must be coordinated by the Employment Center of the Personnel Services Division. The "direct hire," which refers to cases in which a department or other prospective employer has identified a particular candidate for a job opening, continues to be a problem. Departments may recommend candidates to be considered but job openings must be publicized. One of the greatest difficulties with direct hires is employment of persons who do not have the qualifications called for in our Personnel Classification System. One practical example: If the University's specifications for a secretarial position call for typing skill of forty words per minute and a person who types only twenty-five words per minute is hired in that classification, in the eyes of our federal brothers our new standard for that classification becomes twenty-five words per minute and we henceforth cannot refuse an applicant for a similar position because he does not meet the forty-word-per-minute standard.

I thank departmental chairmen and search committees that have maintained an equal opportunity posture in seeking candidates for faculty positions. Please make special efforts to generate applications from qualified women and minority group members.

One other point: Departmental chairmen and supervisory personnel understandably do not wish to lose good people, but unless we keep promotional opportunities open for all staff, we do not fulfill a responsibility to provide equal access to career ladders within the University. Job "posting," as the advertising of vacancies is called, is required.

Effective August 8, the National Labor Relations Board certified the Laborers International Union of North America to act as the collective bargaining agent for approximately 285 staff members, principally in Plant Operations and Food Services. The first meeting with the union took place this afternoon. The University will bargain in good faith. We have an upper limit to the resources available to the University and must live within that limit.

We now have in operation a network of five staff advisory councils that allow representation of supervisory and non-supervisory personnel in all areas of the University. From these five councils will be drawn a campus-wide staff advisory council. This campus-wide council will provide three staff representatives to the Community Affairs Board that became active last year.

Several substantive improvements in personnel policies have come from suggestions made by the several councils. The non-faculty staff of the University is an important Vanderbilt constituency requiring the attention of administrative officers and faculty alike. Many of our staff have long belonged to the University family and identify strongly with the University. As I did last year at the opening of the fall semester, I shall address staff members next week, in three meetings, a week from today, two in the afternoon and one at 10:00 P.M. to catch the night shift. Your support of the new staff council advisory system is important. The effectiveness of all of us ultimately depends on the effectiveness of the rest of us.

If you gain the impression that there is more to my job—and yours—than direct educational effort, you are correct. Through a variety of means of communication I will report and inform about University matters during the coming year.

The End of a Century, 1972–1973

❦

In 1972 I continued the practice of meeting with successive groups of staff employees, the meetings timed to mesh with employee shifts. I declared at the outset, as I had to the Faculty Assembly the week before, that "the effectiveness of all of us ultimately rests on the effectiveness of the rest of us."

On September 7 three sessions were held, one at 2:00 P.M. and another at 3:30 P.M. in Underwood Auditorium and a third, for the convenience of hospital personnel, at 10:00 P.M. in the old Vanderbilt University Theater on Garland Avenue, not yet removed to make way for Light Hall. To acknowledge and encourage recognition of the importance of the work of the University's several thousand nonprofessional personnel was a prime goal. It was a goal not everyone was sure could be achieved or was worth the effort, even those concerned about the spread of labor union organizing activity among University employees.

In addition to speaking in various ways about the oneness of Vanderbilt—the ultimate dependence of all the University's other personnel on the work that those being addressed do—I said,

I also get satisfaction from the fact that last fall the Board of Trust elected a new member who used to be on the grounds crew here at Vanderbilt. Bishop Joseph Johnson of the Christian Methodist Episcopal Church became our second black trustee. He lives now in Louisiana. From hearing him talk I can assure you that he remembers his days here as a worker as well as his days, later on, as a student.

Last spring, 203 members of the staff were honored at a luncheon in Branscomb Quadrangle. They were persons who had worked ten years or more for Vanderbilt. They represented over three thousand years of combined service—over fifteen years each, on the average. Sometimes on an athletic team there are "unsung heroes"—players who are sometimes not noticed in the press as much as a few of their teammates, but who are nonetheless important—essential—to the team's victories. We like to sing about all our heroes at Vanderbilt. Don't ever think that people don't know that you are around. They do and I do.

We have made several efforts in the last year to improve communications. The information newsletter, *News and Views,* has been sent to your homes so that you will be sure to receive a copy. A series of staff advisory councils has been established. There are five such staff advisory councils now active, one each (1) in the Medical Center, (2) in the Schools and the College, (3) in the general administration, (4) in Plant Operations, and (5) in Food Services. The members are listed in the program for this meeting. By the middle of this fall, all of the councils should be operating with elected members. We then will be able to establish a campus-wide staff advisory council, drawing representatives from each of the five councils.

Last year a new organization was set up on the campus called the Community Affairs Board. Its purpose is to provide a place where any matter affecting the University can be discussed, studied, and recommendations about it made. It has some more specific responsibilities as well. Along with members from the faculty, student body, and academic administrative ranks, there are to be representatives of the rest of the staff also. There will be three staff representatives chosen from the campus-wide staff advisory council, thus bringing together in one place participants from all segments of the campus, and symbolizing the unity of our community. There is no doubt in my mind that the staff advisory councils can provide a type of effective communication that we have not previously achieved at Vanderbilt. Already their suggestions have produced good results. The change in policy by which a person going on vacation can get an advance of his vacation pay—rather than having to wait until the end of the pay period—was the result of one suggestion. Also growing out of discussions in a staff council was the change in medical insurance policy that now permits a claim to be made for professional fees charged following an accident, whether the medical service was rendered within a hospital or not. Formerly, only charges billed through a hospital were reimbursed. I expect us to lean heavily on the staff councils for advice and recommendations in forming University policies and practices that are of direct importance to your daily lives.

A major matter of concern and attention during the coming year will be our health and hospitalization insurance. We are like other organizations—other universities, and other types of organizations as well—in that we face rapidly rising costs for health care due to inflation but also due to improved kinds of equipment and medicines that are used in diagnosing and treating illnesses and injuries.

Let me talk a minute about how we came to the most recent increases in the monthly Blue Cross-Blue Shield premium. Vanderbilt was notified in June of a 78 percent increase in premium. Immediately we began to look for alternatives and invited other companies to make proposals for our coverage. We did not succeed in finding a better alternative, but in the course of the discussions we were able to get the premium increase reduced from 78 percent to 40 percent. And I can report that the previous annual limit of $7,500 on the amount of major medical benefits that could be paid in one year has been removed, and beginning on September 1 the full $50,000 of major medical coverage is available during a benefit period. This may be small consolation to the family that must now pay $7.31 per month more for coverage—but that is less than it started out to be, and less than it might have been.

It seems clear that our system of health and hospitalization insurance must be modernized. During the next twelve months we shall be re-studying our present plan, re-examining our whole approach, including considering the possibility of a pre-paid health plan to cover general health care costs as well as the types of costs covered by our present plan. The staff advisory councils will be consulted fully as these studies go forward.

There was more. I repeated some of the reports and comments I had made on August 31 to the Faculty Assembly about equal employment opportunity and Vanderbilt's employment and promotion procedures, the University pledge to bargain in good faith with the Laborers International Union of North America that had recently been certified to act as a collective bargaining agent for 285 staff, chiefly in Plant Operations and Food Services, and other personnel matters. I ended by saying,

To attract students, to attract faculty, to attract doctors and nurses to the hospital, to interest private individuals and organizations in giving money to Vanderbilt, to compete successfully for government grants, Vanderbilt must be well run, must be well managed. You are at the heart of that business—how well Vanderbilt is run. You not only do a job you get paid for, but you also make it possible for young people to get an education, for important scientific knowledge to be discovered, for sick people to get well, and much more. All the rest of us thank you because no one of us can do anything without the rest of us.

❧

Vanderbilt is a younger institution than some of the other prominent private and public universities in the United States, but its founding in 1873 had immediate importance for Tennessee and the surrounding states. When the centennial of its founding was celebrated in 1973 on March 17, the date of Commodore Cornelius Vanderbilt's initial financial commitment one hundred years before, 124 members of the Vanderbilt family came to Nashville for a celebration. I spoke at the Centennial Service of Commemoration in Benton Chapel.

One hundred years ago this morning the future seen from the ground on which this chapel stands seemed sure to bring a grievous testing of human capability. Tennessee had been sundered more severely than any other state by civil war. It had experienced secession within secession. The South lay pauperized, humbled, bewildered by its new condition, and fearful of tomorrow. The great market crash of 1873 led to a national financial panic. Wars, revolutions, conquests on continents beyond the seas held no comfort for anyone who faced the future from this place on the city's western border.

In this bleak setting the titan of American transport founded a university in a place to which he would never travel. The response hereabout was fervent, one writer in 1873 proclaiming with what I assume was unconscious humor that "Tennessee Methodists ought to give Commodore Vanderbilt a free pass on the Old Ship of Zion."

The healing, cosmopolitan duty imposed by our founder—to strengthen ties among the geographical sections of our common country—has been done. Students from fifty states and a hundred nations and dozens of religions have come to Vanderbilt for study. Her graduates have gone forth to every part of this now United States and to all parts of our globe, applying their trained talents and fulfilling the founder's goal with everlasting life.

Commodore Vanderbilt once said, "Though I never had any education, no man has ever felt the lack more than I have, and no man appreciates the value of it more than I do and believes more than I do what it will do in the future." He felt that way because increasing the power of the human intellect increases the power of the human being. The intellect is the central concern of Vanderbilt University. It is not our only concern, but just as the power to reason is a distinguishing human attribute, enhancing that power is the central mission of a university. . . .

No valid distinction separates highest human values from highest powers of the human mind. Morality and ultimate realism are one. Moses came down the mountain with commandments for conduct that are utilitarian rules. They did not come to him in isolation from the human condition to which they would apply. Morality and ultimate realism coincide. That is why commitment to reason is the heart of this university and its quest to help people help themselves become more effective, productive, useful, moral, spiritually fulfilled, happy.

Higher education in America began in small denominational colleges offering classical subjects. During the middle of the nineteenth century the purposes of higher education were radically expanded with accompanying alterations in the scope and shape of institutional life. The modern Western diversified university not only instructs but also trains for the professions, stimulates skepticism, sponsors inquiry, honors invention, and encourages its graduates, its faculties, itself, to apply the fruits of intellect to the world outside. That kind of university evolved during almost precisely the hundred years that constitute the life of Vanderbilt.

Vanderbilt remains the only such private university in the central South, the great region bounded by the Ohio and Mississippi Rivers, the Gulf of Mexico and the Appalachians. It is yet this area's only university, public or private, in the select Council of Southern Universities and Association of American Universities. Last year Professor Sutherland of Vanderbilt's Department of Physiology won a Nobel Prize, the first ever awarded for work in an institution in any of the states of the old Confederacy. This year Dr. Stanford Moore became our first alumnus to win a Nobel Prize. Most important of all for its past and its future, Vanderbilt is today a place of authentic intellectual freedom.

America is already in a new stage of educational development, and I believe Vanderbilt's form and substance will change more swiftly and profoundly in the years ahead than in the years behind. Our world is more intricately interlinked, our problems more acute, their solutions more complicated, and the consequences of failure more devastating than ever before—and this cheerless condition of our culture is significantly a product of the uses of the mind. Our provost uses a phrase, "the consequences of knowledge." If the consequences of knowledge are intractable crises in energy use, environmental deterioration, population growth, ungovernable metropolises, and unsatisfiable expectations generally, is it not sensible to fear rather than foster the mind? We do have much to fear if we do not do what we ought to do. But we cannot by act of will stop human minds from working, nor should we if we could. Our Creator saw to that. We can put our minds to better use, and it is to that unrelenting toil that this university dedicates itself anew.

During the thirty months of centennial celebrations that follow today, our faculties will carry forward the search for new knowledge and for paths to better education and its use. Our freedom to fashion Vanderbilt's future beyond 1973 will differ much from that of 1873. No college or university can ever be an island to itself again. These institutions are the seminal elements in a knowledge culture, a new worldwide culture, whose underlying faith assumes the efficacy of knowledge—in caring for the ill, in lifting national income, in spreading wealth, in sustaining peace, in advancing any national purpose, including going to the moon.

We are one part in a large structure of national intellectual resources. What we do and how we do it will be of consequence to our neighbors in Nashville, to the people and government of the commonwealth of Tennessee, to all our nation, ultimately to other peoples as well. As one consequence it will be wise as well as inevitable for them to have something to say about what we do and how we do it, and for us in turn to help to mold the larger systems of which we are a part.

Speaking of the University

Vanderbilt's strength throughout its life has flowed from many sources. Generations of faculties, students, former students, trustees, administrative officers, staffs of many kinds, private supporters and friends of many kinds, public programs and policies of many kinds have helped to build its strengths in many varied ways. But its merit originated in the strength of its origins, in an idea conceived voluntarily by one set of men, brought to robust life by a gift offered voluntarily by quite a different man, in the classic spirit of American civic responsibility. We are grateful for both the idea and the gift this day.

❧

The Thirtieth Triennial Meeting of the Council of the United Chapters of Phi Beta Kappa met at Vanderbilt on August 9, 1973, in response to an invitation of the University to do so as part of Vanderbilt's centennial recognition. I was invited to speak at a dinner session in Branscomb Quadrangle, which seemed a good occasion—after opening jocularity—to speculate on the irony that "the large challenge to knowledge in our time derives from the dynamic interplay between knowledge as a cause of contemporary human distresses and as a way of mitigating or eliminating them."

It strikes the ever-present man and woman in the street as a curious irony that with all the money, time, and energy that have been spent on research, teaching, and education in our country, we are beset by hosts of new internal and external problems, and, not only that, our problems seem more than ever to defy solution. The same curious irony also impresses the person at the taxpayer's window, in the legislature, in responsible corporate and labor leadership, and even those on college and university boards of trustees.

If the economists are so great, why can't we control inflation? If the engineers are so great, why do we have so much pollution? If the political scientists and moral philosophers are so great, why do we have a Watergate? If the physicists and chemists are so great, why is there so much unutilized waste in our society? If the professional training of social workers, lawyers, and physicians is so great, why do we have horrendous problems of overloaded welfare roles, overloaded court dockets, and grossly unattended health needs in our population? Some may even have the temerity to ask, if our professors of English are so great, why have the diction and syntax of the country deteriorated so, you know, like abominably?

Those questions, however, constitute only part of the equation. We have a reciprocal process in which scholarly inquiry (sometimes heavily subsidized toward reaching specific targeted objectives) not only may succeed in achieving whatever purposes it pursues but also can create new conditions that may themselves lead to new problems. The classic illustration still strikes me as the best because of its simplicity. The sciences of medicine and public health have been applied with stunning success in reducing disease and death rates and prolonging life all around the world. The humanitarian and social values of doing so have been beyond question. But the fact is that the resulting population growth has brought herculean problems in its wake.

Related, but more difficult to fathom, is the impact of knowledge-bred technocracy on our social systems, on our capacities for self-government, on other human institutions, and on the psychological strength and stability of individuals. Incredibly swift transport, enormously varied and instantaneous communications, the unprecedented mobility of populations, and increased affluence above the margin of necessity—all phenomena that stem ultimately from the new knowledge produced by scholarship—have had a profound impact on the historically stabilizing influences of societies all around the world. Among the stabilizing influences affected have been religion, family structure, affection for locality, social custom, historical teachings, conventions of the market place, and the socializing influence of education, whether in a tribal ritual or a public school. And these profound changes have an obvious direct impact on personal values, loyalties, incentives, creeds.

Less subtly, we sometimes see an astonishing positive correlation between, on the one hand, economic development and what is called a rise in the standard of living, and on the other, growth in anti-social behavior—such as violence, crime, family disruption, drugs, idleness, loss of self-reliance, loss of self-respect.

The very idea of "progress" itself is automatically called into question. "By their fruits ye shall know them." Leaving aside the fruits that are sweet, sufficient fruits have been bitter to produce a new kind of latent challenge to the processes of knowing to which most of us here have devoted our lives.

You will notice that I have said nothing of the sweet fruits of knowledge, the enormous positive social and personal advances the planet and its inhabitants have enjoyed. Nor will I tonight. Nor have I, except briefly, acknowledged in this group, where it would be uniquely appropriate, the sweet fruits of seeking and acquiring knowledge, those marvelous endeavors that are rewards in themselves for those graced to achieve them. Rather, I invite attention to what strikes me as an inevitable skepticism, close to antagonism, in our society toward our scholarly business.

The dangers to scholarship obviously have origins other than those I have yet mentioned. Let me illustrate with four more, quickly, even though doing so cryptically incurs the risk of misinterpreting the significance of each.

First, the high rewards of specialization in systematic inquiry have often led to dissociation between the results of inquiry and the consequences of those results.

The high rewards of objectivity in systematic inquiry have often led also to an intensified distinction between the processes and the consequences of study.

The End of a Century, 1972–1973

The point is not that there is conflict between specialization and systematic inquiry on the one hand, and the quality of the scholar's intention, esthetic values, or ethical concerns on the other. The point is simply that a dissociation between these two broad categories of intellectual attention has increasingly developed.

Second, this dissociation has occurred at a time when internal developments in the "knowledge industry"—if you will tolerate that blasphemy—introduce quantitative factors of such significance that those dimensions of quantity change the very nature of much of the intellectual effort that is called scholarly and nowadays leads to knowledge. Librarians know what I mean. The huge amounts of quantitative data, the enormous volume of commentary, and the associated costs of handling both, make research scholars, research libraries, and research institutes very different from what they once were. Desirable efforts to integrate data, to relate disparate processes of inquiry to each other, and to reach competent conclusions resting on comprehensive knowledge, all create problems for the scholar that he did not encounter in an earlier time that was also a simpler time.

Third, in addition, the results of scholarly research carried on or originating in universities and colleges affect drastically a society's economic life and consequently its changing structure of occupations. At the same time, there are intimate and often static linkages among educational programs at all levels of schooling, from kindergarten through graduate school. Meshing a society's educational system, very difficult to alter quickly, with that same society's rapidly changing occupational requirements, poses severe demands. The debate on behalf of "career" education versus education intended to generate more general qualities of personality and intellect is one manifestation of the difficulty. This is especially so when the more general education does not always demonstrate that those who pursue it gain the incentives, abilities, and rewards associated with productive labor. The problems of maladjustment derive not only from the nature of our swiftly developing knowledge systems. Failure to adapt satisfactorily is also blamed, understandably if heatedly, on the educational community, although in truth there is no consensus outside the educational community as to the educational goals to be sought.

Finally, one more illustration of another kind of underlying cause of the challenges to knowledge. The enormous increase in the proportion of the population pursuing college and advanced higher education has altered the basis of the popular perception of scholars. So has the increasing intimacy between faculty members who have worked with others in other reaches of society since World War II. Alas, the proximity of so many to the court has inexorably led some to conclude that the emperor's nakedness on occasion is more reality than illusion. The protective insulation of unfamiliarity has been diluted.

My lugubrious message says two things. After several thousand busy years, the human intellect has brought us to a state in which the human race and its planet may no longer be compatible. This condition is an inherent challenge to the intellectual community, and it comes at a time when that community is enormously burdened by new and complex conditions in which it works.

The meaning of this message for us in college and university scholarship can hardly be fully discerned. I leave you, however, with four things that I believe to be inescapably true.

A topic of recurring discussion in our world these days is autonomy, authority, and accountability. We customarily applaud institutional autonomy, decry authority from without that dilutes it, and readily see the virtues of being accountable largely to ourselves. In fact, none of us in our individual academic roles has ever been fully free to do whatever he wished, nor should we be. The autonomy of our institutions has been and will continue to be invaded by many forms of external regulation, public and private, academic and non-academic. The expectations of Phi Beta Kappa itself constitute an influence in the internal affairs of a college.

Whatever else may be said, colleges and universities in years ahead will be held accountable, in the largest and deepest sense of social utility, by the society that supports them. Free choice of individual intellectual activity and conditions of more general unfettered intellectual freedom will be ensured only as long as they are supported by a social consensus.

That means to me that each scholar in his own socially sensitive, enlightened, chosen way must offer his talents to the understanding and solution of the difficulties that face humankind, difficulties that in toto are objectively unique in our known history.

An inevitable consequence will also be the imposition by society of controls over itself, we hope sufficient and sufficiently soon. The world of knowledge can contribute especially to the design of those self-controls, whether in avoiding material waste, or supplying essential needs, or ennobling human incentives, or deepening human compassion, or creating the inspiration of beauty, or helping us to do justly, love mercy, and walk humbly with our God.

Finally, *if the ways of scholarship are to be challenged, it is essential that they be defended in the highest councils where social decision-making occurs.* If the ways of scholarship are to be altered, it is essential that wisdom prevail in those same councils, whether they be of formal government or of community opinion. The world has already come into the ivory tower. For a generation scholars have increasingly left the tower to do business in the councils of the community. We will need to do that more, and to do that more effectively, in the times ahead if the challenges to knowledge are to bring forth the community's best response.

SEVEN

A New Placidity
1974–1975

BY 1974 THE CLIMATE ON AMERICAN campuses had changed markedly. A new calm prevailed. Drafting for military service had been stopped in 1973, withdrawal of U.S. troops from Vietnam had been steady, and "student activism" had declined, developments seen by many as closely related.

I continued to feel it useful to Vanderbilt to speak away from Nashville, some example events during 1974 and 1975 being the Tenth Anniversary Celebration of the Consortium of Universities in Washington, D.C., a conference at the John F. Kennedy Center at Harvard on political finance (a subject about which, as a political scientist, I had published in the past), the Annual Trustees Dinner of the Savannah Country Day School in Savannah, Georgia (from which Vanderbilt received a welcome number of good students), the Friends of the Library at Duke University, commencement exercises at Duke, Middle Tennessee State University, and Southwestern at Memphis (now Rhodes College), and the memorial service in Miami for Earl Sutherland, Vanderbilt's first Nobel Laureate.

As always, many invitations to speak locally came during these years, one being to address the American Surgical Association, meeting on the campus, and another to speak to the Nashville Chapter of the Financial Executives Institute, the thrust being the similarities and differences among the financial management needs and practices of universities on one hand, and profit oriented enterprises on the other.

At the spring 1975 meeting of the Board of Trust, Sam M. Fleming succeeded William S. Vaughn as the Board's president. Mr. Vaughn, a graduate of the class of 1923, had been the first student to earn all A's since the letter-grading system was introduced, had been the Founder's Medalist and a Rhodes Scholar, and had subsequently enjoyed a brilliant business career. When elected President of the Vanderbilt Board in 1968 to succeed Harold Vanderbilt, he was the chief executive officer of the Eastman Kodak Company. His tenure as president included extraordinarily difficult years of campus tension, during which his poise, wide-ranging experience, intellectual powers, and sagacity made him of prodigious value to Vanderbilt, and especially to me.

Vanderbilt celebrated the centennial of the campus on April 28, 1974, the hundredth anniversary of the laying of the cornerstone of the principal building constructed by the University, known simply as Main Building and later called College Hall until renamed Kirkland Hall. The celebration was held in two places, in Benton Chapel and by the main north door to Kirkland Hall beside the 1874 cornerstone. The celebration was designed to honor a segment of the University's citizens who often seemed to my colleagues and me to be insufficiently recognized, to be taken for granted: the nonacademic staff, especially the nonprofessional nonacademic staff, a long and wide line of loyal persons of competence and good will who from the beginning had been essential to the institution. Others deserved recognition, too, in commemorating the acquisition and development of the physical campus, but we thought it an especially suitable time to sing of the unsung.

A principal speaker for the occasion was Joseph A. Johnson, Jr., bishop of the Christian Methodist Episcopal Church. In 1953 Bishop Johnson became the first black student admitted to Vanderbilt. He was the first black student to earn a Vanderbilt degree, bachelor of divinity in 1954, and the first to earn a Vanderbilt doctoral degree, doctor of philosophy, in 1958. When Bishop Johnson died, I said, in part, in speaking at his funeral in Shreveport, Louisiana, September 29, 1979:

On April 28, 1974, we celebrated the centennial of the laying of the cornerstone of the first building constructed for Vanderbilt University. Taking part were descendants of persons who were responsible for the founding of the University, and for providing the land, and representatives of students, faculty, staff, alumni—of all who make up the University.

Bishop Johnson spoke for the trustees. In doing so he recalled that in 1939 he had worked on the campus as one of the grounds crew. It must have been in the fall of the year, because he told of stuffing leaves into big gunny sacks. From that recollection he then reflected—and he did it again on a later occasion in one of our Board meetings—on his own experiences: of handicaps and yet opportunities; of discrimination and yet progress; of injustice and yet recourse; of discouragement and yet determination; of unfairness and yet hope. All these contrasts and more he had felt throughout his life—his life that was demanding, striving, hard working, educated, tolerant, deeply religious, his gloriously fulfilled and rewarding life.

Bishop Johnson's role in the centennial celebration could be read as a sign of significant change at Vanderbilt—insufficient change, surely, but nonetheless in the right direction. Walter R. Murray, the University's first black trustee, a young alumnus elected in 1970, later noted that the first black student to become Homecoming Queen (Joey Gaudin) was chosen in 1971, that the first black student to become president of the Student Association (that is, the student body) (Larry Wallace) was chosen in 1971, and that Bishop Johnson was also elected a trustee in 1971, to become Vanderbilt's second black trustee. Mr. Murray believed that the pioneering significance of the three 1971 selections warranted more publicity than they had received. I would have welcomed more notice of the progress but also found a positive sign in the fact that the innovations were taken as a normal development.

My own remarks on April 28, 1974, in Benton Chapel, went as follows:

This day we express our appreciation of those who have designed, built, and cared for this campus over the past century. No single person or group of persons among us can alone be, or make, a university. No few persons or groups created Vanderbilt. Our university was wrought in the hearts and by the hands of many.

And a university in its daily life is a place of many mansions. There is no science without a laboratory, no fine arts without a gallery, no medicine without a hospital, no astronomy without an observatory, no baseball without a diamond, no drama without a theater, no chapel services without a chapel, no lecture without a classroom, no faculty without offices, no scholars without books, no books without libraries, and in a university like Vanderbilt, no students without residence halls, dining halls, meeting places, working places, playing places. A university is not just its grounds and buildings, but they are vital to its quality and in shaping its life.

The mood, style, and manner of every institution are implied by the architecture, the planting, the spaces, the cleanliness, the efficiency, the care and concern that are shown in the way things look and work. No student ever forgets them. And they are a large part of the world in which the rest of us who also help to make up the University daily live.

A century ago today, the cornerstone of Kirkland Hall was laid. The centennial of the campus that we celebrate this morning honors those who have built this campus and cared for it with their talents and energies and thought for one hundred years. The generosity of successive generations of members of the Vanderbilt family, one of whom is among us now, has provided much of two necessary ingredients, leadership and money. But these alone do not make a university, nor do teachers and students and research workers and chancellors by themselves, nor all together, make a university. There is no university without those who put stone beside stone and brick upon brick in grand design, and make paths of beauty out of stubble fields.

Among us this morning are one-fourth of a hundred men and women who have labored in Vanderbilt for one-fourth or more of its century of life—including one at their head who has given himself to this institution for much more than one-half of its life, and for nearly three-fourths of his own.

Willa Cather said that to be dissolved into something complete and great is happiness. A university does not become great without those who are a part of it. To be part of a university is more than simply being "in" the university or "with" the university. One does not become part of an institution without rigorously applying his skills and talents, and without loyalty of spirit, in the continuing enlargement of the depth and breadth and merit of what the institution does. The works and glories of the human race that are achieved through institutions grow from common effort, from the collaborative, coordinated labors of many. The things we do in our life together at Vanderbilt all differ from each other, yet all are necessary to each other.

A New Placidity, 1974–1975

Yesterday's burdens may have seemed heavy. Tomorrow's obstacles may seem high. But we at Vanderbilt draw strength from the continuity of the University. A few things were started one hundred years ago. Many small things were among them. They have builded on each other to add steadily to the greatness of an institution. The evidence and the reward are found in the achievements of those students who have come searchingly to us and gone forth as more fully educated, better people. The evidence and reward are found in every contribution to human welfare coming from the scholarship and skills of Vanderbilt's faculties. Some of the little things—the normal things—you and I did during this past week will have effect one hundred years hence, as we create a university to be here one thousand years more.

Someone said to me the other day that people do not differ so much in talent and capacity as they do in purpose and determination. He said that an ordinary person enchanted with a purpose can achieve extraordinary victories. In writing a book, or teaching a student, or healing a patient, in planting a tree, or laying a walk, or constructing a building, or in creating places to work that are pleasant and useful, and sometimes even beautiful, in all these things we create something more or better than it was before.

It is accurately said that we individuals are happiest when tested almost to the breaking point and do not fail. Many at Vanderbilt over this century now gone must have been happy. A university of merit is born of much pain and sacrifice. Yet we who are privileged to be part of it are truly graced.

John Masefield, the English poet, has written lines now famous, that pay tribute to English universities and are true of true universities everywhere:

There are few earthly things more splendid than a University. In these days of broken frontiers and collapsing values—when every future looks somewhat grim, and every ancient foothold has become something of a quagmire, wherever a University stands, it stands and shines; wherever it exists, the free minds of men, urged on to full and fair inquiry, may still bring wisdom into human affairs.

Each of us makes a difference. All of us together make a university. It is to the continuing creation of this University, Vanderbilt, that we rededicate ourselves this centennial morning.

We were sentimental that day and after moving to the cornerstone of Kirkland Hall acknowledged the presence of William B. Tigert, great-grandson of Bishop Holland McTyeire, first president of the Board of Trust; of Mrs. James Sartor (Carolyn Southgate Sartor), great-granddaughter of Mrs. William Elliston (Elizabeth Boddie Elliston), who donated some of the land for the original campus; of Wilbur Foster Creighton, Jr., grandson of Wilbur Creighton, who was responsible for the foundation of the building whose beginning was being celebrated; and of Dr. Thomas Fite Paine, who rededicated the cornerstone that his great-grandfather, Bishop Robert Paine, had laid a century before.

❧

Even university educators can hope that the theme of some occasions will require attempts at humor rather than a summons to duty or pleas for gold and wisdom. When it was decided by admirers of Vanderbilt alumnus and trustee Dan May, class of 1919, to recognize his long, constructive, unselfish career of community service by giving a dinner in his honor, I was asked to preside. Dan stipulated on agreeing to the event that humor and joy, not maudlin celebration, must prevail. Dan knew and retained so many jokes that his grandson, Willy

A New Placidity, 1974–1975

May Stern, prepared a volume of them, published in 1993, *There's an Old Southern Saying . . . the Wit and Wisdom of Dan May.*

The dinner was held in the downstairs dining room of the University Club on the Vanderbilt campus May 27, 1974. There were eight scheduled speakers during the evening before Dan had a chance, among them Governor Winfield Dunn, Mayor Beverly Briley, and Chancellor Harvie Branscomb. A number of volunteers also offered adulatory comments following the scheduled speakers. I presided and early in the evening expressed appreciation to Dan on behalf of all for giving us the opportunity to celebrate him.

In the accurate dictionary meaning, we are "Maying" tonight. It means "the celebration of May Day." May also means, I report to you: the springtime of life, the prime, the heyday; it means can; it means maybe; mayhap it may mean, too, may fly, may pole, may pop, mayhem, but best of all it means May Queen. And while the Queen of the Mays is not here in person tonight, I propose a toast to her health and happiness, and to the good fortune enjoyed by all her subjects: to Dorothy! [Here I referred to a letter to Dorothy drafted by Alf Sharp and being circulated for all to sign.]

For those who do not read their scripture regularly, let me remind you that Dan is one of the twelve tribes of Israel. Dan is, in fact, the northernmost city of ancient Palestine—which of course makes him a Danyankee. Now, a Danite is a member of the tribe of Dan, and it is my great hope that by virtue of this evening we outlanders here can all be considered Honorary Danites.

No philosophy of education, that, but the calls on a university chief executive go beyond the academic, which this night's events well illustrated. After all others, except Dan, had spoken, I made a presentation to Dan on behalf of those assembled and others who could not attend.

Speaking of the University

Before we ask Dan to say whatever he would like, I want to make a presentation to him on behalf of the group who are here, and of others who could not come but wished very much to. . . .

On the Monday of May Day at the Rotary Club [when Dan was honored], Cecil Wray and Harvie Branscomb and I met afterward to discuss arrangements for tonight. I asked whether we were going to give a gift. Cecil said no. [Son] Jack had been consulted. He had said Dan already had two of everything and Dorothy didn't want him to have three. I said I thought it a shame not to give Dan an appropriate memento of his night with the Honorary Danites. They said, all right, we commission you to get it. I said I am going to New York this week, and with your power of attorney and financial backing, I will. . . .

I had a terrible time and saw nothing that struck me as appropriate. . . . Time finally ran out . . . and the young lady who had been helping me said . . . "Why don't you just get him a hippopotamus?" I said, "But what does my friend Dan May in Nashville have to do with a hippopotamus?" She said, "You can find a connection. A hippo is a big beast with room for almost anything." So I came away with a hippopotamus, and have spent the last four full days trying to find a connection between Dan and this second largest of jungle beasts. . . .

I have consulted seven encyclopedia volumes, five nature books, four technical treatises from the J.U.L., 109 issues of the *National Geographic*, ten anthologies of poetry, two dictionaries, three joke books, *Bartlett's Quotations* and *Rodale's Word Finder*, six volumes of Rudyard Kipling, and two books of Christian prayer.

Did you know:

that the hippo can wiggle each ear separately, whirl them around independently of each other: and often does?

that he has a stomach of three sections but no appendix or gall bladder?

that in historic times the hippo was widely distributed over large parts of Palestine, including the part known as Dan?

A New Placidity, 1974–1975

that according to Hans Frädich and Ernest M. Lang, writing in Grizimek's *Animal Life Encyclopedia*, vol. 13, section 4, page 115, zoo keepers can tell when a female is in heat: "The male remains in the female's stall and smacks his lips"? . . .

that the elephant's intestinal track extends about 90 feet but that of the hippo about 180?

that the Emperor Augustus in Rome had a hippo in his animal collection that lived forty-three years, from 29 B.C. to 14 A.D.?

that a one-year-old hippo brought to the Memphis zoo in 1914 was still alive in 1963?

that there are two types of hippos, pygmy and regular—that the pygmy hippos occur in West Africa, and the regular hippos in lots of places?

that T. S. Eliot wrote a poem around 1920 called "The Hippopotamus" in which he said, among other things:

> The broad-backed hippopotamus
> Rests on his belly in the mud;
> Although he seems so firm to us
> He is merely flesh and blood.
> . . . .
> I saw the 'potamus take the wing
> Ascending from the damp savannas,
> And quiring angels round him sing
> The praise of God, in loud hosannas.
>
> Blood of the Lamb shall wash him clean
> And him shall heavenly arms enfold,
> Among the saints he shall be seen
> Performing on a harp of gold.

And did you know that the tanning of a hippo skin takes at least six years? After that it is as hard as a Tennessee rock and about 1 3/4″ thick?

About his hide, listen to the poet Hilaire Belloc:

Speaking of the University

I shoot the Hippopotamus
with bullets made of platinum,
Because if I use leaden ones
his hide is sure to flatten 'em.

And so here we are with Dan and a hippopotamus. All I can say, Dan, is that anybody who has learned as much during the last four days, and listened to as much in the last twenty minutes about hippopotamuses as we have tonight, in order to make you a present, must love and admire you very much. I hope you will make this hippo a mascot member of the tribe of Dan to remind you of this evening we have spent together.

Dan then kept the group in extended laughter. Dorothy permitted him to keep the Steuben hippo, and he would display it when playing the recording of the evening's shenanigans.

❧

In the summer of 1974 a special meeting of the Vanderbilt Board of Trust was held at The Cloister on Sea Island, Georgia, to contemplate a new capital fund drive. "Fulfilling the Conception of a Grand University" was the title of a report to the trustees as groundwork for the discussions. As a result, a new fund drive was begun formally in 1977 and ended in 1981, raising $181.4 million against the original goal of $150 million. Preparing for the drive necessarily required much of the time of many colleagues, and of my own time, during those years. We had a staff conference with robust trustee participation at Montgomery Bell State Park February 22, 1975, to address "Where We Go From Here," only one example of many preparatory exercises. Before (and during) the campaign I often spoke on behalf of the University's appeal in Nashville, but especially around the nation.

As always, however, there were other meetings at which remarks were expected. Five spare examples: on November 25, 1974, the first meeting of the Friends of the Library was held, the Friends having been founded recently on the initiative of Jean Heard and others; on February 8, 1975, a centennial symposium sponsored by Vanderbilt's Centennial Fellows Program and by the Alpha-of-Tennessee Chapter of Phi Beta Kappa was held in Underwood Auditorium on "The Structure of Learning and the Structures of the University"; on February 23, 1975, a portrait of Dr. Frank Luton was unveiled in the Sloan Room of the Medical Center; on March 24, 1975, I presented Willy Brandt to an audience of 5,600 in Memorial Gymnasium, his first appearance in the United States since leaving the chancellorship of the Federal Republic of Germany; and on April 7, 1975, I addressed what became a highly technical discussion of university administration by members of the Southern Association of College and University Business Officers, during which I relayed a favorite comment of one of our financially successful Vanderbilt trustees about the efficiency of profit enterprise: "A great deal of mismanagement can be masked by a 10 percent annual growth in sales."

On October 12, 1974, Max Milam was inaugurated as president of the University of Nevada in Reno, at ceremonies marking the centennial of the University. I was invited to speak.

Of the need for universities to anticipate the future, I said, "By looking back, we know the difficulty of looking forward."

As I look back, I find no prediction made in the 1870s of the avalanche of inventions and social innovations that characterized the years after the University of Nevada and Vanderbilt were founded, inventions and innovations that had profound impact on the societal institutions, on the cultural values, on the intellectual insights, on the scientific advances, on the occupational patterns, and on the educational expectations that largely mold a modern university's life. When this University in Nevada was conceived, there was no barbed wire, tractor, hybrid corn, cotton picker, corn picker; no telephone, phonograph, electric light, motion picture, x-ray; no automobile, diesel engine, induction motor, automatic pistol, steam turbine; no airplane, radio, television, photocopier; no calculating machine, cash register, or computer; no antibiotic drug, nuclear fission, electron microscope, tracer isotope, subcellular research, nor any of a multitude of other creations including contraceptive devices, modern weaponry, altered political institutions, and vastly sophisticated systems of knowledge that make ours literally a new world, and our universities deeply different institutions from the four-year colleges and their preparatory schools of a century ago.

If it was impossible in 1874 to foresee what would come in the decades ahead, how can we expect to do so now on an infinitely more complicated and swiftly changing planet? If we have difficulty forecasting the evolution of our dream to 2074, at least we can examine our condition in 1974 from which it will evolve.

Our national and world circumstances today are directly and chiefly a product of our advances in those scientific and classical studies, military tactics, and branches of learning that are "related to agriculture and the mechanic arts," to encourage which Congressman Justin Morrill introduced his bill [in 1862, that founded land grant institutions like this one]. We have succeeded too well in some compartments of life, and too little in others, and the dangerous conditions in which we live in 1974 are the paradoxical result.

I do not propose to inventory the world's woes and . . . trace their origins to the science-based technologies of the nineteenth and twentieth centuries. . . . But as we rededicate ourselves this day to this university, and as we applaud its new leadership, it is proper to

A New Placidity, 1974–1975

seek to understand the tasks they have ahead. I wish to do this by identifying certain dangerous qualities of our present life, and then suggest their implications for universities in the decades before us.

It is easy in the comfortable circumstances of a university like yours and mine to forget that every one of us here, regardless of origin, color, race, or ambition, is in privileged circumstances. We are all well-fed, well-housed, well-clothed—that is, well-clothed when we want to be. But one anomaly of our dangerous condition is that people go hungry in the United States. I do not mean that some percentage of an anonymous population is undernourished. I mean that pangs of hunger gnaw at identifiable individuals, persons possessed of names and families and even ambitions, who are your and my close neighbors here in the United States.

Hunger in the United States results from inadequate distribution of food stocks that are available. But in [some other nations in] the world at large, the problem is not alone one of distribution but of the physical sufficiency of food and feed production to feed a recklessly expanding world population. Many nations face the most difficult problems of food supply in a generation.

The ironies of our intellectual progress are abundant. As our universities look ahead to another century, let us reflect that in the western world we have spawned not only a civilization that is in aggregate results unprecedentedly productive of material welfare and cultural richness, but also one that burdens its members with a heavy freight of psychological strains. I read the other day of a report on mental illness among Eskimos [in the *New York Times* of July 15, 1974]. It began:

> Social dislocations caused by the intrusion of Western ways upon the simpler hunting and fishing society of the Far North have been followed by a severe outbreak of mental illness, suicides, and murders among Eskimos, according to mental health experts.

Economic development—a much sought goal all around the world—ironically is often accompanied by growth in social distresses. An astonishing, unhappy correlation can often be observed between, on the one hand, economic development and what we call a rise in the standard of living and, on the other hand, growth in anti-social behavior—violence, crime, family disruption, drugs, idleness, collapse of social institutions, loss of self-reliance, loss of self-respect, and more. The very material productivity that has been a distinguishing characteristic of the Western world, and especially of the United States, breeds human problems as it satisfies human wants.

In these very recent months, we might well be worried over the decline of man-hour productivity in the United States. Our vaunted capacity to increase steadily the material products Americans can produce—with the same amount of effort—has recently stalled, while productivity in some other nations has continued to climb.

This is a matter of concern for those who value a healthy American economy, but it is of special significance in a world of rising expectations everywhere. Whatever their other fruits, the material products of efficient and productive technologies are being demanded by almost all peoples almost everywhere on the globe. And that fact breeds political, social, and economic issues of vast complexity. For just as our nation a century and a decade ago could not continue in peace half slave and half free, our nation and our world in the century ahead will not exist in harmony half rich and half poor, half well-fed and half hungry, half in health and half in disease, half satisfied and half distressed, half with hope and half despairing.

Moreover, we have a world of generic conflicts born of conflicting goals and values. We want both abundance and conservation of resources, production without contaminating side effects, security—personal and national—without cost and with unrestricted freedoms, and as always we want both liberty and order.

Skepticism or distrust of established social institutions has in these past few years been repeatedly expressed in polemical debate and sample surveys. The United States government as a whole, corporations, the military establishment, the churches, the public schools, the professions, the labor unions, not least the colleges and universities, these and other traditional anchor points of American society have been declared either inadequate to meet contemporary needs, or to be suspect in motive, or both.

In 1974 we are beset by extraordinary problems that will consume us if we do not resolve them satisfactorily. I doubt that our predecessors of 1874 anticipated World War I or World War II. The real World War III is more likely to be a conflict between the whole of mankind and the oppressive, interconnected, worldwide threats to our existence, than it is to be a world conflagration of people against people.

Even so, the potential for that universal holocaust abides with us always, and its terror is enlarged by the chance that it can be provoked by a more superficial human error than has ignited some of our needless international conflicts in the past.

I read a startling sentence last week. The sentence said: "There is nothing in nature to prove that it cares more of our human species than for daffodils." That sentence opened a book by the editors of Time-Life Books called *Vanishing Species.* The human race is certainly not currently a vanishing species, but it is clearly an endangered species. Can we save it? Can universities help society to meet this extremity that they had a part in creating? If so, we must go about it differently from the way we have up to now.

This is a formidable challenge. To emphasize that fact I go back to three years before Vanderbilt was founded. The man who would become its first chancellor, Mr. Garland, gave a report in 1870 to the General Conference of the Methodist Episcopal Church, South. He said in part:

> Never was there a greater mistake than that which is becoming so prevalent at the present day, that mere intellectual

culture is of itself adequate to exalt the virtue and secure the happiness of a people. It was never so at any period of the world. . . . Education was never more widely diffused throughout the United States than now. Never was there more ado about it. Never were institutions so multiplied. Learning was never more highly valued and sought after, as a means of reducing the laws of nature, and the properties of matter, to human control, and contributing to national and individual wealth and power. . . . Has the virtue of the people increased with their knowledge? Are our public men more patriotic, more self-denying, more honorable, more true to compacts, and more trustworthy than they were fifty years ago? Are the morals of the people improved? Is there less of crime and lawlessness in proportion to population? Alas! to all such inquiries there comes up a negative response which is well-nigh universal. And yet education is, with a vast number of persons, the agency which is to bring us to the perfectibility, so called, of our nature. . . .

Mr. Garland was arguing for education under the sponsorship of the church he dearly trusted, and from which his new university would part company four decades later. I find little evidence, however, that the formal secularization of many of our colleges and universities can be truly charged with the present intensified form of the difficulties Mr. Garland observed over a century ago. Yet it is abundantly clear that the relationship of "intellectual culture" to moral values and to socially useful purposes remains today a crucial issue to every university's future, and ultimately to America's destiny.

I propose seven working assumptions with which our universities should begin the century ahead. And the eighth assumption is that the seven should not be taken for granted.

First, there is no justification for believing that through some

wondrous working of a natural order all our problems will successfully work themselves out. We may up to now have paid heavy social costs of certain kinds for the benefits of industrialization and
advanced technologies, but naive, maudlin, anti-intellectual know-
nothingness will not help us now in eliminating those costs or
avoiding others in the future. Trained intelligence and humane and
aesthetic sensitivities, inspired by one's faith and a golden vision of
the unity of man, are required if we would match the magnitude of
our problems with ways to moderate or solve them.

This means that the purposes of universities and of university
education go beyond the personal benefits that may accrue to students. A nation must look to larger and more general societal objectives of higher education: to make a better culture, a more tolerant,
just, productive, benign civilization in which people can live peace
fully and seek their own fulfillment in ways at once satisfying to
themselves and supportive of opportunities for others.

We in higher education—as individuals and as institutions—
are a privileged minority. We are obligated to justify the privileges
we enjoy.

A *second* postulate follows: Universities must continue to contribute to increasing the production of socially desirable goods and services in this country and elsewhere.

So does a *third:* Whatever volume of goods and services is forth-
coming around the globe, more equitable distribution everywhere
will help ensure both our domestic tranquillity and the modern reality of what the United States Constitution calls "the common
defense."

And, *fourth,* as contributors to increased material productivity
through science-based, industrial technology, and as major sources
of social thought, those who work in universities must accept responsible concern for the full and the ultimate social consequences
of what they do. Our margins for error and self-indulgence are
steadily narrowing.

Speaking of the University

Intellectual capacity distinguishes the human from other forms of life. The first concern of a university is the enhancement of that power. But a university must also be concerned with ultimate results. How could it be otherwise, in a year in which both a President and a Vice President of the United States have been forced from office in disgrace?

It is absurd—I offer my *fifth* assumption—to suggest that rationality and morality impede each other, that rationality somehow eschews values. Very much the contrary; in the human conduct they commend, ultimate realism and highest morality are one.

When [John Charles] Fremont and [Kit] Carson explored the open spaces of the Great Basin and the Sierra Nevada, they were helping to open up what in their time was called "the New World." The record of our continental pioneers has celebrated their self-reliance in the hostile regions they entered, and also the virtues of the uninhibited personal independence they in consequence displayed.

We now have a new kind of "New World." The self-reliance now required calls more for ability to function in interdependence with others than with independence from them. In this new world, says my *sixth* assumption, we will not preserve our personal prosperity, nor freedom, nor privacy, nor opportunities for personal development by fleeing from the complex, frustrating, mystifying political issues and organizational demands imposed by national and global distress. Every human being needs private satisfactions and personal certainties to maintain equilibrium. But these individual satisfactions are not enough to save an endangered species.

I believe that our evolving dream must, *seventh* and most important of all, help prepare us for an even newer world, hardly now envisioned. The annual consumption of world resources may one day reach a stable plateau. Limits on the availability of nonrenewable resources do exist. Even with unlimited energy, the capacity of our globe and its inhabitants to tolerate material production and consumption would have limits. We will not be able, then, to count on the stimulus and anesthesia of ever-expanding material gratifications to help maintain our physical and mental health. We will need the wit, ingenuity, imagination, and resourcefulness—the wisdom—to gain for ourselves human satisfactions in more subjective modes, and to unprecedented degrees, from other realms of individual behavior. And that will be the newest world of all and the greatest test of our universities and ourselves.

❧

On May 18, 1975, Miles College, in Birmingham, Alabama, held its sixty-fourth commencement exercises. It was a traditionally black institution in whose affairs Vanderbilt trustee Bishop Joseph A. Johnson, Jr., was active. It had dedicated leadership, about which I knew something from colleagues in the Ford Foundation, which had made several grants to the college. I was happy to accept the invitation to speak at commencement. At one point I observed:

Few college presidents can report as many new, meticulously designed, concrete academic programs as I have read in the most recent annual report of your president, as you work in building a "non-traditional black college" adequate to the non-traditional requirements of the last quarter of the twentieth century.

I reported that I had lived in Alabama for three years after World War II, 1946–1949, and could not help contrasting the conditions of public life then and in 1974.

Anyone who does that will be deeply impressed with the effective power of people that is evident in the history of our Southern section during these recent years, years that are, in fact, the lifetime of most of you who are being graduated today.

Speaking of the University

The range and speed of change in Southern politics have been startling. Political reforms whose pursuit two or three decades ago seemed fruitless or endless have been widely attained. The political life of this state and of our region has been modified in fundamental ways. Unyielding, intractable, seemingly unsolvable problems of political organization, of political power, and of human behavior have given way. Those who aspire to make structural changes in our society can take heart.

Poll taxes as a prerequisite for voting were long decried as an obdurate obstacle to an open suffrage, and in some states it seemed that they were as permanently fixed as the stars in the sky. Poll taxes have now been abolished everywhere.

In my native state of Georgia, a county unit system of voting, under which the urban areas of that state were massively handicapped in the selection of statewide officials, seemed to be an eternal feature of the state's political life. After all, the public officials who might be influential in its removal were the very officials elected under the system itself. The Georgia county unit system is now gone.

Gone also all across the South are all legal and most extra-legal restraints on voting by black people.

Gone is legalized segregation, once a pervasive and inflexible characteristic of our society.

Gone is the old legislative malapportionment.

Gone are other ancient shackles imposed on the minority political party across the South.

The most distinctive political feature of the Old South was the one-party system dominated by the Democratic party. That system is so radically altered that in 1972 all eleven former Confederate states voted for the Republican presidential candidate. At all political levels across our region, Republican candidacies and officials are sufficiently numerous to constitute a revolution in the conditions of twenty-five years before. Winston County was for years the *only* Republican county in Alabama. Voting shifts within as well as between the parties signify a vastly more independent politics than prevailed during the decades dominated by the one-party system.

Many changes have occurred that many people like you and me hoped for, and few expected.

Most important of all, black citizens and their interests are no longer simply the objects of reaction in Southern politics, the ploys of demagogic debate. Across the South, blacks now constitute an affirmative voice whose importance is reflected in the number of ballots they cast and in the deference shown that fact by candidates of whatever color.

These changes came about through the power of people, people like ourselves. These changes came about through the actions of individuals: political activity at the polls; judicial activity in the courts; legislative activity in state capitals and in the Congress; tenacious, courageous, peaceful, patient assertion of rights at lunch counters, in buses, in the streets, on lonely country roads. These changes came about through individuals with purpose and determination acting effectively wherever public opinion and public policy are influenced.

I followed that effort to cultivate perspective by warning against the debilitating fear that we cannot do much about the difficulties that plague us, that we have lost control of our destiny. I enumerated and described at some length the litany of the world's woes of social dislocation and resource waste that had emerged during the previous six decades and warned against the assumption that "through some wondrous working of a natural order our problems will all work themselves out," adding, "That reminder is surely not needed here."

And then, to close:

Your faculty, your president, your trustees, and you new alumni may often truly wonder whether the dawn will follow the night. But it will, on this campus, and in our nation, and around our world. It will just take you and the rest of us working relentlessly together.

§

As excerpts in earlier chapters will have made clear, my reports to meetings of the Faculty Assembly were customarily comprehensive and often detailed—and too long for many to be included in this book. My reports to the Faculty Senate were also often long and detailed, a standard agenda item being a report on actions taken "by the University," meaning the appropriate authorities, on senate recommendations of the previous academic year, and another addressed to unfinished business from the previous year, or years. My report to the senate of September 11, 1975, ran to about four thousand words, or thirty-five to forty minutes (if no allowance is made for interruptions by questions, or murmurs of doubt or approval, or sometimes even mirth). I hesitate not to include more of these recurring, major efforts at faculty communication and consultation, but their mood and substance, if not their topics and details, tended to be continuous. At this meeting, for example, my remarks reported approval by the trustee Executive Committee of an "in-residence" academic title (e.g., Musician-in-Residence); of an amendment to the grievance procedures approved for inclusion in the *Faculty Manual;* and of a lengthy report on proposals that had been made to improve the University's—especially faculty—committee structure.

After introductory comments:

As I said last year, university committees pose a dilemma. On the one hand, there should be suitable opportunity for faculty to have a voice in university matters that are not already and automatically under faculty control. On the other, the voice is heard only through sacrifices of time and labor, not unattended by the tedium of detail and the frustration of wheels that turn slowly by the nature of the machine. Nevertheless, I believe we have successfully found new provisions for responsibility and improved communication, and some safeguards against overlapping efforts.

Then followed some fifteen minutes plus of excruciating detail about committee functions, subject matter, and structure, all directed toward improving the value and satisfaction of faculty participation in university matters in which the faculty was not already dominant.

I then addressed other matters and finally a concrete suggestion made in a letter of August 27, 1975, from the chairman of the Faculty Senate, Professor Jean Leblon,

that I consider discussing such issues as will receive priority in your future deliberations with the Board of Trust and the administration of the University, inasmuch, let it be understood, as you deem such topics timely and advisable.

I responded:

As I have thought back over the agenda of meetings of the Board of Trust and its Executive Committee, and actions taken by them, in recent years, the bulk of the items that have come up can be classified in four categories.

The four were: first, standard, recurring, and predictable matters (e.g., approval of faculty promotions and annual school budgets); second, unpredictable matters (e.g., controversies over student publications, responses to lawsuits, and use of unanticipated bequests); third, continuing matters of several years duration, frequently discussed in sundry forums, often recommended by a school or by the senate itself, on which action fortuitously became possible (e.g., appropriations to meet a school's long advocated space needs or creation of a program center requested by a school such as the Center for Industrial Water Quality Management in the Engineering School); and, finally, there are always matters that may not fall into the above categories but on which the chancellor's recommendation or emphasis may have influence with the trustees.

There was more, but this senate meeting closed with what was then a customary invitation:

You senators will have a chance to speak with our trustees yourselves during the fall meeting of the Board in October. As is our custom, the trustees will be inviting members of the senate to have lunch on Thursday, October 2, in the Faculty Dining Room of Rand Hall. We hope all of you can come.

☙

Vanderbilt's three formal occasions celebrating the centennial of the founding of the University were concluded October 3, 1975. A large convocation was convened in Memorial Gymnasium. Symbols of the University's origins were displayed or invoked, among them the charter of August 6, 1872, from the Minute Book of the Chancery Court in Nashville, and a paperbound book, the official account of the "Dedication and Inauguration of The Vanderbilt University," the ceremonies that began October 3, 1875.

Individuals were recognized, including trustee William S. Vaughn, who had just completed seven years as president of the Board of Trust and Dean of Alumni Madison Sarratt. John Horatio Clagett was the first student to register at Vanderbilt, being number one in a hefty leatherbound volume in which every student signed his name during the University's first thirty-five years. Mr. Clagett had no children, but his great niece was present, and her daughter, Lillian Harpole, was present as a member of the freshman class from Roanoke, Virginia, and was asked to stand for recognition.

Two visitors spoke. The president of Yale had spoken at the celebration of the twenty-fifth and the fiftieth anniversaries, and this time Kingman Brewster, the current president, spoke. His focus was largely American. The second speaker, Dr. Soedjatmoko, a widely respected world intellectual, had served in the United Nations and been Indonesia's ambassador to the United States. He was deeply knowledgeable of the United States and was invited to speak as one who looked with knowledge at us from afar.

My own substantive remarks were brief and preceded the two speakers.

At the centennial of the founding, attention focused on the origins. At the centennial of the campus, attention focused on those who have built and cared for the physical facilities. Today, the centennial of the University, we would be in touch with the future, with our purposes and duties, with the academic and intellectual university, with the teaching and learning for which it was founded and built.

A university's duties derive from accelerating accumulations and changes in what we think we know—from the interpretations we place on our insights and the explanations we give of the origin, nature, and destiny of the universe. Our duties are not prescribed alone, however, by the state of knowledge, but also by the qualities of the people who come here to study, to search, to learn, and to make the results useful to themselves and others. The meaning of universities, their grand design, is found in the ways that knowledge and people act and react with each other, and with the societal conditions, the human conditions, in which people live.

The interactions are increasingly intricate. Permutations occur increasingly fast. The relevant context is increasingly the whole world. The requirement that our insight go beyond the observable and logical is increasingly great. The stress on social institutions and the impact on individual personalities are increasingly heavy. And the inevitability that assumptions and values will be questioned rides tandem with the human need for stability in assumptions and values.

Universities must help create harmonious balance between humankind's unlimited capacity to cause change and the limited capacity of human beings to accommodate to change. It is not changes wrought in technology so much as [the resulting] changes in human relationships, values, and the aspirations that flow from them that make the situation in which universities now live. Universities have in our past been such enduring institutions as to be viewed as permanent. But if they would now continue to serve and see their values survive, they must increasingly enlarge their understanding of knowledge, its uses and consequences. To that purpose we are giving our attention today.

EIGHT

Inexorable Change
1976–1977

THE FIRST OF VANDERBILT'S ANNUAL
Parents Weekends was held in February 1964. I was
asked to speak to an assembly of our visitors that year
and annually for the next dozen years until the format of the
weekend was changed. Jean and I would normally greet the vis
itors at a reception following the program. When a special dinner was held in 1989 celebrating the twenty-fifth anniversary, I
was invited to speak again and gave an overview of the quarter-
century experience. The remarks I gave on April 2, 1976, seem
best to reflect the spirit the talks tried, each time, to convey,
and also to signal changes that had occurred in the campus climate by the late 1970s.

This thirteenth annual Parents Weekend has been initiated, organized, and carried out by students. . . .

Last year at this time all four of my wife's and my children were
in college, in four different colleges in fact. Two of them were graduated last May and two others are still enrolled. I speak to you tonight, therefore, as one who has on other occasions, on other campuses, sat out there where you are sitting. I share the pride, anxiety,
curiosity, and mystification that every parent feels at one time or
another. I have an additional perspective, too. My concern must

of necessity extend beyond my own children to yours as well. And there are nearly seven thousand students altogether at Vanderbilt. . . .

I have been thinking lately about two aspects of the current Vanderbilt scene, about two qualities that characterize campuses generally across the country. One of these is the so-called "apathy" among students. The other is the discussion of why go to college at all.

Student activism is surely less in evidence than it was five or ten years ago. Extracurricular student interests have changed. Ten years ago, during the course of a single year several outside speakers invited by students themselves would attract several thousand listeners each at Vanderbilt. Few speakers do so now. Student participation in off-campus community activities has declined. Political demonstrations are less frequent. More time now goes to the books.

It took Jean's and my two 1975 graduates longer to land jobs than either of them found comfortable. My mailbox has its share of letters from perplexed parents wondering why their children cannot gain admission to law or medical school. A senior woman student asked me the other day, jokingly but seriously, what can an English major do after graduation? All of these conditions ask What is college for, in 1976?

First, student moods. I am not so concerned tonight with how campus attitudes today compare with earlier times. I think it is useful to ask, however, how good a predictor campus attitudes at any time are of behavior in later life.

It is often commented nowadays that our present students are lamentably passive and fatalistic, concerned with training for a profession or finding a job, interested in economic security, and turned inward intellectually. The turn toward hobbies, crafts, cultural activities is noted. Political complacency is deplored. It is even sometimes suggested sadly in campus newspapers that students have lost a certain amount of virtue because they listen more attentively now to teachers and parents than they did a few years ago. Vanderbilt has many diverse groups in its student body and many universities are different from Vanderbilt. Nonetheless, comments like these describe the general style and mood of contemporary undergraduate life, especially in contrast with four, six, and eight years ago.

My wife called my attention the other day to a detailed article published in a national magazine. The article silhouettes the college generation of the decade 1930–39. The description of young people's attitudes was derived from extensive interviews with a variety of persons on and off campus all across the country, plus a systematic nationwide sample survey conducted among students. I was intrigued because many of the general characteristics prevailing on campuses in the 1930s parallel those perceived as prevalent today. Moreover, as you and I know well, this generation of the 1930s later became an older generation of the 1940s, 1950s, 1960s, and 1970s.

George Weller wrote a college novel that was published in 1933, called *Not to Eat, Not for Love*. It likened the undergraduate to some snakes that Ralph Waldo Emerson had encountered while making his way to Cambridge in 1834: "four snakes gliding up and down a hollow for no purpose that I could see—not to eat, not for love, but only gliding. . . ."

The survey that Jean ran into found the 1930s college generation to be fatalistic.

> If we take the mean average to be the truth, it is a cautious, subdued, unadventurous generation, unwilling to storm heaven, afraid to make a fool of himself, unable to dramatize its predicament. It may be likened to a very intelligent turtle, skeptical of its biological inheritance, the shell, but determined not to be a bull, a bear, or a goat. The turtle has security. . . .
>
> Security is the summum bonum of the present college generation. This may be convicting the average undergraduate of having good sense, yet security is usually thought of as the

ideal of middle age. Yearners for security do not set foot on
Everest or discover the Mountains of the Moon. They do not
even defy the racketeers and start new wet-wash laundries.
They want a haven in a . . . job that is guaranteed to be safe
and permanent.

The generation of the 1930s skipped central Africa's Mountains of
the Moon and chose instead as its target the moon itself. And it
started a lot of enterprises a lot more complicated, productive, and
useful than wet-wash laundries.

Briefly, other features of the 1930s students:

Experimenting with Leica cameras, rushing for the Berkshire
snow train, Ping-Pong, squash—the popularity of all such diver-
sions increased during the decade by leaps and bounds.

Religion, as an institution, had "taken a back seat."

On drinking and sex . . .

> Less flamboyant drinking is the present-day rule; there is
> no prohibition law to defy, hence one can drink in peace. As
> for sex, it is, of course, still with us. But the campus takes it
> more casually than it did ten years ago. Sex is no longer news.
> And the fact it is no longer news is news.

I found the following paragraph about that earlier generation especially intriguing for us tonight:

> The family as such is no longer an object of derision, as it
> was in the early twenties. Fathers and mothers are listened to
> once more, at least in the East and in the Middle West. (The
> Pacific Coast universities, which lag behind the colleges of the
> East, show less evidence of respect for parental dicta, but even
> on the coast the tide is beginning to turn.) Deference to the
> advice of father is part of the general yearning for security
> among the young. It is also part of a world hungry for cer-

tainty. And as the world wags, so wags the undergraduate, who can usually be counted on to follow the [fashion].

The American colleges have always followed the fashions of the country at large and are still doing so. . . .

For your amusement, I report that the picture of students in the 1930s was put in contrast to students of the 1920s, who were described as possessing "general disrespect for all constituted authority. Iconoclastic, exhibitionist, ignorant, raucous, socially irresponsible, and self-indulgent. . . ." To any of that college generation among us, I apologize.

The points I make are two. As we think about characteristics of the present student generation, remember that while we shape our future, the future also shapes us. Attitudes displayed by a college-age generation are not very good predictors of how they will react to the responsibilities of later life. For those who are worried about the present, that may be a comfort. For those who are happy about the present, that may be a warning. . . .

The student of the 1930s was worried about getting a job, as are many seniors this year: [The] law schools are overcrowded, and the undergraduate knows it." The law schools and medical schools and a lot of other graduate and professional schools are crowded in 1976.

I was accosted by a recent Vanderbilt graduate at an alumni meeting in St. Louis Wednesday night. She said that Vanderbilt not only had not prepared her for a job but had not told her how to go about getting one. I asked whether she had sought help from our Career Planning and Placement Service. No, she did not know there was such an office. She opined that the faculty was at fault for not having directed her to it. The conversation was good-humored and I understand the young lady has a good job. But if Vanderbilt failed her, it was not in not requiring her to take a pre-vocational course of study, not in the fact a faculty member did not direct her to the available student counseling facilities. The University's failure was in not stimulating the qualities of mind that would have led her to discover those facilities for herself. . . .

As it has ever been, a college campus is more an assured place of opportunity than of reward. I remember a commencement speaker who once said that a student who completes his course should not think of himself as better than someone who has not. He should simply realize that he himself is better than he would have been had he not finished that course.

College can offer no guaranteed solution to its students' problems. A college degree cannot be a life insurance policy against future risks. All it can do is to help a student equip himself to meet better whatever comes, help him to enhance his possibilities.

In the years between Catherine the Great's marriage to the heir apparent to the Russian throne and her own accession to the throne, she filled the days with reading. She read everything she could get her hands on and became one of the most knowledgeable and articulate devotees of the eighteenth-century Enlightenment. As empress, her days were filled from early to late with activities of state, but her thought and action for the rest of her life were profoundly influenced and steadily refueled by those early years of study and reflection.

College is a place of rare opportunity. Four years are not a long time, but they offer opportunity in a remarkably protected environment to indulge one's interests, to try options, to do almost anything that a civil society will permit—all without much hazard. And the glory is that different people can do different things.

🌿

The Southern University Conference was an encompassing organization of institutions that met on April 23, 1976, at the Williamsburg Inn in Williamsburg, Virginia. I was invited to speak on "Imperatives for Higher Education in the South," but I added "and Elsewhere." The conference's focus of concern was education in the Southern region. I invoked contrasts between 1976 and the state of Southern graduate education as I had found it in 1961 and reported in a talk at Oak Ridge, Tennessee, to the Conference of Deans of Southern Graduate Schools, in which remarks I had reported bleak conclusions about the region's graduate education.

That lugubrious exercise [in 1961] succeeded in demonstrating by various measures that we in Southern higher education had many imperatives then for the immediate future. Now, fifteen years later, we can note advances, small though they be, and varying in significance though they are.

In the Keniston Report, drawing on opinions of academic departmental chairmen collected in 1957, only 3 percent of arts and science departments that were ranked among the best in the land were located in the eleven former Confederate states. The Roose-Anderson report of 1969 showed 5 percent of the programs rated among the best for effectiveness of doctoral programs and 8 percent rated among the best for quality of graduate faculty to be located in those states.

Three percent of the 1950–59 members of the National Academy of Sciences were from these Southern states; in 1975 the proportion had risen to 6.5 percent.

Three percent of the members of the American Philosophical Society in 1960 were from the South; 5 percent in 1974.

In the listing of over fifty Americans who had won Nobel Prizes in the sciences prior to 1961, I could discover none who I thought was connected with an institution in the eleven Southern states. Among the thirty-eight Americans receiving Nobel Prizes in the sciences between 1961 and 1974, I found one Southerner.

In the years 1948 through 1958, the South, with a quarter of the nation's population, awarded 9 percent of the nation's graduate doctoral degrees. In 1971–72, the South, still with the same percentage of the nation's people, graduated 17 percent of earned doctoral degrees.

Given the fact that the eleven states used in this analysis do hold a quarter of the nation's population, these percentages are still depressingly low. And, by some other measures, we have fallen behind. Six of the forty-one United States universities in the Association of American Universities were located in the South in 1961. Eight United States institutions have been added since then, none of them in the South.

This kind of volunteered proclamation of regional deficiencies seemed to some to be unnecessary, not helpful, and gratuitous, but on this and other occasions I felt that we of and within the region could be its most useful critics. And there were hopeful signs, and also larger issues beyond regional borders.

But we are edging up, nonetheless, and perhaps in the fundamental economic strength of the region is to be found the greatest long-range portent. I will use just one indicator, per capita personal income. Data are conveniently available for the "Southeast," our eleven states minus Texas plus Kentucky and West Virginia. In 1950, per capita personal income in the Southeast was 68 percent that of the nation. By 1960 it had risen to 73 percent, and by 1974 to 85 percent. The average national rate of increase between 1950 and 1974 was 5.52 percent for the nation and 6.50 for the Southeast.

If our focus here were solely the South, I would argue now that the third century of American Independence will be distinguished by a massive emergence of the region from the shackles of its inheritance into the major locus of the nation's economic, social, and cultural strength. The first eighty-five years of the first Southern century after Independence were spent in slavery and in slavery to slavery, and the last fifteen years in unhappy adjustments to freedom. The first eighty-five years of the second Southern century after Independence were spent in a dying resistance to freedom, and these past fifteen years in a glorious although as yet incompletely fulfilled adjustment to its realities.

The weight of our own past has been lifted, and we are now fortuitously spared many of the old and new burdens of the older and newer regions of traditionally greater American prosperity and prominence. Our Southern resources of land, water, minerals, climate, location and people—and the good fortune, in new perspective, of previously limited economic development—will make the third century of American Independence not only the first century of Southern freedom, but also the first century of full Southern participation in the rewards and shaping of the national life. As the East dominated the growing years after 1776, and the West the growing years after 1876, the South stands to do so in the growing years before us now. But there is something more important before us today. . . .

Our greatest imperative [in American higher education] . . . is not greater financial support, nor relief from misplaced regulation, nor more advances by statistical measures, nor other such things. It is very different, it is deeper in ultimate significance, and it is worldwide.

That imperative is to fortify the liberal tradition. We have a liberal crisis in our world, meaning both in our world of intellect and on our planet. It is a crisis of diverse origins and it strikes at the modern home place of the liberal intellect, colleges and universities.

The liberalism of which I speak had its origins in England in the seventeenth century. Since then it has had a complex and uneven development, a development occurring chiefly in Western Europe and the English-speaking world. Whatever its varying manifestations, liberalism has connoted and sought to advance free expression of individual personality. It has connoted and sought to enhance the belief that people can make that expression valuable to themselves and to society. It has connoted and sought to enlarge support for those institutions and policies that protect and foster both free expression and confidence in free expression.

What we call liberal education is closely connected with this concept of liberalism. Liberal education is more than a diversity of subject matter. It is more than a roving interest that explores many reaches of individual behavior and collective experience. It is breadth of curiosity and also openness of attitude. It is the search for relatedness and the capacity for comprehensively integrative thought. These qualities may be found among individuals who work in all categories of intellectual effort. Liberal education seeks to forge the vital combinations of creativity and conformity, of skepticism and constructive purpose. It seeks independence of judgment tempered by regard for the independence of judgment of others. It combines a respect for intuition, and awareness that much is yet beyond human comprehension, with commitment to reason. It adds a sense of responsibility and purpose to the indulgence of personal intellectual purpose.

Not much of our planet has embraced the tenets of classical liberalism nor been exposed to the opportunities of liberal education. British imperialism spread an important but thin veneer of both to parts of distant continents, including this part of this one. Here in Virginia, Mr. Jefferson set the basis for the university he founded. The university

> will be based on the illimitable freedom of the human mind. For here we are not afraid to follow truth wherever it may lead, nor to tolerate error so long as reason is left free to combat it.

We have a liberal crisis this day partly because of confusions in the concept of intellectual freedom, with a consequent wavering in allegiance to it, and partly because of an explicit assault on the root concepts of liberal thought.

I wish to describe five episodes in what I deem to be ascending order of significance for the liberal crisis. I do not draw my conclusion that we face a liberal crisis simply from these episodes, but I offer them to you as a way of illustrating conditions that I think we all must recognize as intruding generally into our lives and into our society. . . .

This past February 18, Secretary of the Treasury William E. Simon addressed the New York Chapter of the Public Relations Society of America. Speaking of the private enterprise system, the private economic enterprise system, he said as follows:

> One way to ensure our freedom is through education. As public relations professionals, you counsel corporate leaders who provide millions of dollars each year to educational institutions and foundations. It is fundamental to America's strength to continue that generosity. I would advise, however, that you counsel your bosses and your clients to take a close look at the teaching policies of those schools and foundations being considered for corporate gifts. Find out if the subjects of that generosity are really assisting in the fight to maintain our freedoms or if they're working to erode them—and urge that judgments be made accordingly. Otherwise the largesse of the free enterprise system will continue to finance its own destruction.

This understandable sentiment poses a dilemma. It is not a new one. It is one always with us. Surely it is reasonable for a donor to expect that the recipient of his generosity will help to encourage the conditions that the donor considers made the generosity possible in the first place. And surely freedom must not be the author of its own destruction. But the important aspect of these remarks is the misconception expressed by Secretary Simon: he speaks of the "teaching policies" of our educational institutions. That concept of teaching policies—the concept that attitudes toward social phenomena among faculty and students are or can be set by the institutions themselves—is simply not applicable to a free university, nor to a democratic society, nor to the liberal tradition.

Every university of true quality has persons on its faculty with widely differing views of the American economic system, of our social heritage, of our political institutions, of how individuals can best cope with the pressures of contemporary life, of how our nation can best move to become a better one. A university could not attempt to have a teaching policy in the sense Mr. Simon has implied without attempting to curb the free thought and expression of its members. Moreover, it may be well to remind ourselves, a society that cannot tolerate intellectual freedom cannot long tolerate a free economic system either. . . .

My second case is perhaps more an enigma of freedom than a confusion about it. It grows from the expansion in recent years of legally protected freedoms of expression.

Hard core pornography and savage brutality have grown malignantly on the esthetic landscape—on street corners, in cinema houses, on the air waves, on the printed page—and there are many who, thinking they recall Voltaire, will defend to the death their right and the right of others to indulge them.

We are justified to have concern for what our visitor who will be with us tonight [Norman Cousins] has called in the *Saturday Review* [September 20, 1975, pp. 4–5] a major national problem, which he describes as "desensitization": annihilation of the concept of privacy, the premium on shock and revulsion, the corruption of human feelings, enfeeblement of the concept that there is, indeed, such a thing as good taste. One is forced to wonder, with *SR*, why the freedom of the press sought by the founders of the republic to prevent every tyranny over the mind of man should require public use of language and pictures that are both offensive to human sensibilities and devoid of useful content. Public access to certain broadcast channels, currently required as a condition of license, attracts uses in New York City that surely contribute to no conceivably useful public purpose. This enigma of freedom has deepened much in our generation. The perplexing lack of restraint that produces it ironically poses a threat to the very liberal intellectual tradition that seeks to guarantee rights of free expression.

Now a third, still different case.

Education has been viewed in our society as a guarantee of improved opportunity, an avenue to self-development, self-advancement, personal fulfillment, a principal instrumentality of social mobility.

There now appears an incipient threat to the liberties of liberalism on which such opportunities ultimately depend if the social consequences of the American educational system are misunderstood.

Education at all levels in the United States has manifestly functioned to prepare persons for the labor force, to improve their opportunity for economic success, to enhance their individual development. But it is now argued by some that the record demonstrates that our educational system principally fulfills the class interests of "capitalists" and their allies. A recent review in *The Chronicle of Higher Education* summarizes the conclusions of a new book, *Schooling in Capitalist America* [by Samuel Bowles and Herbert Gintis], as follows:

> No doubt our political ideology emphasizes freedom of choice, open competition, and distribution of income and status according to personal merit. But, in reality, class, color, and ethnic origin bulk larger than individual effort and talent when prize-giving time rolls around. . . .
>
> [The] message is unambiguous: It is fruitless to expect education to alter existing distributions of income and wealth or even to discriminate fairly according to relative ability.

Speaking of the University

I read this review not long before reading a report entitled "Higher Education and Social Mobility: A Promise Still Kept," a paper presented by E. I. Holmstrom at the Annual Meeting of the American Association for Higher Education, in Chicago, March 1976. The first paragraph of the conclusion reads thus:

> To summarize: Just over half the students entering the nation's four-year colleges and universities in 1968 were first-generation college students. Four years later, these first-generation students received nearly half the baccalaureates awarded to their class. Thus, in a short period, higher education institutions provided the means of upward social mobility to over a quarter-million students—many of whom were, at the time of college entry, "disadvantaged" in status. In the four college years, these students improved their status and their prospects; in spite of a crowded college labor market, they nonetheless had enhanced their competitive position for a better job and stable income.

My concern here is not which interpretation is correct, or whether the conclusions are reconcilable. Rather, it is another conclusion related by the authors of *Schooling in Capitalist America*. I have not read the book, but apparently the authors point to the social and educational systems of the Soviet Union and other socialist countries—far removed from Western liberal traditions—as affording superior opportunities for individual self-development. The facts would seem to be precisely the opposite. Hedrick Smith in his current, comprehensive, descriptive analysis of *The Russians* concludes that "variations in the quality of Soviet education are so great that both Soviet and Western scholars now suspect that the educational system is rigidifying and reinforcing the class structure of Soviet society."

Those who offer the Soviet model as a way to improve American education, imperfect as our system is, propose the dilution of liberal freedoms. When one includes the character of explicit ideological indoctrination, the Soviet educational system seems by far more a mirror and perpetuator of existing political values, social mores, and class structure than does the educational system of the United States.

Liberty breeds inequality. A system of liberal education opens opportunities to create inequality as well as to overcome it. Any formal educational system in any culture, moreover, can at best be a partner in shaping the society that supports it and that it serves. Expecting more from institutionalized education than it can deliver is a dangerous confusion in the analysis of freedom and can become a peril to intellectual liberty.

In the fourth episode I cite, the threat lies not in confusion but in clarity.

Universities, colleges, schools are accustomed to threats to their intellectual freedom from without. During recent years, we have experienced a new threat from a new quarter—this time from within. This is a threat to the essential requisite of a true university: its forum for free exchange of information, ideas, and conclusions.

The simplest invasion of intellectual freedom—not to allow freedom of expression—occurred on some of our campuses in the late 1960s. The right to obstruct public speakers has continued to be asserted spasmodically on some campuses. Defenses of a selectively open platform discouragingly turn up where the platform has traditionally been freest. We have curiously moved from a state in which the gravest threats to the university's true spirit were from without to one in which there are grave threats from within.

My illustration comes from Yale. There are others one might use, at least one I know about in the South, but I choose Yale because there the issue has been stated clearly and faced squarely.

A controversy arose because certain students, holding deeply held convictions, refused by disruptive processes to let a visiting speaker, who held contrary views, speak.

The speaker who was denied the opportunity to express himself held what is currently an unconventional view of "racial equality," stemming from debatable conclusions he had reached about genetic inheritance.

After the episode a Committee on Freedom of Expression at Yale was formed. It issued a report in January 1975. The report exposed a deeply important difference of view toward campus intellectual freedom that is found not only at Yale but elsewhere in our land. There were thirteen members of the committee. All agreed except one. The dissenting member put at the beginning of his statement this illuminating paragraph:

> The majority's theory is a simple one: a university's primary purpose is to discover and disseminate knowledge; free expression should always supersede any other values which might conflict with it. I would challenge this theory on several fronts.

This dissenting member closed his statement as follows:

> In sum, I agree that free expression is an important value, which we must cherish and protect. But it is not the only value which we uphold. Either in our society or in our universities. Under certain circumstances, free expression is outweighed by more pressing issues, including liberation of all oppressed people and equal opportunities for minority groups.

A quotation attributed to Voltaire says: "I do not agree with a word that you say, but I will defend to the death your right to say it." Here, in a time of peace—at least peace as we have customarily defined it—is an explicit challenge to the primacy of that concept.

My sentiments at this point are like those of the limerick:

> God's plan made a hopeful beginning,
> But man spoiled his chances by sinning.
> We trust that the story

Inexorable Change, 1976–1977

Will end in God's glory,
But at present the other side's winning.

Now to the fifth and final case.

A chilling vision of the condition to which a Western liberal democracy can come is provided by recent experiences at a college called the Polytechnic of North London, founded in 1971. This condition I offer as symptomatic of attitudes widely in evidence in the United States and abroad. It is described in an article appearing last December [1975] in the *Newsletter* of the International Council on the Future of the University. The authors call The Polytechnic of North London

> a laboratory for studying the strategy and tactics of the modern revolutionaries of the Far Left. As a microcosm it reflects the inability of many liberals to defend their basic values and structures—either through naiveté, cowardice, or ineptitude.... There is an urgent need to raise the general public's level of awareness to such trends, in order to generate some appropriate response for the defense of democracy.

The disruptive tactics pursued at the Polytechnic are rooted in the dogmatic Marxist concepts that "academic knowledge and academic standards are merely a part of bourgeois ideology, serving to bolster up the authoritarian and exploitative structures of capitalism." Academic standards have been attacked at all levels in the institution. A Communist Party student shouted in one academic meeting, "All academic standards are political constructs which have been used to undermine the due processes of democracy." In one debate, a visiting speaker, severely heckled, asked one tormentor: "Where in the world is there greater tolerance than in Britain?" and received the reply: "You are the one who counts tolerance a good thing. I don't."

The authors of the article from which this description is drawn put the matter this way:

> Western liberal democratic societies are now confronting an extreme form of the classical liberal dilemma. Are we willing, on both national and international levels, to take the steps necessary to defend our liberal institutions? The defenders of tolerance must now move to the attack.
>
> But these are not the objectives of an educational program that merits the designation "liberal." A precise and inclusive statement of the genuine objectives is elusive, but it is not difficult to list some of the central elements. They clearly include: the ability to identify and to define a problem; the skills necessary to acquire, to assess, and to analyze evidence; the sensitivity to recognize values and to understand if not always to reconcile conflicts among them; the capacity to exercise critical judgment and to tolerate uncertainty; the competence to achieve precision in thought and in expression. The liberal arts are . . . "the arts of thought, perception, and judgment." They do not depend upon any restricted subject matter, literary or scientific. Although experience and tradition indicate that some subjects are better adapted to these objectives than others, their pursuit may draw fruitfully upon any aspect of human vision, experience, or action.

Here the dilemma is plain: Can we preserve freedom without destroying it?

The implications are far-reaching. Charles Frankel in a different connection put it thus [*U.S. News and World Report*, March 8, 1976]:

> The most important [trouble], to my mind, is the outbreak of irrationalism in the world—the "counter culture"—which says that something one feels deeply and emotionally is not to be denied. "Letting it all hang out" becomes more important

than discussion, facts, tolerance or reason. This creates an atmosphere in which democracy cannot function well. So our first great problem, I think, is to recapture our old faith in reason, tolerance, and humanity.

"To recapture our old faith in reason, tolerance and humanity." Professor Richard Morris of Columbia in a book called *Seven Who Shaped Our Destiny* [1973] analyzes the personal qualities of Franklin, Washington, John Adams, Jefferson, Jay, Madison, and Hamilton. What he says about these American Revolutionaries is profoundly important to our present crisis in liberalism and to higher education's present imperatives:

> What gave the American Revolution its distinctive character was its sense of legality and moderation. The Seven Founders rested their cause upon charter rights, the English common law, and the British constitution.... Without a leadership committed to government by due process of law and to paying a "decent respect to the opinions of mankind," the American Revolution could have taken a more ominous turn; it might well have drifted down the road pursued not long thereafter by the French Revolution, whose initial thrust it had inspired. France's revolution was also rooted in legality, but it soon repudiated moderation and made a shambles of that very legality.... In France the very notion of constitutionalism was discredited beyond recognition. With its streak of demagoguery, its implacable spirit, its taste for bloodletting, its conviction that it had a corner on virtue, the French Revolutionary leadership could not, happily for America, be matched by the more moderate, responsible, and less vindictive stewardship of the American Revolution.
>
> Opinionated the American leaders indubitably were, but none could be accused of that fanatical dogmatism that has so often been the stamp of the revolutionaries who followed.

Theirs was indeed a fortuitous conjunction of character and destiny, which left its stamp of moderation and legality both on the Revolution and on the Constitution which was its ultimate achievement.

It is precisely the qualities of rationality, patience, tolerance, moderation—and the sense of independent honor and spiritual humility without which they do not exist—that are endangered in our present world—our world of intellect and our planet.

Two hundred years ago the American dream was born, or at least christened by faith in the new continent's future. As I encounter sensitive observers from other Western industrialized nations, and from developing nations in the Third World, I sense, and they frequently say, that they are deeply anxious over the United States' loss of confidence in itself.

The indisputable fact is that we are no longer so sure of ourselves, so persuaded of our virtue, so expectant of our future, so poised before uncertainty. Our domestic difficulties are intractable. They pose a greater threat to our future security than does any threat from outside. We have had a bewildering misadventure across the seas. We acknowledge now that political democracy and the rule of law are not exportable graces that mankind in all conditions is able and should be eager to embrace. . . .

What should we do?

Andre Sakharov, the Soviet physicist, won the Nobel Peace Prize in 1975. His Nobel Peace Prize lecture—read for him in Oslo by his wife, because he was not permitted to leave his country, and his wife was fortuitously already outside it—is a remarkable explication of the interdependence of progress, peace, and human rights. We must not forget this interdependence. Without all three, no one of them—not progress, nor peace, nor human rights—will survive. To understand the interdependence is essential to the preservation of liberal values, as liberal values are essential to fullest realization of mankind's dreams of harmony and plenty.

We must, first, without equivocation or delay, satisfy more effectively humankind's basic wants, including his hunger, his material needs, his needs of feeling and spirit. It is not necessary here to catalog human requirements and expectations. But it is important to recognize that the liberal values we cherish flourish more easily in a time of growth and plenty, in a time of "progress," in Sakharov's word. We on our planet must cope with changing and perhaps diminishing sources of energy. We must cope with changing and probably in some sectors diminishing consumption of resources. We must face the need to alter patterns of satisfaction. As we do these things, the stresses on freedom—economic, political, intellectual freedom—will be great.

So be it. We must solve whatever must be solved, do whatever must be done. We must again "move forward with strong and active faith." That is as true today as it was in April 1945, when Franklin Roosevelt wrote his last speech: "The only limit to our realization of tomorrow will be our doubt of today."

And, second, our vision must be enlarged by the knowledge that our liberal values were seeded and brought to fruition in special circumstances in the English-speaking world. Our planet harbors cultural diversity of greater depth, range of difference, and durability than we have recognized or conceded in our first two centuries of Independence. Simultaneously, the world's interdependence across these cultural diversities continues to intensify. We will need to extend our understanding of uniqueness. The world, as well as the United States, must be made safe for differences.

This is an awkward and demanding requirement to assert as part of an argument to protect and extend liberal values, values that have grown from circumstances and rest on cultural inheritance and social consensus far from universal.

Nonetheless, finally, in our own culture, and wherever else we have the chance, free inquiry, free thought, freedom of expression must be nourished and protected. All mankind in common aspires to liberty—that flame of hope burns in us all. "The defenders of tolerance must move to the attack."

Freedom is its own reward. But also guarantee of freedom for the human intellect is the surest hope that the majestic powers of humankind's unique resource, his mind, will be brought in full power to humankind's own service.

The fruits of freedom will not ripen automatically. They need more than faith and will. They must be nourished and protected by reason, by understanding, by self-restraint, by tolerance, by moderation, and also by relentless vigilance, by tactical skill, by supremely sophisticated intelligence, by implacable resolve.

If we succeed in these things, we will meet successfully the most important imperatives for higher education in the South and everywhere else.

❧

The years 1976 and 1977 were like all others in requiring—or so I judged—a wide range of talks to diverse audiences in scattered places, including the Council on Foundations meeting in Atlanta, the commencement exercises at the University of Connecticut in Stoors, the Third Judicial Circuit Conference in the Academy of Music in Philadelphia, the Martin Memorial Lecture at the Clinical Congress of the American College of Surgeons meeting in Chicago, the National Forum of the College Entrance Examination Board in New York, talks at two preparatory schools in Dallas (Hockaday and St. Mark's), plus others, and the inevitable goodly number in Nashville and on the Vanderbilt campus, including the ground-breaking for the new Vanderbilt hospital and the ceremonial meeting of some 144 United Nations diplomats in Vanderbilt's gymnasium on June 17, 1976, during an unprecedented excursion away from New York on a one-day visit to Nashville. They came from nations that included 98 percent of the human race.

But our main focus must stay on education closer to home. On May 28, 1976, I spoke to the Board of Directors of the Alumni Association in the faculty dining room of Rand Hall about the membership and work of the Board of Trust, both of which had changed substantially in recent years. Here is what I said, reconstructed from notes for the meeting.

It was suggested that I discuss the Board of Trust, its composition, how it works, how its functions have changed over the years, its significance in the life of Vanderbilt. I welcome the suggestion because all these things about the Board have been changing in recent years, especially the last twenty, and may continue to do so. The Board is important to Vanderbilt, and why it is important is not always understood well by some of the University's varied constituencies, especially among those not experienced with governing boards of charitable institutions, corporations, or banks. There is for some a "cloak of mystery" about the Board's work.

Let me speak first of the composition of the Board. Twenty years ago its membership was all men, all white, and all "mature" in age. All came then from the worlds of business, finance, law, and publishing except one—John J. Tigert, president of the University of Florida and a descendant of Bishop McTyeire. There were no doctors of medicine.

There were less than forty members. Listed in the 1955–56 Bulletin were thirty-nine members, thirty-one including the chancellor plus eight life trustees. Prior to 1950 there were no life trustees [those elected after age seventy are now so designated, thereby creating vacancies], meaning there could be very little turnover in the Board, and consequently the Board was smaller. Chancellor Branscomb proposed creation of the category of life trustee. Presently there are fifty-one trustees, (including Mrs. Harold Vanderbilt): thirty-two "regular" and four young alumni trustees, plus the chancellor and fourteen life trustees. Seven are women; one is black; the members range in age from twenty-two to eighty-two with four in their twenties, four in their forties, twelve in their fifties, sixteen in their sixties, and fourteen seventy or over (with one unknown!). The majority have had much experience in business, finance, and the professions (four practice law) but eight have had significant experience in teaching and administration in higher education, seven have had significant government or political experience, two have been active in the arts, and others have had experience in publishing, philanthropic foundations, and welfare activities.

Twenty-seven of the fifty-one live currently in Tennessee. The rest live in ten other states. Forty-six of the fifty-one attended Vanderbilt, four winning a Founders Medal (Messrs. Waller, Vaughn, Moore, and Roberts). Seven have law degrees, four have Ph.D.s, two have divinity degrees, and two are doctors of medicine. Half a dozen have master's degrees (M.A., M. S., M.B.A., M.F.A., etc.). There were four Rhodes Scholars (Branscomb, Vaughn, Price, Cuninggim). Of the fifty-one, twenty-six were nominated originally by the Alumni Association and twenty-five by the Board's own membership committee. Now, how do these members, how does the Board, do Vanderbilt's work?

I recall my surprise in June 1963 when my colleagues and I presented the budget—my first—for the coming year to the Executive Committee. The attitude was explicit. If the chancellor recommends it, there is no need to discuss or debate it. That was an attitude whose inherent wisdom and good taste I devoutly applauded, but mostly to myself, because it did not reflect adequate trustee involvement to protect the University's (and, incidentally, my own) interests. The trustees then had two principal committees, the Finance (meaning Investment) Committee and the Executive Committee, the latter empowered to act between the semiannual meetings of the full Board. In addition there was a committee on Board membership, one to recommend members for election as officers of the Board, a Medical Center Board, and a Committee for the Joint University Libraries on which Vanderbilt named trustees to sit.

I then described the committee structure in place in 1976: the six noted above, plus nine others, committees for Academic Programs, Alumni and Development Affairs, Audit, Buildings and Grounds, Business Affairs, the Hospital, Institutional Relations, Naming of Buildings and Spaces, and Student Affairs. After discussing the significance of these committees for trustee understanding of the University and the exercise of their powers and discharge of trustee duties, I moved to the innovations that had been introduced since 1963 in opening Board meetings to observers:

The Board approved five procedures for opening meetings to more persons from the campus and increasing the flow of information, as follows:

1. The agenda for meetings of the Board of Trust and of the Executive Committee will be made public in advance.

2. The chairman and chairman-elect of the Faculty Senate and the president of the Student Government Association and an equivalent officer of a graduate-professional student body will be invited to attend Board meetings as observers.

3. At each semiannual meeting of the full Board, a thirty-minute period will be scheduled for faculty and thirty minutes for students to address topics of their choice. Priority will be given to the Chairman of the Faculty Senate and to the President of the Student Government Association and equivalent officers of graduate-

professional school student bodies, with others scheduled on the basis of first-come-first-served.

4. Following each day's meeting of the Board and of the Executive Committee, appropriate officials who were present will be available to report and discuss actions taken at the meeting.

5. Trustees will give increased attention to inviting faculty and students to meetings of Board committees such as Academic Programs, Student Affairs, Buildings and Grounds, and Business Affairs.

The five procedures are in addition to three that have been in effect for some years and will be continued, as follows:

1. Continue to invite faculty and students to contribute to the Board's discussion of particular topics.

2. Continue to invite representative faculty to lunch with the Board at the time of the fall meeting and students in the spring.

3. Continue to issue press releases on actions appropriate for public announcement.

The Board specified a trial period of two years for these procedures.

I then described how the various committees functioned with respect to frequency of meetings, formality of procedures, the ways committee recommendations were subsequently handled, the time required for committee work, and the like. I tried to emphasize the extent of change in Board accessibility to others than trustees, noting that only twenty years before the only person not a trustee admitted to Board meetings was Madison Sarratt, who had once been acting chancellor and was at that time admitted in that capacity.

There was in those years, as before and since, skepticism among some of the importance of trustees. They do not control course content, curricula and degree requirements, research content, normal faculty appointments, and certainly not the views expressed and actions advocated by students, faculty, and chancellors. So I discussed the significance of trustees.

The Board's significance stems significantly from the fact that it is there. Even though its power in many matters is only technical, or latent, its presence is influential. The Board's ultimate powers may be lost on many in the University community, but it is not lost on the chancellor, who must assess—one hopes correctly—the limits of the patience and tolerance of those with ultimate formal responsibility.

Trustees are often of substantial help, technical and otherwise, to University officers in matters of real estate acquisition, floating of bond issues, influencing legislation and public policies, building construction, judging public opinion, interpreting the University to outside constituencies in specific matters of controversy, and more generally to act as a shield and help in developing a wider understanding and acceptance of "the nature of a university." Trustees are often notably valuable in raising money from others for the institution as well as in giving it themselves.

The trustees of Vanderbilt, it is crucial to recognize, constitute the unity of the institution. They are the place where ultimate responsibility for the institution and its welfare resides. They have the responsibility to see Vanderbilt as a whole, very important in an institution that is largely self-governing through a system of widely dispersed powers. Because of that, they can also be and sometimes are a locus of innovation, to say nothing of an aid to executive leadership when the institution is attacked from without. The trustees symbolize and can provide the legal and functional continuity of the institution.

❧

At the Annual Alumni Luncheon in Rand Hall May 14, 1977, the day after my meeting with the Alumni Board, I spoke of two major steps that had recently been taken toward the further advancement of Vanderbilt, "a major change in the executive organization of the University" and launching "the largest campaign for private funds in Vanderbilt's history."

The change in executive organization completed by the trustees two weeks ago yesterday, April 29, creates, for the first time in Vanderbilt's history, the office of president of Vanderbilt University. Traditionally the presiding officer of our trustees has been called president, that is, president of the Board of Trust. Under our new arrangement, to become effective later this summer, Sam M. Fleming, our distinguished president of the Board, will take the more conventional title, chairman of the Board, and the titles of Sartain Lanier and Hugh Luckey will be changed from vice-president to vice-chairman. The duties of these three trustee officers will remain unchanged.

When he comes this summer, Emmett B. Fields will become the first president of Vanderbilt. He is, in my judgment, the best person in the country for the position. Since 1975 he has been president of the State University of New York at Albany. Before that for six years he was vice-president and dean of the faculties of the University of Houston, and before that for nine years he was dean of Vanderbilt's College of Arts and Science. He earned his master's and doctor of philosophy degrees, in history, at Vanderbilt and will come to us this summer as professor of history as well as President.

Under the new arrangement, the chancellor remains the chief officer of the University. By delegation from the chancellor to the president, the president will be the chief administrative and chief academic officer of the University. The other general officers will report to him, and those who have been called vice-chancellor in the past will be called vice-president. The new president will be a member of the Board of Trust and will report on his responsibilities to it, his point of communication with the Board being the chancellor.

Inexorable Change, 1976–1977

The chancellor has been elected to two newly created positions, executive vice-chairman of the Board of Trust and executive vice-chairman of the Executive Committee. The chancellor will be chairman of a newly created Board Committee on University Planning and Development.

This change is similar to changes made in a substantial number of complex private universities in the United States during the last twenty years. In deciding what we should do here, we examined the experience of several of those universities in detail. Some four years ago, I first asked trustees to begin considering how the executive structure of the University could be made more effective in light of the University's changing circumstances. In April 1976, the Board of Trust authorized appointment of a committee to examine the matter in consultation with various groups within the University. Last October the Board authorized creation of the new position. Its definition, duties, relationship to the chancellor, relationship to the Board, in fact the very titles to be used, have all undergone change during the long and thoughtful consultative processes, both within the Board and beyond it, that led to the action on April 29.

Why did I, and then the trustees, think this change desirable? I argued four principal reasons, with abundant illustrations: (1) Vanderbilt's growth during the previous fifteen years in size and complexity: the size of the physical plant up by 50 percent, the number of students up by 63 percent, the number of faculty up by 84 percent, the operating budgets up by 500 percent; (2) the increased expectations imposed on Vanderbilt from inside and outside the University during the previous fifteen years (such as mounting legal actions, increased governmental regulation, changes in accounting and information systems, increased faculty and student consultative processes); (3) Vanderbilt's tradition of deep involvement of the chancellor (and often his wife) in the detailed life of the University, of

257

which abundant illustrations came easily to mind; and (4) Vanderbilt's transition, amidst the Southern region's emergence in social, economic, and cultural strength, to a new level of realistic aspiration:

We of Vanderbilt must in that massive national evolutionary change pursue relentlessly and tenaciously our determination to become a premier world center of learning. A conviction of communal urgency, not of institutional vanity, compels us.

Vanderbilt must perform better each of its several educational missions. For pedagogical reasons, and for financial reasons too, our old habits will often not be good enough. Vanderbilt is at the threshold of major development. Its traditional regional roles have already expanded to ones of national and world leadership in some of its undertakings. The requirements of our society . . . call for far better service from Vanderbilt in the years ahead than it has ever given before.

I urged that in the five years remaining until I reached retirement age, during at least four years of which the $150 million fund drive would be underway, my time could be focused to best advantage on measures of institutional evolution and development and the financial means to make them possible. [I did not predict so at the time, but within two years the merger of Peabody College with Vanderbilt occurred and by 1981 the Blair School of Music was added to Vanderbilt.]

After expressing the University's profound gratitude to the assembled alumni for all they do, near the end I did not fail to assure the faithful that "I would mislead you if I gave the impression that the $150 million goal is the full measure of our needs."

Inexorable Change, 1976–1977

On November 11, 1977, the Fifth International Congress of
Verdi Studies attracted visitors from near and far to the campus of Centre College of Kentucky, in Danville. The session I
addressed met in the college's magnificent Regional Arts Center, which I took as a symbol of the energy, imagination, and
effectiveness of the long leadership by the college's president,
Thomas A. Spragens. I had been asked to speak on "The Importance of Liberal Education" and did so, in part, as follows.

The quarterly journal of the Association of American Colleges
is called *Liberal Education*. Brown University has just published a 141-
page book of essays by selected alumni "on the purposes and content of a liberal education." The most recent issue of the *Educational
Record*, a periodical publication of the American Council on Education, carries an article with a typical title, "Needed Changes in Liberal Education." I counted upwards of twenty books on my home
bookshelf that address issues of liberal education in some explicit
way. Definitions and prescriptions flow annually and torrentially. If
the subject were *not* important, we surely would not be dwelling on
it again this afternoon.

I shall refrain from drawing another new definition of liberal education and from prescribing the contents of a curriculum that
would assure arrival at the freshly defined state of grace. Definitions
often depend on one's perspective. The egg's definition of a chicken
is a mechanism for reproducing eggs.

Let us come from another direction. Let us ask how we in our
society are failing, and let us ask what capacities we need to develop
through education in order to reduce our failures. Our American
heritage is one of Western liberal values, values rooted in concepts
of liberty, of the significance of the free expression of individual
personality. The education needed for such a society to be prosperous, secure, fair, and free is our subject.

One perception of our problem is provided by Leonid Brezhnev, general secretary of the Soviet Communist Party [quoted in *The Ten-nessean*, October 5, 1977]. Last month he assailed "prominent leaders of the capitalist world" for using the issue of human rights as the main thrust of what he called an "ideological crusade" to sow distrust and hostility toward Socialist countries.

"It seems," he said, "that from the standpoint of our class adversaries, Soviet citizens should evidently be granted only the 'right' to fight against the Soviet state, the Socialist system, so as to gladden the heart of the imperialists." Then he went on the attack. "What real rights and freedoms are guaranteed to the masses in present-day imperialist society?" he asked.

> The "right'" of tens of millions to unemployment? Or the "right" of sick people to do without medical aid, which costs a vast sum of money? Or else the "'right" of ethnic minorities to humiliating discrimination in employment and education, in political everyday life? Or is it the "right" to live in perpetual fear of the omnipotent underworld of organized crime and to see how the press, cinema, TV, and radio services go out of their way to educate the younger generation in a spirit of selfishness, cruelty, and violence? Propagandists and ideologists of capitalism cannot deny the fact that socialism has long cured these social sores.

The qualities of liberal education that are distinctive and important in our time are inextricably bound up with the values of Western liberal social thought. I do not refer to "liberal" in the political sense of "left" or "right," but in the sense of the classical Western liberalism that originated chiefly in England in the seventeenth-century and that has been profoundly influential in Western Europe and the English-speaking world—but not very much anywhere else.

The liberal tradition has had varying manifestations, but whatever forms it has taken, it has connoted and sought to advance free expression of individual personality, and the belief that people can make that expression valuable to themselves and to society. It has connoted and sought to enlarge support for those policies and institutions of society that protect and foster both free expression and confidence in free expression.

Yet, it is prudent and important to remember, only a minority of the world has adopted the tenets of classical liberalism or been exposed to the opportunities of liberal education. Liberal education is the exception, not the rule, among world educational objectives.

Remember the indictment of our culture laid down by Chairman Brezhnev. Now hear what the American journalist Robert G. Kaiser says in his current book about educational objectives in the Soviet Union [*Russia—The People and the Power*, p. 482]:

> In the West we put great faith in the civilizing value of education. Our confidence that education enhances respect for liberal ideals is shared by some of our experts on Russia, who have predicted that the Soviet Union will become more liberal as its educated population grows. The nature of Soviet education suggests that this assumption is overly optimistic. . . . The way it is organized . . . would seem to discourage the spread of liberal values.
>
> Like so many aspects of Soviet life, education is highly formalized and narrowly practical. Its goal is not to produce men and women of great intellectual breadth, originality, and creativity. On the contrary . . . Soviet education is supposed to supply the country with specialists who can make it work, specialists with limited competence in narrow fields.

Our challenge is to sustain the freedoms of classical liberalism, to assure the human rights we cherish and proclaim, and simultaneously to make our society successful. A liberal, democratic society cannot be like the man who said he leaned neither to partiality nor impartiality. It must be decisive in its determination to succeed. If our society is not a satisfactory and rewarding place to live for all large categories of our people, the liberal values of freedom that we cherish will not survive.

American society is now dangerously uneven in the prosperity and sense of fulfillment present among its citizens. Groups are incapsulated by poverty, shortage of education, cultural deprivation, and, in some instances still, by race, which added together so severely limit their opportunities as to put them and their children at a continuing, oppressive disadvantage.

The indicators of American social pathology are abundant and sadly familiar: adult crime, juvenile crime, syndicated crime, violence, drug abuse, mental illness, corruption, and more, including—in my view at least—the breakdown of the traditionally central institution of our culture, the family.

Beyond such measures of social distress as these, however, are issues of energy, environmental contamination, world economic interdependence, arms control, population control, food supply, international war and domestic tranquillity, and the ironic struggles for separate group independence and identity in a world of increasing pressures toward interdependence and mutual reliance.

Toward the end of *Macbeth*, Shakespeare has Malcolm saying that if he had the power, he would

Pour the sweet milk of concord into hell,

Uproar the universal peace, confound

All unity on earth.

In 1977 we might easily conclude that some hidden power, lacking the "King-becoming graces," is at work beyond our ken to uproar peace and unity among us humans.

Let us on this lovely college campus keep perspective. Far more persons in the United States receive advanced formal instruction outside liberal arts colleges and universities like Centre and Vanderbilt than within them. Liberal education is only one range of educational opportunities offered by our society through its colleges, universities, proprietary schools, industrial and labor union training programs, military schools and other forms of adult education. Yet liberal education exerts a decisive influence in our society. Its future adequacy in helping to meet the requirements of our national condition is of overwhelming and unique importance. We cannot be like the man who fell from the top of the skyscraper and as he passed the tenth floor said, "All well so far."

The desirable goals of liberal education are numerous. I offer you three, however, that I think must be more fully realized than at present if our difficulties are to be successfully attacked, and if the incredibly interesting, rewarding, diversified, creative, enriching elements in our culture—of which we must be especially aware this afternoon in this place—are to survive and flourish.

All three of these goals call for a more comprehensive understanding of the human record and of human beings.

Let me introduce the first by what strikes me as an extraordinary report.

The famous British Fabian Society was founded in 1884 by a group of intellectuals who over many subsequent decades exerted profound influence on the development of social and economic thought in Britain and who were crucially influential in the rise of the British Labor Party. George Bernard Shaw, Graham Wallas, H. G.. Wells, G .D. H. Cole, and of course Sidney and Beatrice Webb were among the conspicuous members.

Lord Ritchie Calder, now dean of science writers in the United Kingdom, was secretary of the Fabian Society in younger years. I am told that not long ago, at a meeting on the campus of the California Institute of Technology, Lord Calder said that in all the Fabian Society discussions in which he had taken part, over the years before World War II, about the future of Great Britain, not once did anyone envision Great Britain without the Empire.

Our education must develop the instinct and capacity to examine our most fundamental assumptions—not to destroy them, but to understand them, and to be able to act effectively in the circumstances to which those assumptions are pertinent. The capacity to look at ourselves with the same lens through which we look at others—and through which they look at us—is essential. It is especially crucial on our twentieth-century planet of material interdependence and of incessant interaction among radically different systems of cultural values and among newly assertive national entities.

Our education must also develop a reach that extends beyond the narrow confines of that conscious reason that is an inherent part of the very Western philosophical tradition from which our liberal educational values spring. Persons attending a Conference of Verdi Studies know well that some roads to perception and insight lie outside the realm of deliberate thought. Humankind's powers of reason may be at work in all that humans do, yet they are not all that is at work in what humans do.

Thus, one goal of liberal education that for the survival of our liberal values must be achieved is capacity to examine and understand the confines of our own cultural inheritance. This goal is especially important in our world of increasing ethnic consciousness. In our world, I recently read in the *Annals* of the American Academy of Political and Social Science [September 1977, p. 1], "Ethnic differences are the single most important source of large-scale conflict within states; and they are frequently instrumental in wars between countries as well." To cope constructively, especially with ethnic conflicts, educated people must be able to see themselves as others see them.

I frequently think of the priests, one Anglican and one Roman, good friends who met regularly for tea, and as the church bells rang calling them to their separate evening prayers, one said to the other, "Ah, now we must part, you to worship the Lord in your way, and I in His". . . .

Liberal education needs to strive to create a second quality: the capacity to make choices. The capacity to make choices requires, first, acknowledgment of the need to do so, and second, ability to weigh relative merits.

In many of our national social policies in recent decades we have been caught in a philosophical dilemma. We have become aware of the importance of social environment in influencing the behavior of individuals and in determining their social lot. So we have adopted policies that recognized these influences external to the individual, without always anticipating the accompanying consequences of those policies and making the tough choices needed among the resulting benefits and evils. The dilemma to which I refer reaches into programs of public welfare, unemployment compensation, rehabilitation of criminal offenders, protection of juveniles, and into many other areas of social subsidies and regulation.

A recent study [reported by Nicholas Pileggi in *New York*, June 13, 1977, p. 38] was made of 4,857 young people 15 years of age or younger who were arrested in New York in connection with violent street crimes such as murder, assault, armed robbery, and rape. In the nearly five thousand cases—the arrested person in none of them being over fifteen years of age—only 113 of the juveniles were institutionalized in any way, only 79 of those being sent to secure training schools.

Another recent report from New York referred to over 2,500 youngsters ten years old and under who had been arrested for major crimes such as murder, manslaughter, assault, robbery, burglary, and grand larceny.

The plight of those youngsters is tragic. The fate of their victims is more so. One tragedy does not justify another. A liberally educated society must be able and willing to grapple with such social ambiguities and with the tormenting conflicting incentives that arise among humane people in a society conscientiously seeking to address the needs of all its inhabitants.

The third goal I emphasize is ... [the capacity for] integrative thinking. [Harlan Cleveland observed in the April 1977 David Dodds Henry Lecture at the University of Illinois] that the world increasingly requires people to think about an enormous range of interrelated fields in order to operate effectively in any one of them. The great unreported crisis is the issue of how colleges and universities that are built on a proliferation of valuable but narrow expertness will respond to the judgment of irrelevance that may be laid on them by students and employers who sense, though often only vaguely, a need for more integrative thought.

The highest road of liberal education is toward this capacity for integrative thought. To conceive liberal education as embracing a preference for arts and humanities and the wordier social sciences on one side, over physical and biological and more systematic social sciences on the other side, mistakes the point. Liberal education does not conflict with vocational or professional preparation. It enhances the capacity of individuals to prepare for and practice whatever vocations they select.

Liberal education must prepare people to view the world and themselves whole.

It must, in fact, go beyond creating an integrative intellect to help create an integrative spirit. Barbara Ward once said, "We will have to learn to love each other, or we will all perish." The profound Indonesian humanist, Soedjatmoko, has called for the "articulation of a new inner vision of man." Liberal education will find its most important meaning in its contributions to the interior harmony of individuals and the harmonious unity of the human race.

So, on this splendid occasion of celebration this afternoon, you have let me say these things:

Liberal education is important because it is both a child and a parent of the liberal values of our free society.

It is important as it equips us to meet better than others will do the complicated, interrelated dilemmas of our contemporary world.

Liberal education can prepare us better to do this if it creates a greater capacity to understand the established assumptions under which we live; if it enlivens the habit of making decisive, painful choices among conflicting desirable goals; and if it helps to develop the capability for integrative thought and spirit that view as a whole the issues that confront individual human beings and the corporate body of humankind.

NINE

Diversity in a University
1978–1979

WHAT BECAME VANDERBILT'S medical school was in existence long before the University itself was created. Both before and after Vanderbilt's founding it had many prominent alumni. One of the modern loyal ones has been Dr. Thad M. Moseley III of Jacksonville, Florida, a graduate in the medical class of 1943 and father of two sons who were graduated from Vanderbilt, Thad IV in 1972 and William A. in 1975. In 1978 Dr. Moseley, who was then president of the Southeastern Surgical Congress, invited me to speak at its meeting in the Fairmont Hotel in New Orleans on February 20. Part of what I said focused on several issues that would still be of concern to the Clinton administration fifteen years later.

Thad has instructed me that you are the "working surgeons" of our region and, as such, I conclude you are important influences in the communities that taken together make up the American Southeast. In consequence, although I believe I am the only civilian on the program, you and I have many stakes in common as we view the present and prospective conditions of our section of the nation.

Moreover, Vanderbilt has been graduating doctors of medicine since 1875 and nurses for many decades. We have missions with the same ultimate purpose as yours: to bring always improving health care to people who need it. The title I have given to these remarks is "The Newest New South." I speak with a recent report on the rural South in mind, a report entitled *Increasing the Options.* The report was made a year ago by a task force [organized by the Southern Regional Council] of which I was chairman, comprising some twenty-five Southerners, from all sectors of our society, including the present Secretary of Commerce, the present Secretary of Labor, and, less actively, the present president of the United States. What I shall say is stimulated by currents in our lives in the American Southeast that this task force encountered, and that I think have great meaning for ourselves individually and for our communities.

I have a medical steppingstone to my topic. Dr. G. Canby Robinson was Dean of Vanderbilt Medical School from 1920 to 1928. Recently I read an address he gave to the Southern Medical Association in November 1924, meeting on that occasion also in New Orleans. I believe I could read his remarks, which were entitled "The Influence of Environment in Medical Education," to you this morning and you would not detect that they were delivered fifty-four years ago.

Dr. Robinson addressed, for example, what he called "one of the most serious medical problems of our day. I refer," he said, "to the crying need of rural practitioners."

Or, for another example, he said, "We hear complaints that modern medical education is more concerned in developing scientists than it is in developing physicians."

And, listen to this: "Medical education, in the technical sense, occupies the years of study and guidance prior to the practice of medicine, but in reality medical education is a lifelong process."

Dr. Robinson also found occasion to allude to "large expenditures for hospitals and laboratories," a subject on his mind no doubt because he was then supervising the construction of a new medical education building and hospital at Vanderbilt, as indeed his successors in Nashville have again been doing during these last three years, half a century later.

Dr. Robinson's 1924 address illustrates the tenacity of many fundamental conditions—in this instance health conditions. . . .

My words this morning are two. First, our newest new South has come a long way. We have made great advances on many important fronts. Second, we have a long way to go. Many frontiers of need remain to be conquered.

As the United States was struggling four decades ago to come out of the Great Depression, President Franklin Roosevelt described the South as "the nation's number one economic problem." In that simple phrase he summarized social and political as well as economic conditions that had been evident for a century. The South then lagged behind the rest of the nation by almost every standard. Monumental changes have occurred since that time. . . .

I then outlined some of the important features of the changed Southern scene . . . making the point that much of the weight of the past had been lifted and that a new era was coming for the region.

Southern resources of land, water, minerals, climate, location and people—and the good fortune, it would seem in this new perspective, of previously limited industrial and other economic development—can make the years ahead ones of full Southern participation in the rewards and shaping of the national life.

I take heart from surveys of opinion that report that despite the inferior rankings by objective social and economic measures that still remain, "Southerners are more satisfied in almost every respect than their counterparts in the rest of the country" with their personal lives. . . .

The South's progress, however, has been uneven, and that takes me to my second word for the day.

Diversity in a University, 1978–1979

Many people and places have been left out of the advances reflected in the general measures of progress for the region as a whole. And the rural South, especially, has dragged behind. Again, let me use only one indicator to suggest a very complex condition.

In 1974, 45 percent of those Americans defined by the census as "poor" lived in the South, way and again a higher percentage than the South's proportion of the nation's population. Of those Southern poor, a substantial majority lived in non-metropolitan areas. And, among those poor in the non-metropolitan South, it is crucially important to know that in 1974 about 15 percent of whites were below the poverty line but 44 percent of blacks were below the poverty line.

Rural development is among the South's main unfinished tasks. The rural South lags behind Southern urban areas, and it lags behind rural areas outside the South in many dimensions of human satisfaction and development.

Because of the unevenness of economic development, far too many people in the rural South are poor, have inferior educations, suffer from poor housing and nutrition, and receive inadequate health services.

Rural problems therefore stand at the forefront of our unfinished business. And of course rural and urban problems are intimately related. The migrations of rural and urban Southerners that began after World War I to cities outside the region contributed more significantly than any other single factor to the growth of the huge concentrations of persons now living in the non-Southern metropolitan areas, including their ghettos. The intimate connection between the rural South and the urban North has become increasingly apparent to students of urban problems.

And, so, with all that has been accomplished, there is much yet to do.

The Task Force on Southern Rural Development to which I referred addressed most important aspects of Southern rural life, including health. It depended heavily on specialized studies, and to close these remarks, I suggest some of the conclusions of those studies that were concerned with health care.

Health problems are more severe in Southern rural areas than elsewhere. The rural South has higher infant and general mortality rates, higher incidences of restricted activity because of health problems, higher incidences of most chronic diseases, lagging nutritional levels, and fewer patient-care physicians in relation to the population. And, moreover, the health of rural Southerners is adversely affected by a large number of important conditions that make improvement difficult.

Rural residents are less often covered by private health insurance programs, and the plans they do have are less comprehensive than those of urban residents.

The coverage of public programs is less extensive in the nonmetropolitan South than in other areas.

While a greater proportion of rural residents is elderly, and Medicare has been of considerable assistance to them, the program sets lower reimbursement levels for physicians practicing in rural areas.

Medicare also makes it difficult to develop clinics staffed by nonphysician health professionals who can deliver a limited range of health care in isolated rural areas.

Health professionals risk professional isolation in rural areas.

The scarcity of health professionals causes those who do locate in rural areas to be overworked and to have limited time for their families and for recreation and professional activities.

Because a minimum population is required to support a physician, low population densities make the establishment of traditional solo medical practices difficult.

The establishment of rural medical practices can be more expensive. Start-up costs are often increased by the need to build facilities that, in urban places, are usually already available.

Diversity in a University, 1978–1979

Rural areas often lack the cultural, entertainment, educational, and housing facilities many health professionals want.

Prevailing medical specialization means that fewer doctors are available to rural areas because rural population densities are not ordinarily great enough to support specialists.

There are no simple, certain ways to overcome these difficulties.... But among the approaches that could prove useful, let me suggest five.

First, the financing of rural health care requires change.

Advocates of national health insurance argue that such insurance would especially benefit rural residents who have inadequate coverage under private health insurance and public programs. They would urge that specific features ensure that fee schedules for physicians should reward rather than penalize physicians for practicing in under-served areas, provide reimbursement for services of non-physician health professionals, and recognize community-sponsored rural health centers as eligible for direct reimbursement.

In the absence of a national health insurance program, it is argued that current programs could provide needed relief to rural residents if rural health centers were designated as participating providers under Medicare and Medicaid, with adequate reimbursement and inclusion policies.

Second, in the spirit of Canby Robinson, greater emphasis is urged on training physicians and other health professionals specifically for rural practice. Special programs should acquaint medical students with rural health problems and medical practice, and states should support the establishment of health education centers and family practice residents in rural areas and give greater support to the development of broadly trained non-physician health professionals.

Third, it is argued that attention should be given to changing the nature of rural practice. The following components for a rural health system have been suggested:

Group practice should be established where needed to prevent social, cultural, and professional isolation and overwork.

Nurse practitioner clinics with backup part-time physician support should be organized within smaller communities that cannot support or attract groups of physicians.

Programs should be adopted to help meet the start-up costs of establishing rural group practice.

A system for rural health care should extend care into remote areas, through outpost clinics or the use of mobile facilities, and should relate to hospitals, laboratories, and specialists in rural or urban areas.

And, as always, special provisions should be made for the continuing education of health professionals engaged in rural practice.

Fourth, the content of rural health care should be modified. Rural health care practice surely needs to be concerned with environmental health and preventive medicine. A primary concern by physicians and others for providing high quality medical care sometimes stands in the way of attention to environmental health problems and related community affairs. Publicly or privately supported community organizations can help to address these needs and to bear the costs of community outreach programs needed to improve rural access to medical care, especially to meet the dental care and mental health needs of rural people.

Rural areas have a much higher proportion of elderly, and the incidence of chronic conditions or confinement to bed is greater in the rural South than other areas. Emphasis is therefore needed on home health services for the rural, homebound elderly.

Because of low educational levels, many rural residents are unfamiliar with good health habits. Effective patient health education, including provision of printed materials and visual aids, should be a part of rural health care.

Fifth and finally, special measures need to be taken to improve health care for Southern rural minorities, usually but not always black minorities. Affirmative action in health training has attracted relatively few members of minorities into the health professions. Not only should nondiscriminatory practices be enforced in the delivery of health care services, but over the long haul the number of minorities trained in all the health care professions must be increased.

I sometimes tried to close speeches on somber subjects on a lighter note. This time I said I had just received a signal from someone dear to me in the audience, indicating it was time to close, which opened an opportunity to quote the epitaph on the tombstone of an elusive waiter: "Bye and Bye, God caught his eye."

§

As is surely true for all university chancellors and presidents, I received invitations to address college and university graduating classes. I felt it an obligation to show the flag for Vanderbilt whenever feasible, especially in an educational setting. From 1963 on I spoke at some forty commencements, almost all while I was still in office, in addition to the twenty at home.

It is surely a burden to prepare and deliver a speech, but I always thought the burden was greater on the young graduates who had to sit still for commencement orations. I was invited to speak at the commencement exercises of Morris Harvey College in Charleston, West Virginia, on May 7, 1978. Now the University of Charleston, the institution then had some 1,700 students. I tried a new tactic. After opening sentiments of appreciation, I asked President Tompkins's permission to invite, first, the members of the graduates' families to stand, so that the graduates could applaud them, and, second, the faculty, staff, and trustees of the college to stand, so that the graduates, with their families joining, could show appreciation to them. Then:

If you women and men who are soon to be graduated are like other graduating classes I have known, this Commencement speech looms as the final obstacle standing between you and your degrees. . . . Surely this is one day that the prayer to the sun by Piet Hein is justified:

> Sun that givest all things birth
> shine on everything on earth!
> If that's too much to demand,
> shine at least on this our land.
> If even that's too much for thee,
> shine at any rate on me.

The sun is shining on you today, and what I worry about on such a day is that the sun does not shine so clearly or brightly on some other men and women of your age elsewhere in our world.

I would like to ask Michael L. Garcia to stand, and to remain standing. Now would Linda Sue Whittaker stand, too. and James D. Eplin. Finally, where is Laura Elaine Morrison, would you please stand? [These four members of the graduating class, doubtless mystified, rose.]

I do not know any one of you four graduates individually. . . . I picked your names at random from the commencement program, but I do know that you and your classmates are a highly privileged minority.

I want to ask each of you four who are standing to accept a new name for the next few minutes. As I give it to you, you may be seated. Mike Garcia, I am going to give you the temporary name "Menak Sartono," a resident of Jogjakarta, Indonesia. Linda Lou Whittaker, we will call you "Kisum Chunder," who lives in West

Diversity in a University, 1978–1979

Godavari District, India. Jim Eplin, your name for the next fifteen minutes will be "Ali Ahmed," from near Kano, Nigeria. And Laura Elaine Morrison, yours will be "Salvadora Pallares," of Cayambe, Ecuador. Let us imagine that you Morris Harvey graduates might have been these four people. I have only partly created them for our purposes this afternoon. Let me tell you a bit about each of them.

Menak, you are a native of the city of Jogjakarta, which is in central Java in Indonesia. You work in a silver factory, as an apprentice to an artisan who embosses with a hammer and sharp tools, with enormous skill, intricately designed historical scenes on flat plates of silver with highly decorative results. You ride your bicycle back and forth to work over bumpy, muddy roads, as does the master craftsman whom you seek to emulate. You were hit by a car five years ago and have limped ever since. You are a Buddhist and have been favored with formal schooling equivalent to the first four grades in the United States, and the person you are learning from earns in real income less per hour as a talented, trained artisan than a student of Morris Harvey did if he or she clerked last summer in a drug store.

Kisum, you are a Hindu who lives in West Godavari District in the state of Andhra Pradesh in the southeastern part of India. You live with your husband and five children near a canal that irrigates the rice fields on which your family and your parents and your husband's parents depend. They have worked many years to improve production from the new strains of grains that have been developed in the Philippines and elsewhere for growing conditions like yours, and to improve processing, storage, and marketing, too. The battle is a hard one: the monsoon on which agriculture throughout your country annually depends often does not come. Diseases attack the new grain. The costs of commercial fertilizer and equipment keep rising. The population to be fed increases inexorably—your country's population grows by one million people every month. You seldom go to the nearby village of two thousand persons and you have never been more than twenty-five miles away.

Ali, you are a nomad, a Muslim, a native of northern Nigeria called a Hausa, living near the important, thousand-year-old sub-Sahara city of Kano. You ride for a living, tending cattle mostly. But you and your family also have sheep. Your schooling came from your family and tribal traditions. You fear and do not know how to prevent the drought, which comes often. And you hear that your country has more people than any other in Africa, with more every year, and that black oil comes out of the sea along your country's coast six hundred miles away and makes a few city people wealthy, your country stronger, and your country's political leaders strangely ambitious. And you ride and look forward to the great celebration, Id el Kabir, held once a year in Kano, where you can watch a reen-actment of medieval pageantry which is the only formal theater you see.

And Salvador, you are an Otavalo Indian with four children liv-ing in a mud and thatch two-room house in the Andean highlands of Ecuador outside the town of Cayambe. Although Otavalo Indi-ans are relatively prosperous, and your father owns his own land, your husband works on an hacienda owned by a family in Quito, and for a wage far smaller than that of the Indonesian silversmith. You and your husband are both Roman Catholics, and you live with snow-capped peaks all around you in one of the most spectacularly beautiful places in the world, but the most visible testimony to the quality of your life is that almost every Sunday your husband is found by the road where he has fallen drunk on his way home from a long Saturday night at the bar in Cayambe, where he drinks a raw fermented intoxicant called chicha. You have been too tired, or busy, or bored, or maybe, as they say, "borracho" yourself, to keep him home, or to get him home before he fell.

Menak, Kisum, Ali, Salvadora: You have much in common, in addition to being unlike the people of your age who are here this

278

afternoon in the spring 1978 graduating class of Morris Harvey College. You four share the fact that you, as well as they, are a big part of the world of us Americans. Yours and the other developing countries represent at least three-fourths of the people and three-fourths of the nations of the tightly interconnected world of which Morris Harvey, and Charleston, and West Virginia are a part. You four lead moderately fortunate lives in your native lands, yet you share in acute form in each of the world's triad of decisive issues that will ultimately determine the kind of future we all have. Those issues are growing population, inadequate food, and unassured reserves of natural resources, including energy.

These problems are closely interwoven with each other. Where each of you lives, overpopulation is a tragic reality, or a hovering, growing menace. In 1900 the world had about one billion six hundred million people. In 1970 it had about three billion six hundred million. It may have around seven billion by the year 2000, twenty-two years from now. . . . Overpopulation in your developing countries finds its most primitive consequence in starvation. Hundreds of millions of people around the world go to bed hungry each night, and at least seven hundred million are seriously malnourished. Well over one billion do not have access to safe drinking water. In fact, water supplies are increasingly being depleted and subterranean water tables lowered. Forests are cut down and the soil is mined. And more subtly, although sometimes more brutally, the future of innocent individuals is threatened by the dislocation of their social systems.

The changes wrought in this perplexing world have also upset religious teachings and community customs, creating an environment of unsure values, of cultural insecurity, in which fear and bewilderment sometimes immobilize ambition, sometimes unleash destruction.

The chances you four residents of Southeast Asia, India, Africa, and South America have for better nutrition, better education, better income, better health, for greater meaning and satisfactions of all kinds in life, ultimately rest on finding the social and political ways to solve problems of population growth, of food supply, of resources and energy. And so do the chances that we here this afternoon can have more satisfying and more secure futures. For, be in no doubt, we in the United States, with our intricately and delicately balanced interdependent social system of inordinately high consumption and cost, are ultimately as vulnerable as any people anywhere to the consequences of world overpopulation, world starvation, and the diminution of world resources.

Surely no graduate of Morris Harvey in 1978 needs instruction that we humans literally have one world. If two world wars and several other wars in this century, along with recurring world economic crises, including our present one, have not taught all of us that, at least the world's energy condition will have induced understanding of that fact here in the state of West Virginia.

I like another little verse [by Piet Hein] called "Mankind":

> Men, said the Devil,
> are good to their brothers;
> they don't want to mend
> their own ways, but each other's.

We have a better chance to mend our own ways in our country, to contribute significantly to solving the world's terrible triad of problems than Menak, Kisum, Ali, and Salvadora have of doing so in their countries. We have more resources and more time and more margin for error to work with. What we need to do will not be easy. It is always true that, "Problems worthy of attack prove their worth by fighting back." But we in America have a privileged chance to fight back ourselves. We have not always acted as though we understood the unity of the fate we share with the rest of the world. Our official financial aid to developing nations in recent years has regularly been a smaller percentage of our gross national product than that of the great majority of industrialized nations. Yet we have, for the moment at least, capacities greater than those vouchsafed to much of the rest of the world.

We have our own frontiers of need within the United States, too—pockets of city poverty, of rural hopelessness, of racial bias and handicap, of psychic pain, and more. We are guilty of the greatest waste of all (in any faith it must be a sin)—our failure to justify fully the majestic good fortune and opportunities afforded by our incomparably blessed nation.

E. B. White wrote:

> When I arise in the morning I am torn by the twin desires to reform the world and enjoy the world. This makes it hard to plan the day.

I hope, henceforth, each of you will find it hard to plan every day of your life. And I hope the Common Father of us all will bless you every day of your life.

❧

Madison Sarratt died March 24, 1978. I spoke about him at Vanderbilt's Annual Alumni Luncheon in Rand Hall on May 20.

The humor, patience, realism, and understanding of Madison Sarratt made him the best-loved person in Vanderbilt's history, and account for the affection toward him that thousands of alumni have carried with them wherever they have gone as long as they have lived.

When I was installed as chancellor October 4, 1963, Madison Sarratt was then vice-chancellor emeritus and dean of alumni. He made remarks on behalf of the installation committee, during which he said, "At Vanderbilt chancellors are durable—vice chancellors, indestructible."

Speaking of the University

"Indestructible" is indeed the meaning of Madison Sarratt. I think that what makes him indestructible is not his well-known name, nor a beautiful and useful building named for him, but something that everybody wants to be. He was wise, and his wisdom touched us all. It is not fashionable to talk about being wise any more. If youngsters use the word "wise," it is likely to come after rather than before: That was a good race, time-wise; or he is a good student, science-wise; or, believe it or not, she is a pretty girl, face-wise.

But Madison Sarratt knew what it meant to be wise. In an old file in the Vanderbilt archives there is an undated speech of his, probably written in 1958, entitled "The Bewildered Undergraduate." He linked undergraduate confusion to a tendency that he saw toward early specialization—often caused by the desire to get out and get a good job. And in this context he wrote:

> Knowledge, factual, extensive, and accurate, thus acquired does not necessarily lead to the understanding of meanings which we call wisdom. . . . Knowledge must become the servant of wisdom. I recall that some historical character when riding used to wear only one spur because, he said, if one side of the horse went forward the other side was unlikely to stay behind. Knowledge and wisdom should thus be related.

He knew too that understanding meanings, gaining wisdom, was not necessarily a classroom matter. He said once, "I know of no schoolroom where character is developed directly." He did not, however, hesitate in his own classroom to teach wisdom—which I see as part of character (another old-fashioned word but important nonetheless).

He stood for principles against prejudices, and learned in over sixty-one years of service to Vanderbilt students that the young often throw out the baby with the bath. He once said,

Diversity in a University, 1978–1979

Don't let prejudices harden into principles if you would avoid frustrations and bewilderment. Avoid also the other extreme of the cult of the open mind—those whose minds are so broad that their brains spill out. It's a fine thing to have an open mind so long as it is not open at both ends.

He recognized "the right of every college boy and girl to make fools of themselves while they're young"—and he was not above helping them do it to make his point. Joe R. Hendrickson, who was an instructor in civil engineering in 1933, remembered such an event. One afternoon during Prohibition days when the home brewers on campus were less than under control, Dean Sarratt, according to the story, started a rumor that "Revenoors" were going to inspect fraternity houses for "signs of pollution operation" that afternoon. The rumor spread rapidly in Old Science Hall, and in forty-five seconds one laboratory and one classroom were completely empty. The students, the professor recalled, ignored the doors and scrambled out of the ground-floor windows, overturning at least one professor in their flight. There was no inspection, of course. But we can assume that Sarratt offered the fraternity men what is now called "a moment of truth" . . . and a step in the process of wisdom.

He saw that the educational system itself was not always wise or according to nature, and this is expressed in a letter of 1936:

> Youth is a time for action, and age for reflection and contemplation. Our educational system reverses the order, and we force, with some success, thought, reflection, and contemplation upon young students. These outbreaks [this was 1936] are the young savages reverting to the natural order of development. . . . The bull frog wears the tad-pole's tail for a considerable while after it becomes a bull frog.

Mr. Sarratt liked to think of Vanderbilt as a great river: "It is the same river but it has grown deeper and wider and with more force since it has gone along." But even though this university is deeper and wider, he saw in his wisdom that the generations on the river are much the same. He summed it up in an article written for the *Alumnus* in 1961:

> No matter what the times are like, or what generation we are considering, the Vanderbilt student is a young person who is restless, seeking new ideas, new experiences, new horizons, new opportunities—but he will return in twenty-five years to deplore the behavior of youth and to complain about the political, economic, and religious views we are teaching his children.
>
> All in all, the college students of every generation turn out mighty well considering what they have to put up with for four years [in their] teachers, preachers—and parents.

Madison was not misled or intimidated by other persons, no matter how formidable. Once, referring to the creators of Vanderbilt's most famous literary tradition, he said: "I had the other end of the Fugitives. I had 'em in math."

One day Mr. Sarratt was walking with one of the leading figures on the campus, an important colleague who was a large woman: tall, big-boned, and heavy. They approached a door, and she hurried to open it for him saying "Age before beauty." In a whispered aside, Madison commented promptly. "Grace before meat."

For about ten years before his final illness, as some of you younger alumni will remember, Madison used to sit in a metal porch chair—he was living in Building C on West Side Row—and watched the students pass on the shortcut through his yard. He called it the Hypotenuse Trail. He was no doubt "reading rabbit tracks," the term Miss Jane Sutherland remembers that he used for sensing what was happening or going to happen. Many students stopped to chat or to ask advice; so did many others of the faculty and staff. Dean K. C. Potter tells about grumbling to Mr. Sarratt one day, as they sat beside the Hypotenuse Trail, about all the trials and doubts and low pay of a dean involved in student affairs. Dean Sarratt stopped him short: "Oh, yes, but you are just like me. You are doing what you want to do."

I want to put that observation alongside a quotation from William James that Sarratt was fond of using: "The great use of life is to spend it for something that will not end with it." To do what you want to do, for something good that will endure—that is the example and end of wisdom. I believe that Dean Sarratt, in his sixty-one and a half years at Vanderbilt, lived what he said and made it a living part of Vanderbilt.

In those same remarks at my installation, Madison Sarratt recalled that, toward the end of the $30 million campaign the year before, one of his colleagues said "that if at a dinner someone accidentally struck a water glass with a knife Sarratt would rise and begin to speak." I am confident that, water glass or not, he rises in our minds and speaks to us here today.

🌹

In the many speeches alluded to in the Preface that I made each year to Vanderbilt clubs around the country I naturally emphasized the University's connection to the location of the meeting. I would report campus occurrences and University achievements of local interest, and was not above mentioning University needs that I thought would be understood by the attentive faithful. In Louisville, Kentucky, on February 7, 1979, I did a full share of the usual, but also at the outset explained the title I had chosen for the remarks, "A Place to Come From."

I came to this title and this subject by way of two books. One is the recent novel with the provocative title, *A Place to Come To*, written by one of Vanderbilt's distinguished alumni, Robert Penn Warren. "Red" Warren's setting is in part Vanderbilt and Nashville, but, more importantly, his theme, as I perceive it, is the need and search for enduring human relationships, for roots and the continuity that they imply. That theme is not unrelated to a university's mission, to Vanderbilt's mission. We humans with all our deep diversities are, nonetheless, all ultimately of one fabric. Every university has a part to play in weaving and mending that fabric by helping to create a community of rationality and integrity, which is also a community of common interests that extends from the past through the present to the future.

The second book that prompted thoughts about "a place to come from" was published a month ago by the Vanderbilt University Press. It is called *The Vanderbilt Campus: A Pictorial History* and was written and designed by Robert A. McGaw, Secretary of the University. Bob McGaw has been a Vanderbilt administrative officer for thirty-one years and his life has been close to Vanderbilt since childhood. He has become the chief identifier and preserver of our traditions—of our architecture, of our archival documents and photographs, of our institutional paintings, of our trees, of our place names and University symbols—in short, of our campus. In Bob's splendid picture book—with almost 250 photographs, maps, master plans for the campus, and other illustrations—we are moved from Vanderbilt's beginnings to its present, a guided tour of buildings, greensward, walkways, persons, events, and the hopes and accomplishments that these things signify.

It is in our nature, I think—at least I know it is in my nature—to associate in a significant way an event in time with the place where it occurred, to put a revelation, a feeling, a memory in a certain place. Our minds are like photo albums. If you will recall something important that happened to you the moment you decided you would go to Vanderbilt, or would try to go to law school, or were elected president of your sorority, or were given that special word by the coach, or had a flash of insight into a tough personal problem, or a flash of insight into yourself, or decided to propose, or to accept a proposal—do you not remember where you were and how you were? Do you see yourself ascending a certain stair, or looking at the sun through a particular tree, or gazing out a particular window, or walking along that special path, or sitting at a desk or on a bench that ever remained memorable, or walking along a beach or over a mountain or looking at a fading sky? . . .

So the preservation of places is in a sense the preservation of our identity, an assurance that something of us and something we believe in goes on. At Vanderbilt, with all the new buildings and changes over the years, we have always been concerned with this kind of preservation—as Bob's book testifies. Interest in preservation of historical sites has been growing in the United States for two decades, and public policy has supported it. Last month we received notice that old Mechanical Engineering Hall, built in 1888, has been placed in the National Register of Historic Places by the United States Department of the Interior. The nomination was made by the State Historic Preservation Officer because the building, believed to be the first one in Tennessee designed for engineering education, is significant to Tennessee history. Other Vanderbilt buildings already in the National Register are the Fine Arts Building—to some of you "the old gym"—and the first dormitories, five of six remaining, that are known as West Side Row.

But even as we have preserved, so also have we built to meet new needs—all the while trying to bridge between the old and the new, trying to retain the distinctive mood and feeling of the campus, as I think we did in the Sarratt Student Center completed five years ago.

There are a number of new constructions on campus. Mayfield Place for housing two hundred undergraduates was completed in the fall of 1977, and recently the architects received an award for excellence in design from the Tennessee Society of Architects. These twenty units on the south edge of the campus commemorate

George R. Mayfield, the well-remembered professor of languages who came to Vanderbilt in 1903 as a graduate student and taught for almost half a century. Rudolph A. Light Hall—named for our late alumnus, faculty member, trustee and benefactor—is the new $13 million medical education building on the south side of Garland Avenue. It was completed last year, as was the $2.5 million Lilburn C. Langford Auditorium, adjacent to it. Next to both is the new $45 million replacement hospital that is scheduled for completion in the summer of 1980.

On the other side of the campus the outward signs of current change are less visible. Although virtually unaltered on the outside, Neely Auditorium has been converted to a flexible and inviting theater that has added to the art of drama for students. Also unseen from outside are important changes for psychology and geology in the Stevenson Center. The openness of the campus has been preserved by building underground the new $1 million addition to the Nursing School's Godchaux Hall. And there is renovation to be done. In Alumni Hall, it is already underway, with beautiful results.... We will soon proceed with a long-planned-for outdoor track, and we are going this year to construct new playing fields south of McGugin Center.... By all of this, I mean to suggest that Vanderbilt as a place, a physical entity, changes and yet remains the same. What shapes the changes is not a desire to be bigger, but to be better. Buildings are but signs of the intangible: the values of education. They are the locus where learning in its many forms can take place for students—and for faculty, too, who are not only teachers, but also scholars....

❧

Long before I was invited to come to Vanderbilt, I knew of the historic distinction of George Peabody College for Teachers, across the street from Vanderbilt on what was said by many to be a more impressive campus. Peabody had an important heritage. It was one of the prominent teacher training institutions in the nation and before World War II was in many ways comparable to Vanderbilt in the recognition accorded to it. Constructive cooperation had been achieved between the two institutions. The Joint University Libraries, the product of a formal agreement in 1936, was the most important both in symbol and in function. Other cooperative relationships and divisions of labor existed. Peabody-Vanderbilt relations were discussed in higher education and foundation circles outside of Tennessee, with examples of their successful collaborative efforts and yet unrealized possibilities often cited. Financial as well as educational considerations periodically spurred discussion of how the institutions might be brought into more productive and economical collaboration. Sometimes someone might dare to speculate (I inferred usually in private) on the desirability of making the two into a single institution. There had been a joint study of possible new relations between the two institutions during 1961 and 1962, under a $50,000 grant from the General Education Board, but before I arrived in 1963 neither institution had found the proposals acceptable.

Before taking office at Vanderbilt, I had concluded that among many people of crucial influence in Peabody's affairs any initiative by Vanderbilt that could be interpreted as a move to dilute Peabody's independence would be vigorously resisted and would deepen endemic feelings of fear and suspicion. Over the years after I took office at Vanderbilt, I told each of the three successive presidents of Peabody that as long as I was in office at Vanderbilt, Vanderbilt would initiate no action looking toward merger of the two institutions. We would continue the cooperative efforts already in place as long as they were satisfactory to both institutions and would negotiate others Peabody initiated or found agreeable, but any discussion of a merger would have to be initiated by Peabody.

In 1978 President John Dunworth of Peabody asked that discussion of a merger be commenced among a small group of representatives of the two institutions. After a normal experience of ups and downs, and eventually a debate about the matter in the media, conditions were agreed upon in the spring of 1979 for Peabody to become part of Vanderbilt on July 1, 1979.

Peabody's board met on April 27, 1979, in the Kennedy Center on the Peabody campus, in a session preparatory to a vote on the proposed merger. I was invited to address it. Vanderbilt's board was in session at the same time. Both boards acted at that time to bring the institutions together on July 1.

Here were my informally delivered comments to Peabody's trustees of April 27.

I appreciated the suggestion yesterday that came from Chairman [Robert] Gable and President [John] Dunworth to come to meet with you today.

The initiative for this prospectively important move for both institutions came from Peabody. We welcomed it then and welcome it now. If it should work out that later today you take action that gives us at Vanderbilt the opportunity to take action that would lead to joining our two institutions, I think the Vanderbilt Board of Trust will be enthusiastically affirmative.

I think it would be a fair question for you to ask me why Vanderbilt is interested in this prospective merger. It is a question that we have asked ourselves, too. It is a proper question that we should ask ourselves and that you should ask us, and it is a question that is enormously important to the future of Vanderbilt as it now exists and to the future of George Peabody College for Teachers.

I think we are all aware that over the decades these two institutions have been side by side—some seven decades now. The development of each of them has been substantially influenced by the development of the other. Vanderbilt has consciously sought to be complementary to the programs at Peabody, and Peabody has sought to be complementary to the programs at Vanderbilt. We have had a remarkably extensive record of cooperation that has been, from our point of view at least, extremely effective. Some of these relationships have in fact served as models to be emulated in other parts of the country.

Why, then, if we have had these seven decades of successful joint activity would Vanderbilt be interested in the union of the two institutions? I suppose we have various perceptions of this question. I can speak for myself only, I suppose, but in truth I think the views that I have are shared substantially by my colleagues at Vanderbilt.

I think the root of our understanding is that we have in the United States and in the Western world a knowledge-based civilization. The distinctive characteristic of the times, and of our society, is the extent to which knowledge determines the nature of our lives. It has not always been true that the impact of science, technology, and other forms of human inquiry have so shaped daily lives as is true of our civilization. We are a knowledge-based, science- and technology-determined society with all of the enormous complications that result from the impact of these forces of modernization on our culture, on our beliefs, on our traditions, on our values, and on our humanistic concerns.

Education, therefore, is the most significant process in our country and in our society. And if there are some remote tribes somewhere who cannot now be called part of this Western culture, they soon will be. The whole world is of a kind that the processes of education are the most important processes that go on. They have a larger ultimate impact on the welfare of human beings than anything else.

Education begins at the beginning, and by the time we at Vanderbilt University receive students for freshman work or graduate work those individuals have been through educational processes— of which we are very conscious—at the pre-elementary level, and elementary and secondary school levels, so that the students who come to us are the products not of ourselves but of others.

The university is the source of the educational process in the United States. Our teachers at pre-college levels come out of institutions of higher education. We turn out a few at Vanderbilt who are declared qualified because of work they have taken at Peabody, but we have not been at Vanderbilt an institution that has, except in very indirect ways, taken part in this vastly important process of pre-college education of people.

We look around the country and even the layman can conclude that the pre-college education is a very difficult business. The old term "blackboard jungle" seems almost archaic now. The layman can at least see the difficulties that are experienced in crowded urban areas, the problems of morale and morality and discipline and mental health and other indices of social disorder that are found around the country, including in our schools. We look at those who come to us at the university and see changes, and we think perhaps we see deterioration, in the qualifications that they bring—at least if you ask them to write or sometimes even to read or to count—and we become very much aware of the critical importance to higher education, as well as to the country more generally, of the processes of pre-college education everywhere.

Vanderbilt has over the years felt excused by the presence of Peabody across the street from coming to grips with these matters as most advanced universities in the United States have. We would not be coming to you with the request that we join up if you had not come to us with the suggestion that this might make sense. It is our view that it makes enormous sense. I have tried to inform myself in recent weeks. Since we began conversations with President Dunworth and his colleagues, I have been given very clear affirmative statements—from people much more knowledgeable than I suppose any of us at Vanderbilt are at the moment—about the kind of educational environment that is, if not optimum, at least highly hospitable and promising for a school of education and human development.

One former United States Commissioner of Education volunteered that Vanderbilt has a Law School, a Management School, a Medical School, a Graduate School (offering the Ph.D. in some thirty-four fields) and a diversified College of Arts and Science. And without knowing anything else about our university than that, he said that in his view of the future, and the way these very difficult and complex problems can be best addressed, it is that kind of campus that offers the interschool, interdisciplinary support that an advanced school of education and human development can best benefit from.

That sounds sensible to me. I would not be able to debate the matter in detail. And I would certainly defer to anyone associated with George Peabody College for Teachers in respect to that judgment, but it does seem to me that, from Vanderbilt's point of view, we have got to face the question.

It is the inescapable obligation of higher education and its universities to address the needs of society, particularly the needs of our own country, and to do so more effectively than we have been doing in the past at Vanderbilt—and perhaps more effectively than has been done in the past at Peabody. I think we can do so through the union of the two institutions. That is why we are interested in this—that is why we are willing to take some risks with you.

I think it would be foolish to suggest that it will be an easy course. It will be a very difficult one. There will be many problems, and not all of them financial ones. There will be financial problems and problems of adjustment. The most demanding requirements of us, should we join, will be in determining the optimum educational programs that should go forth in George Peabody College for Teachers of Vanderbilt University, and in other schools of Vanderbilt. The course will not be easy by any means and it involves a lot of risks for the present Peabody College and the present Vanderbilt University, but it seems to us to be a risk worth taking. The reason it is a risk worth taking is the educational significance of the missions we think we can achieve together.

❧

As true in every year, 1978 and 1979 brought abundant opportunities and obligations to speak: to a conference at the Bard College Center in Annandale-on-Hudson, New York, on "What Ought to be Taught?"; to the Eagle Scout Recognition Dinner at which Vanderbilt Trustee David K. Wilson was made an Eagle Scout Honoree; to a dinner meeting at the Belle Meade Country Club at which Vanderbilt gave to the Hermitage nine pieces of silver that had belonged to General and Mrs. Andrew Jackson and had been a bequest to Vanderbilt in 1918; to the First Annual Symposium at Vanderbilt of a program of the Robert Wood Johnson Foundation that offered Nurse Faculty Fellowships in Primary Care; to the St. John's Dinner Club in Jacksonville, Florida, on "Education in Today's World: The Paradoxes of the Consequences"; to the Symposium on the Holocaust, in Nashville, on Jewish and Christian perspectives; to the Southern Academy of the Letters, Arts, and Sciences, meeting at Vanderbilt; to the Southeast Council of Foundations, meeting in Atlanta; to a National Conference on Organized Crime at the University of Southern California in Los Angeles; and speeches to "Major Gift Kick-Off Dinners" in more than a dozen cities. As usual, the record of talks came to about forty per year.

On June 2, 1979, I spoke at the commencement of Simon's Rock Early College in Great Barrington, Massachusetts. Simon's Rock was closely affiliated with Bard College in Annandale-on-Hudson, whose commencement Jean and I also attended later in the day. Here is part of the Simon's Rock talk:

I read recently that George Bernard Shaw once observed:

The reasonable man adapts himself to the world; the unreasonable one persists in trying to adapt the world to himself. Therefore, all progress depends on the unreasonable man.

Like many of Mr. Shaw's epigrammatic insights, that one is too pat, too simple, too extreme. But there is a continuum, from complacent compliance at one end to irascible irrationality at the other, and choosing the right point along the continuum at which to invest one's strengths and energies—that is, deciding how to invest one's self—requires judgment and sensitivity, and knowledge of one's self.

Our world, in its riches and in its hurts, is a monstrously uneven place. It is, moreover, a place in jeopardy. And everywhere people search for comfort, for hope, for solution, for salvation.

Two weeks ago I was in Denison, Texas, and went to see the house where President Eisenhower was born. It is a lovely, immaculate place, surrounded by a white fence enclosing emerald green grass and attractive planting. In a park to one side is a tall, imposing statue of the Supreme Commander of Allied Expeditionary Forces.

This was a remarkable family. Six of seven Eisenhower sons grew to manhood. Ike's brothers included a bank executive, a lawyer, an engineer, and a businessman, as well as Milton Eisenhower, a public servant of distinction who served as president of three important universities.

Speaking of the University

The house is a State Historic Site. Its present appearance is quite unlike an early photograph that shows a shabby, run-down dwelling with scraggly planting and tasteless appointments. Three railroad tracks run through the neighborhood, one immediately beside the house. Ike's father was an engine wiper with the Missouri, Kansas and Texas Railroad. There are three small bedrooms, two on a second floor connected by steps so steep that visitors may not use them. When the Eisenhowers lived there, one of the bedrooms was rented to lodgers. The circumstances were not propitious.

I thought about the qualities of the country in which these Eisenhower boys became those Eisenhower men. America was and is a land of remarkable opportunity. The achievements of thousands of spectacular people like the Eisenhowers are only the tip of an iceberg. Tens of millions of less visible folk have found material advance and personal fulfillment in our miraculously productive and miraculously free country. I guess it was Aristotle who said, "He who has health has hope, and he who has hope has everything." Hope was justified for Mr. and Mrs. David [Jacob] Eisenhower, parents of seven boys. The Eisenhower story reminded me that hope is the priceless reward of opportunity. It also made me reflect that our world is a very uneven place.

It is hard to know how best to convey the hurtful unevenness of the world. [As I have emphasized on other occasions] perhaps a billion people around the world go to bed hungry every night. At least 700 million are seriously malnourished. Well over one billion do not have access to safe drinking water. A United Nations expert estimates that over 532 million Asians live in "absolute poverty"—most of them in Indonesia, Bangladesh, and India. A study commissioned by the Asian Development Bank reported recently that Asian rural poverty "has considerably worsened in the past decade."

Our own country is not immune. A knowledgeable observer remarks:

Diversity in a University, 1978–1979

It is evident that a permanent black underclass has developed, that virtually an entire second generation of ghetto youth will never enter into the labor force. This means that a large part of the young black urban population will remain in a condition of hopelessness and despair and that the social and psychological costs in wasted lives continues a major tragedy in American life.

One reads that a quarter century ago the rate of unemployment among black young people sixteen to nineteen years old was 16 percent, and then that today it is 36 percent. The comparable percentage for white youth today is 14.

More than poverty can trap people. American state and federal penal institutions—not counting city and county jails—contain some 300,000 prisoners nowadays, and the number has been inexorably rising. President Carter's Commission on Mental Health last year estimated that 15 percent of the U.S. population is affected by mental disorders in any given year. The commission's preliminary report traced many of the nation's mental health problems to the "unrelenting poverty and institutionalized discrimination that occur on the basis of race, sex, class, age, and mental and physical handicaps."

In February, 1979, the *Buenos Aires Herald* estimated that some three to ten persons had disappeared in Argentina each day over the previous three years—many of them never to be heard from. The Argentine Permanent Assembly for Human Rights published a list of 2500 missing persons in *La Prensa* on May 17, 1978. Amnesty International is an organization that won the Nobel Peace Prize in 1977 as a "bulwark" against increased brutality and the internationalization of violence. Its publications report extensive, pathetic, bitter, malignant violations of human dignity and liberty around most of the globe. And then another tearing reality. Some millions of people—yes, apparently millions of people—have been killed in

Southeast Asia since the end of American intervention in Vietnam.

And from another perspective, United Nations statistics in 1970 showed 28 percent of the world's men and 40 percent of the world's women unable to read or write.

Everywhere, individuals are caged by hopelessness—poverty, illiteracy, mental illness, drug addiction, imprisonment, political repression—by anything that smothers hope including loss of guiding values.

The cohesion and continuity of our interdependent world—that world that you can wake up each morning to reform or enjoy, or both—are imperiled by the pervasive infections of hopelessness among large segments of all the world's peoples. We know that the world is jeopardized in other ways too. Growing population, inadequate food, and unassured reserves of natural resources, including energy, constitute a triad of decisive issues that will ultimately limit our future. [As I often emphasize,] on almost every part of the globe overpopulation is a present reality or a hovering, marching menace. In 1900 the world had one billion six hundred million people. In 1970 it had three billion six hundred million. It may have around seven billion by the year 2000, twenty-one years from now. Even if the encouraging signs of declining fertility rates be accurate indicators of the future, under present conditions the world population may not stabilize below eleven billion. This massive overpopulation, especially in the emerging developing countries, finds its most primitive consequences in that malnutrition and starvation that enervate hope. Not only do food supplies not keep up with population growth, but water supplies are increasingly being depleted and subterranean water tables lowered. Forests are cut down, the soil is mined, and in the United States neither we nor our elected representatives will hear our president's repeated warning that we ourselves are on a course of disaster in our refusal to recognize the certainty of [eventual energy shortages]. More subtly, but ultimately more brutally, the future of innocent individuals all around the world is twisted by the dislocation of their social systems and corruption of their cultural heritage.

Changes wrought in this perplexing world upset religious teachings and community customs, producing an environment of unsure values and cultural insecurity in which fear and bewilderment immobilize ambition on some occasions and provoke mindless violence on others.

The spectacle is dreary without even mentioning the black vulture that darkens our sun each day, the potential for nuclear destruction.

The world is monstrously uneven and its existence is in jeopardy. One is tempted to feel about the world as Lady Astor and Winston Churchill did about each other. They served together in the House of Commons and were often at odds. Lady Astor—tart-tongued and American-born—once berated the future prime minister at great length on his inconsistencies and perversities and in exasperation finally concluded, "Oh, if you were my husband, I would kill you." At which Churchill jumped up and said, "Madam, if I were your husband, I would kill myself."

Albert Einstein is often quoted as issuing this warning:

> The unleashed power of the atom has changed everything save our modes of thinking, and thus we drift toward unparalleled catastrophe. . . . A new type of thinking is essential if humanity is to survive.

"The Great American Frustration," Archibald MacLeish has written, is

> a numb, unformed persistent sense like the hinting pinch of pain which is not yet mortal, that we have somehow lost control of our destiny. And not our military destiny only, or our political destiny, but our human destiny as men. It is a sense we have had in one form or another for a long time now, but

not as an explicitly formulated fear until we found ourselves deep in the present century with its faceless slaughters, its mindless violence, its fabulous triumphs over space and time and matter ending in perils that space and time and matter never held.

We continue to struggle, using the tools of our civilization and the social ways we know, seeking roads to peace and better living. We sometimes have encouraging success. But that worry over our destiny, our destiny as humans, makes us now, as ever it has, look beyond our tools and our established ways. Everywhere people are searching for hope, for solutions and salvation.

A campaign has recently been launched under the call of "Here's Life" to raise one billion dollars to finance evangelical work across the United States and on every part of the globe through the Campus Crusade for Christ. One million dollars each is asked from one thousand people. Together they are to constitute "History's Handfold" of persons joining in action decisive to save salvation.

That is only one effort. The nation is undergoing an evangelical rebirth. Not only is our president a "born-again Christian" and his sister a prominent faith healer, but a jailed assistant of a former president conducted revival crusades to bring prison inmates to Jesus, and a former, violent black activist has been preaching his new faith to large audiences and to breakfasts with Christian businessmen. One survey of the phenomenon reports: "Olympic athletes, beauty queens, television and movie stars, generals, politicians, and what must have been more than half the National Football League were all proclaiming themselves converts to evangelism. . . ."

We have had our periods of religious revival before—in the 1720s and 1730s of colonial America and in the two decades following 1790, for two examples. But today Billy Graham stands high in every popularity poll, and the amount of time on local and network television given to religious programs is now immense. The following in this country and abroad that rally behind articulate, forceful, intense personalities preaching a gospel is a sign accurately revealing our times.

Where in all this longing can be found that hope for which hundreds of millions in our uneven world are hurting? How, indeed, shall we spend our days? . . .

Our enormously creative human reason and its associated powers have made our world one of unprecedented satisfactions and unprecedented peril, one of stunning abundance and merciless poverty. For my part, we do not have to choose between the "powers of reason"—to oversimplify for a moment—and the enormously creative strength of spiritual commitment to a goodness that lies beyond. There is hope in both. There is hope too in the very nearness we have to each other, the nearness that threatens us with brutal rivalry and mutual ruin. Our common terror makes us brothers. Perhaps in our age humankind has its first true opportunity to discover what it really is. I close with some lines written by Mr. MacLeish after man first orbited the moon:

> To see the earth as we now see it, small and blue and beautiful in that eternal silence where it floats, is to see ourselves as riders on the earth together, brothers on that bright loveliness in the unending night—brothers who see now that they are truly brothers.

🦋

One of the last talks that I made to a welcoming convocation for new students was on August 25, 1979. It was the first in which I could say that "this year we especially welcome students registered in George Peabody College for Teachers of Vanderbilt University." I also, as always, assured the newcomers that "all the office doors at Vanderbilt have hinges and with a little nudge will swing open"—our open door policy. The bulk of the talk went like this:

We here on the stage are wondering this to ourselves—who is sitting out there tonight in the class of 1983?

Who among you will become Governor of a state, as did Lamar Alexander, class of 1962, who was elected governor of Tennessee in 1978? Who will go to the United States Senate, like James Sasser, class of 1958, who did so in 1976? Who among you will follow earlier Vanderbilt students to become attorney general of the United States, a justice of the Supreme Court of the United States, vice-president of the United States?

Is there present a Robert Penn Warren, winner of Pulitzer Prizes for both fiction and poetry; a Grantland Rice, America's most famous sportswriter; a Stanford Moore, winner of the Nobel Prize for chemistry in 1972; a Dinah Shore, for forty years a national entertainment personality. . . .

When I became chancellor in 1963, a host of business and financial leaders were Vanderbilt graduates, including our nation's most highly respected banker, the chief executive officer of the Eastman Kodak Company, the president of the American Bankers Association, and the chairman of the Board of Directors of American Express. The principal architect of national awareness of Appalachia as a region of national problems and potential was W. D. Weatherford, class of 1899, with two additional Vanderbilt degrees; and, not long before 1963, Will W. Alexander, class of 1912, had died, the white person who probably more than any other during the years between the First and Second World Wars contributed to the amelioration, and I like to think the ultimate removal of the South's racial problems.

Bishops, publishers, editors, network broadcasters, authors, ministers, social workers, librarians, physicians, nurses, engineers, scholars, public officials, college presidents, war heroes, athletes, businessmen, inventive entrepreneurs of many kinds—persons of achievement, of useful and satisfying, effective and rewarding lives, have sat on other opening nights where you sit tonight about to begin life at Vanderbilt.

This past May, at the fiftieth reunion of the class of 1929, the most celebrated member was Morris Frank, the first blind student to attend a Southern university. Vanderbilt alumnus Morris Frank brought the first seeing-eye dog to America and, through this pioneering step and his subsequent organizational work, he brought the marvelous resource of these extraordinary creatures—and the hope they will bring with them—to thousands upon thousands of Americans.

The part and importance of women in Vanderbilt have risen steadily across the years since a single female was pictured among eighteen graduates in the first regular class of 1879. I say "pictured" intentionally because Miss Kate Lupton was not officially listed, and in fact was asked to receive her Master's degree in decent privacy, since Vanderbilt had been founded for the education of young men.

Times change. We have a system by which each year a new young alumnus is elected at the end of the senior year to serve a four-year term on the Vanderbilt Board of Trust. Since the system was initiated in 1969, fifteen young alumni have been chosen by nomination of their peers and election by the trustees. Of the fifteen, nine have been women.

We have a steadily lengthening register of prominent women professionals among graduates from all schools of the University. Last May one-sixth of the Ph.D. recipients, one-fifth of those receiving law, medical, master of business administration and undergraduate engineering degrees, nearly one-third of those receiving master of divinity degrees, and over half the graduates of the College of Arts and Science were women.

I think tonight of some other graduates, too, all of these being recent ones.

Of Bedford Waters, 1970, doctor of medicine, 1974, now launched on a career as a urologist.

Of Perry Wallace, 1970, basketball star, later graduated from Columbia Law School.

Of Larry Moore, 1971, with master of arts and doctor of jurisprudence degrees from Memphis State University, now an assistant district attorney.

Of William O. Nash, 1972, doctor of medicine, 1976, now a surgical resident in New York City.

Of Larry Wallace, 1972, president of the student government association, later graduated from Harvard Law School.

Of Vanessa Rouselle, 1974, now a regional manager with South Central Bell.

Of William C. Campbell, 1974, doctor of jurisprudence from Duke, now in successful law practice.

Of Robert Scott, 1975, who received his doctor of medicine degree last May.

Of Patricia Rogers, 1976, now nearing the completion of medical school.

And of Walter Fields III, 1978, one of those few men elected as a young alumnus to the Board of Trust.

One quality makes these recent graduates of achievement come to mind tonight. They are all black alumni of Vanderbilt. Many other black graduates could be mentioned alongside them, too.

Your predecessors as Vanderbilt students have demonstrated that it is a privilege to be a Vanderbilt student. But being one carries obligations. The obligations go beyond using seriously the time bought for you here—bought by your families, but also bought by the generosity of foundations and corporations and alumni and other individuals (some of them named Vanderbilt) who over the decades have provided the rest of the support needed to make this university possible.

Diversity in a University, 1978–1979

Over the years I have said regularly on occasions like this that we expect our students to have a good time. I do not worry much about your having a good time on the lighter side of things. Most Vanderbilt students do, and doing so deepens their affection for the place. But in a university it is incumbent also to have a stimulating and rewarding time intellectually. You have the resources here to have a good time intellectually.

Our country and our world are confronted by a long agenda of difficult problems that we must cope with somehow—by solving them, or ameliorating them, or transforming them, or perhaps on occasion just by postponing them. Understanding tough problems can bring joy.

We face, you face, tough problems. Let me illustrate.

Throughout most of our national life the marvel of American ingenuity, energy, enterprise and resources has regularly brought forth continuing increases in national productivity, increases not just in how much America produces, but also in the efficiency—the output per hour of effort—with which it produces it. For the three decades after World War II, the steady increase in productivity was around three percent a year compounded. For the past two years, however, the increase was under one percent, and in the first quarter of this year productivity declined by four percent. That is a profound and serious change in our national condition—and it contributes significantly to the plaguing problem of inflation that wracks us every day in universities and throughout the rest of society.

Here is another example of a challenge we, you, face.

Depending on where you come from, you will already be more or less aware that the relations of the United States with its most immediate neighbors, Canada and Mexico, have been changing. Probably unlike any other nation in the world, we in the United States have enjoyed the luxury of not worrying much about relations with our closest neighbors. Those neighbors have worried about those relations, but we have not. That time is now gone and we are not truly sure what to do about it.

Take another case.

Only very recently have large segments of opinion in the United States begun to share genuine skepticism of the validity and efficacy of growth—just plain growth, getting large for its own sake, as well as economic growth and growth in other dimensions of community life. Recently a beginning of understanding has come of the consequences for societies and individuals of rapid growth in science and technology, of rapid "modernization." There was a time when novelty and invention and growth were their own justification. We are now beginning to make social decisions about matters that used to be decided automatically by the inner processes of science and technology and the economic system.

Also, we have a well launched nagging anxiety that I imagine all of us here tonight share about the adequacy of our political institutions in the United States. During the great Depression that began fifty years ago a few weeks from now, we developed deep anxiety about the adequacy of our economic institutions. Now, for the first time since the Civil War, we are wondering whether our political institutions can provide the governance the United States needs for itself, and that the world needs from the United States.

Our governmental system has not coped adequately with issues of which we are daily reminded by the news: inflation, energy, equal opportunity, balance of payments, unemployment, arms control, the Middle East, urban decay, and on and on and on.

Problems like these challenge the wits of us all, but they offer the prospects for you to have an intellectually stimulating and demanding time, which I would call a good time, at Vanderbilt.

I recently read a speech by Ambassador John Reinhardt, speaking as director of the United States International Communication Agency this past June. His title was, "The Real Shortage: Ideas." He said, I am

> concerned that we as a people are not sufficiently preparing ourselves for the world in which we must live. I mean this in

two senses: first, that we appreciate neither the role of ideas nor the force of our own ideas; and second, that we have not the interest, nor the knowledge, nor the skill required to deal effectively with other societies—and at present we are doing far too little to acquire them.

Ambassador Reinhardt's first point

is reflected in the intense focus on self running rampant throughout our society. I doubt that we have ever experienced a more self-centered period in our history. Rarely, if ever, have we witnessed such a wave of interest in, such an overwhelming emphasis on self-understanding, self-awareness, self-gratification. . . .

[T]he point is that we are in serious danger, I believe, of forgetting H. G. Wells's simple but profound proposition that "human history is in essence a history of ideas."

Ambassador Reinhardt described the thousands of students, scholars, and foreign leaders from a variety of influential fields who come annually to the United States to teach and meet their counterparts. He reports that almost to a person they find their experiences exciting, exhilarating, rewarding. But he goes on to say:

They meet stimulating Americans, they are invariably impressed, if not a little bewildered, by the extent of our personal freedoms and our pursuit of individual rights. But they are also disappointed, all too often, by what they consider our inexcusable lack of knowledge about their societies and cultures.

Many of them are better informed about the United States and our history than we.

These college years ahead offer a chance to lift yourself outside yourself. From time to time I go to class at Vanderbilt. I drop in to catch the flavor of your scene. It is one of the easier and more enjoyable things a chancellor can do. I never come away without thinking what a marvelous privilege it is to have this kind of help in taking oneself out of oneself. Courses in the history of social thought in America; in Buddhist art of Asia; in historical geology; in probability and statistical inference; in molecular biology of diseases; in the American presidency; courses in contemporary ethical theory; in African philosophy; in government policies toward business; in Shakespeare; in the forms and techniques of poetry, of prose fiction, of drama; courses in the Greek historians; in computer science; in the biology of man: evolution, heredity and society; courses in frontiers in astronomy; in social psychology; in themes in world religions; in crime and delinquency; in cultural anthropology; and courses in French, Spanish, Italian, German, Russian, Chinese, and other languages. These and a myriad of other courses like them are available to you. Each of you will have your own decisions to make with the requirements of the curriculum you decide to pursue. Gone at the right way, however, every course of study at Vanderbilt offers a chance to lift oneself out of oneself, offers a chance to have an intellectually good time.

Going to college, coming to Vanderbilt tonight, involves risk. Sometimes the way will be hard, lonely, frustrating. But that's the way life has always been.

I close with a quotation I like from Edward Gibbon, writing about Greece:

> In the end, more than they wanted freedom, they wanted security. They wanted a comfortable life and they lost it all—security, comfort, and freedom.... When the Athenians finally wanted not to give to society but for society to give to them, when the freedom they wished for most was for freedom from responsibility, then Athens ceased to be free.

Welcome and good luck.

TEN

☙

Many Constituencies
1980–1981

MY LAST YEARS IN OFFICE increased the speaking requirements. The final phases of the fund drive (that ended June 30, 1981, and raised over $181.4 million) and invitations to give a final talk to familiar audiences, plus regular University requirements on and off the campus, led to something over ninety-four formal speaking appearances during 1980 and 1981. A few addressed a political science topic (procedures of presidential selection), conditions in South Africa (I was then serving on a national commission concerned with them), or a subject from an earlier incarnation (a speech about Frank Graham, president of the University of North Carolina when I was a student), but these came to much less than 10 percent of the total, and some of them were in response to invitations from Vanderbilt alumni.

Some talks on significant subjects were given from notes too cryptic to permit a re-creation—for instance, remarks I was grateful to be invited to make May 10, 1980, to the Executive Committee of the Peabody Alumni Association on "The Future of Peabody," and remarks on May 23, 1980, to the Board of Directors of the Vanderbilt Alumni Association on "Vanderbilt, Higher Education, and the Future." Other occasions called for comments in Benton Chapel in 1981 at a symposium entitled "Surviving the Holocaust—Sane, Alive and Still Human," remarks in Branscomb Quadrangle on "Black-White Relations at Vanderbilt" (a seminar sponsored by the Student Government Association and the Afro-American Association), and, less formally, July 4 comments in 1981 at a neighborhood gathering on Whitland Avenue in Nashville that included many Vanderbilt alumni residents and their guests.

During this period a crucial step was taken in the evolution of Vanderbilt as a fully developed university. The previously independent Blair School of Music became Vanderbilt's tenth school on January 1, 1981. Already possessed of highly successful pre-collegiate offerings, Blair proceeded quickly to develop collegiate offerings and conferred its first degrees, bachelor of music, in 1990.

Universities depend importantly for their success on the respect of devoted alumni, and of others brought by that respect into the fold. Francis Robinson was an impeccable Vanderbilt graduate. He combined exemplary human qualities, including generosity, knowledge, humor, talent, good taste, and an embracing capacity for friendship. He died May 14, 1980, and I spoke of him in welcoming first-year undergraduates in Memorial Gymnasium the following August 23.

In good time you will be graduated, and if you are what your families think you are, and what Vanderbilt thinks you are, and what we hope you think you are, you will join a long line of eminent American citizens who took advantage of their opportunities at Vanderbilt to learn and to become better human beings.

Such a man was Francis Robinson, who was born in Henderson,

Kentucky, in 1910, was graduated from Vanderbilt with a Bachelor of Arts degree in 1932 and a master of arts degree in 1933, and died three months ago in New York. When he was seven, his family moved to Mt. Pleasant, Tennessee, where he lived until coming to Vanderbilt. He did not sing, nor act, nor dance, nor play an instrument, nor conduct an orchestra, but when he died he was completing thirty-three years with the Metropolitan Opera, was called publicly and often "Mr. Metropolitan Opera," and, more important, still was, in the words of one of the world's great prima donnas [Bidu Sayao], "the soul of the Met."

Last December, before he was taken ill, a patron's dinner was given for Francis Robinson on the stage of the Metropolitan Opera in New York. The stage was set as the white and silver Viennese ballroom from Act II of *Der Rosenkavalier*. Those in attendance were the luminaries of the world's greatest opera house. The president of the Opera gave him a silver loving cup, saying, "He has been a man for all seasons with the Met. . . . He has been an administrator, friend and confidant to artists and staff, lay psychiatrist, ambassador, radio and television personality, historian and defender of the faith."

Francis Robinson had learned to do everything of value to the Met, except sing, act, dance, play, and conduct, which one would have thought are the main things necessary to make the Metropolitan Opera. He was at one time or another in charge of press relations, and of the box office and subscription department. He was tour manager for the Met's famous excursions out of New York. He spoke on the intermission programs of the Saturday matinee broadcasts from the Metropolitan Opera House, and in recent years he was the host, as many millions of television viewers know, of "Live from the Met," where he exhibited the qualities that made all who knew him as "Mr. Metropolitan Opera" love and respect him: his profound knowledge of music and opera, his impeccable fairness and honesty, his artistic sensitivity, his unflagging humor, his robust enthusiasm, and his inevitable courtesy. He was an educated human being.

As a Vanderbilt student he majored in German and philosophy. He worked as an usher for theatrical and musical events at the Ryman Auditorium. He worked for the *Nashville Banner* after graduation, first as a reporter and then as Sunday editor, and he also worked as a writer and producer for radio station WSM in Nashville. In 1938 he was invited to go to New York, where his qualities of mind, personality, and character were brought to the service, as a press representative, of some of the most famous figures then on the American stage, including Katherine Cornell. He served three years in the United States Navy during World War II. He worked summers for the Boston Symphony's Berkshire Music Festival at Tanglewood, Massachusetts.

One of Mr. Robinson's passions was the legendary tenor Enrico Caruso, whom he never heard sing except on records. He collected everything he could about Caruso, visited all the Caruso places, and in 1957 published a handsome book, *Caruso, His Life in Pictures.* In 1979 he published another book called *Celebration,* a marvelous book about the Metropolitan Opera.

There is enough good to be said about people, so even with old and intimate friends Francis Robinson never said anything derogatory about someone else. He knew so much about so many famous people under so many different circumstances that some of his friends wished he would write a book about them—that is, a book about the other friends. Someone said to him once, "If you ever write a book, Francis, and tell all you know, you will have to leave town." Mr. Robinson replied, "Oh no I won't, they will."

Mr. Robinson, by temperament and principle, took a positive view of life's vicissitudes and people's frailties—and there are many of both, at Vanderbilt and at the Metropolitan Opera and everywhere else. He did not complain, nor gossip unkindly, nor indict

other people for their failings. An interviewer once challenged him
on this rosy outlook and Mr. Robinson conceded that, indeed, like
the rest of us, he had his grievances, differences of opinion, frustrations, that he found stupidities and imperfections everywhere. "Well," asked the interviewer, "how do you handle them?"
Mr. Robinson replied: "Possess your soul in patience. Do the best
you can."

Somewhere Shakespeare refers to memory as "the warder of the
brain." Mr. Robinson's brain was well-guarded and well-stimulated
by a much-remarked, fabulous memory, a memory that was gifted
but also cultivated. He remembered everything, and equally important, he remembered everybody. As he would walk through the
Metropolitan Opera House at Lincoln Center he called ticket tak-
ers and ushers and sweepers by name, name after name, not only
their names but asked by name about the mother, the sister, the
baby, the husband, the friend. And it was not just that he knew by
first name all the people on stage and off who were important to the
life of the Metropolitan Opera. They knew him. He charmed and
cajoled and humored with an unlimited supply of apt anecdotal recollections. He knew more people better—each along a unique line
of friendship—than most of us ever will.

Also, in his work he drove undeviatingly for perfection. He knew
more about more dimensions of opera than anyone else alive. He
was honored abroad and at home, and in 1972 he received the highest honor in the arts the City of New York can bestow, the Handel
Medallion.

Mr. Robinson was a man of the world, and his small home town
and his university were as much a part of it as any other part of his
world. He was elected a trustee of your university in 1970. When he
died, his pallbearers were not the world's greatest singers, nor music's greatest patrons, as they would have been at his request, but
nine old friends from Middle Tennessee. . . .

You can be what you have the desire and the will to become, and

Vanderbilt is here to help. Remember that one who did not sing, nor act, nor dance, nor play an instrument, nor conduct an orchestra became "the soul of the Met," the world's greatest opera house.

❧

Among many, Vanderbilt is most lastingly known for the Agrarian and Fugitive literary movements. On October 30, 1980, I welcomed a symposium meeting in Sarratt Cinema that marked the fiftieth anniversary of the publication of the Agrarian manifesto, *I'll Take My Stand—The South and the Agrarian Tradition*, a collection of essays by twelve Southerners.

Vanderbilt extends its welcome to all who have come to participate in this fiftieth anniversary symposium. It celebrates an important event in American intellectual history and in Vanderbilt's life. We are especially happy that many distinguished persons have come from distant places to take part.

In the fall of 1934 I went from my home in Savannah, Georgia, to Chapel Hill to major in chemical engineering at the University of North Carolina. Paper was beginning to be made from pine pulp, and it seemed that chemical engineering would offer a young man opportunities in the course of contributing to the slowly growing industrialization of the South. I found myself during that freshman year stealing time from chemistry and mathematics and mechanical drawing to read the history and politics, and sometimes the economics, of our region. It was still a time when, at least where I came from in Georgia, the Civil War pressed heavily on our awareness, and I felt sentimental ties to values and ways of living that had earlier characterized our section, or that we thought had done so. I grew up in circumstances and among people that often made recollections of an Old South appealing.

I moved from engineering after one year to studies more congenial to my interests. I believe it was 1935 that I read *I'll Take My Stand.*

Many Constituencies, 1980–1981

I remember still the sense of irony, enigma, and puzzlement that was stimulated in me by the book. I was drawn to the themes in it by sentiment and consciousness of heritage, and away from it, in those Depression years, by the directions of regional development that seemed called for by the times. I still recall vividly the perplexity with which I finished the book.

I have thought of it since the Second World War while pondering the impact on our world of the enormous technological and scientific advances that have issued forth in these recent decades. We are beset by paradoxes. In our twentieth century we have greater wealth than ever before, yet greater poverty. We have greater productivity than ever before, yet greater inequality. We have greater affluence, yet greater dissatisfaction, more education, yet more ignorance. We have more research, basic and applied, than ever before, yet accompanied by a seemingly greater inability to solve in lasting ways the problems that surround us. And we in the universities are more than anyone else the ultimate originators of scientific discovery and technological innovation.

When Vanderbilt celebrated the centennial of the University on October 3, 1975, we invited two principal speakers. One was the president of Yale, speaking in a tradition that has brought the president of that university to Vanderbilt on important anniversary occasions. The other speaker was the great world humanist, Soedjatmoko, former Indonesian ambassador to the United States and now rector of the United Nations University in Tokyo. We asked him to speak about the paradoxical consequences of knowledge. He said in part:

> We are rejoicing here at a time when vast and rapid changes are taking place . . . in the various ways individuals relate to the administration of their nation, to the ever-growing transnational, regional, and global organizations and institutions that affect their lives so deeply and impersonally, while feeling

more and more in need of the sense of belonging, of the inner security and comfort that identification with smaller social units seems to be capable of giving them.

In part these problems are the result of the phenomenal growth of systematic knowledge itself and the technology it gave birth to during the past two centuries. They have re-shaped the natural conditions of peoples' lives and created a new environment which gives us great power and has opened up unparalleled new opportunities for the fulfillment of our needs, for the enrichment of our lives but also for its destruction. They have at the same time also imposed on all of us the terrible psychic burden of living with continuing and continuously accelerating change as the permanent condition of our lives in directions which seem to escape our control. In principle, mankind should now be able to fulfill all of its material wants. Still, poverty remains the seemingly permanent condition of hundreds of millions in large parts of this globe. We have developed the most sophisticated instruments for the expansion and transmission of knowledge, but the number of illiterates in the world is growing both in relative and absolute terms. We know much more about the individual and human nature through scientific inquiry, but we cannot seem to avoid having to spend a large portion of our resources for armaments, and violence has become our permanent companion in modern life.

I'll Take My Stand addressed a universal condition and not simply a Southern regional one. Three of the twelve writers who wrote the book's essays are attending this symposium: Lyle Lanier, Andrew Lytle, and Red Warren. As I reread their essays, published half a century ago, I was struck that many themes in them, and in the whole volume, run through world issues we face today. The enigmas are universal, and we in the universities are the parents and grandparents as well as the children of the baffling puzzles of human intellect and human destiny that define our world.

The issues that Soedjatmoko addressed are at heart the same with which the twelve Agrarians wrestled. I hope that these three days now beginning will be more than a commemoration, that they will in fact be a further exploration of the most important frontier lying before mankind.

On the second evening of the symposium, the Heards entertained a number of the visitors at dinner before a reception later in the evening at the residence of President and Mrs. Fields. The date was October 31, Halloween. Toward the end of dinner, the doorbell rang and there stood a group of students, the third group that night, proclaiming "trick or treat." We had sent the two earlier groups away with "treats," explaining to our guests the custom, but I invited the third group to come into the dining room to meet our visitors, who included, aside from any 1930 lions of the weekend, Cleanth Brooks and Eleanor Clark. Some of the students thought Jean and I were joking as we called the well-known names of the guests, and some of the guests were kind enough to express enthusiasm for what they declared to be unique in their university experience.

❧

"The Divinity School's Role in the Larger Vanderbilt Community" was the topic I chose when asked to speak on the Divinity School's Forum Series in Benton Chapel on December 2, 1980. I acknowledged that the topic was inescapably important for one in my position, a position in which I could reasonably be expected to know the role in the larger Vanderbilt community of all the components of Vanderbilt, not only of each of its degree-granting schools, but of all else as well, such as the bookstore, the intramural sports program, the Alumni Association, and the hospital, not to mention the intercollegiate sports program.

The role of the Divinity School has, however, distinctive significance. During my years at Vanderbilt the functioning and, in fact, the appropriateness—the legitimacy, if you will—of the Divinity School within Vanderbilt has been questioned and discussed more than that of any other academic unit, and more than that of any component of the institution except the intercollegiate spectator sports. This has been so, I think, for three main reasons:

(1) the periodic public controversies in which faculty and students of the school have been involved, mystifying or outrageous involvements—or both—to some people, including sympathetic persons of reason and good will;

(2) the history of Vanderbilt's relationship to the Methodist church, and the bitter controversy that marked the separation of the two, the feelings about which lasted, I can testify, at least until 1963; and

(3) the philosophical uncertainty over the rationale for having within an institution, conceived as dedicated to the optimum enhancement and exploitation of human reason, an intellectual activity seen to rest on nonrational processes, processes of faith or insight or instinct, viewed as uncongenial to what a university ought to be about.

I have listed these three sources of skepticism of the Divinity School—or, on occasion, hostility to it—in what I think is the descending order of importance. . . .

Many persons whose connections with Vanderbilt go back many decades—although every year their number necessarily diminishes—refer to "the School of Religion." The use of the term signifies, I think, more than out-of-date nomenclature. It harkens back to the old controversies with the Methodist church, but it also connotes a narrower concept—understanding—of the school's missions than I believe members of the school hold, or at least than I hold for the school.

There is an awareness among lay persons that much of the world's brutality—human "inhumanity" to humans—has been in the name of religion, in the name of one compelling, self-satisfying true faith after another. I have been in the Republic of South Africa three times in the last two years. I am just finishing James Michener's *The Covenant*. Much in that nation that you and I disapprove has been justified in the name of "religion" over three centuries. . . .

I then called attention to the religious basis of much conflict in the West and the East—for example, the Crusades, religious wars in Great Britain and Western Europe, and the Muslim holy wars—and the absolutist, authoritarian spine that can run through religious bias in our daily lives.

To many an outsider, many persons concerned with "religion" display in our contemporary society a degree of certainty, inflexibility, moral superiority, intolerance, and lack of self-searching that is akin to the fervor that sends women and men to war against each other in the name of God. Oh, they of too much faith! What, then, is the role of the Divinity School in the larger Vanderbilt community?

A couple of years ago I was moved to flights of oratory at a Divinity School gathering in the Blue Room of the University Club and one of our trustees present was, doubtless because of the lateness of the hour, complimentary. I searched for notes to remind me of those great remarks, and found none. But I found something else—of all things, some seven minutes on the missions of the Divinity School that I presented when Dean Forstman was installed in September of last year, 1979. Reading the remarks persuaded me that, for better or worse, I could probably do worse, but not better, if I wrote or rewrote a new piece for this morning. And inquiry revealed that memorizing the seven minutes of text has not yet been made a degree requirement in the Divinity School—although presumably it has been for some courses—nor as an expectation of faculty employment. So, I want to repeat now what I said then, on September 11, 1979 in Benton Chapel, after which I hope we can have observations from you and discussion among us all.

The missions that fall to Dean Jackson Forstman and his colleagues of the Vanderbilt Divinity School are unending.

The first *Register of Vanderbilt University,* for 1876–77, carries this language:

> The whole end proposed to be accomplished by the Divinity School is to furnish to the Church ministers learned in the Scriptures, sound in doctrine, refined but simple in manners, full of zeal, abundant in labor, direct, plain, and perspicuous in the presentation of the truth, and ready for any field to which the Church may call them.

The *Register* also said:

> Students will have the opportunity of exercising their gifts and graces in social and public worship during the entire period of their pupilage.

I think it significant—I like to think it significant—that at this very beginning of Vanderbilt, the *Register* declared "Ministers of the gospel, of any Church—who are, or purpose to be, devoted to the pastoral work—will be admitted to any school in the Academical and Biblical Departments free of tuition fees." Later language makes it clear that the statement did, in fact, mean "any" church, not just any Methodist church.

Many Constituencies, 1980–1981

The current *Bulletin* states that:

> The Divinity School seeks to fulfill two basic objectives: education of men and women for the practice of ministry; education . . . of future scholars and teachers in the field of religion. . . .
>
> The Divinity School is committed to critical, open examination of the Christian and Jewish traditions, marked by affirmation and appreciation of the abiding strengths and revelatory power of these traditions.
>
> The School is committed to discerning the import of these traditions for church and society and for the lives of individuals. Concretely, this commitment entails the education of men and women who will be effective agents of social change working for a more just and humane society, for the development of new and better styles of ministry, and for leadership in church and society that will help to alleviate the ills besetting individuals and groups.

We in our culture have lived through a century when the ambition of intellect challenged every limit. We here at Vanderbilt live in a house of intellect—a university—where we increasingly aspire to reach and explain all the universe and all life. Yet as long as we cannot comprehend a beginning or an ending, of time or of space or of life, we will seek answers outside our powers to reason. That means our clergy have a difficult job and our theologians a permanent one.

The task of the minister and the task of the theologian were more self-evident, more a part of peoples' daily being in the early millennia of the human experience, when the most that people were conscious of was what they saw, felt, smelled, heard, tasted.

More than now, humans turned to their religious interpreters seeking protection against the mystery of illness, against the unexplained death, the unpredicted storm, the uncontrolled drought, the beast, the foe; seeking help in getting food from the forest, in getting harvest from the soil, in having a healthy child, a longer life, victory in war, bounty in peace; seeking understanding that would avoid misfortune, would bring good grace, and most of all would explain the caprice of life. With the birth of the first human was born the need for comfort and courage, hope and virtue.

Tenets of faith and establishments for worship alter with changes in the human condition. The power of the Creator is manifested in many ways. The longing and search for relation to a universal spirit takes many forms. Through them all runs the striving to connect what is known to what is unknown, what is personal to what is universal, what is self-centered to what is virtuous.

The missions of this Divinity School are at home in this university. There can be a university without a divinity school and a divinity school outside a university, but our Divinity School was begun with the founding of Vanderbilt.

Its missions are University missions: to give intellectual and spiritual leadership to the ecclesiastical and educational institutions for which it trains its students, and which are audience to its scholarship. We have a golden paradox. The University itself insures that the Divinity School's tasks of reinterpretation, the search for new insights, are unending. The scholarship and science that flourish elsewhere within the University steadily refresh the Divinity School's requirement to be modern, its requirement to develop principles of faith and ethics adequate to the always changing setting of our lives.

The task is interesting in a university especially because that institution is variously dedicated to rationalism and empiricism and indeed is one in which the modes of authority are not unknown. Revelatory powers must be strong.

I then closed, saying that the Divinity School's missions are vital, strenuous, endless, and inevitable and that we anticipated with appreciation and enthusiasm the leadership Jack Forstman would bring to those missions at Vanderbilt.

❧

I was persuaded to speak to the Estate Planning Seminar for Women conducted by Vanderbilt in Branscomb Quadrangle on May 23, 1981, the day before the annual reunion. Any university believing in itself strives to help others to help it. I averred that such a seminar for *women* was appropriate.

Women constitute some 51 percent of the United States population. Of Americans age sixty-five and over, 59 percent are women. In Tennessee 60 percent of our citizens sixty-five and older are women.

Women fifty years of age normally have at least one-third of their lives remaining. . . .

Longer life for women, steadily higher educational attainment, smaller families, and increasing numbers of women in the nation's work force—all now make women concerned about matters that they once left largely to men. The orientation, preservation, and disposition of material resources are among those proper women's concerns.

I then described the changing importance of women in the University's instructional programs.

Women are now more than 46 percent of the University's total enrollment. The 3,965 women students enrolled this spring are almost as many as the University's total enrollment two decades ago. At commencement a week ago today, 1,035 women received degrees from Vanderbilt—44 percent of the graduating classes. Seven Founder's Medals were awarded to students earning first honors in their respective schools. Four went to women—in the College of Arts and Science, the Engineering School, the Nursing School, and the Divinity School.

In our Engineering School, 279 (or 26 percent) women were enrolled this spring; ten years ago there were 110 (12 percent). In the Divinity School, there were 58 women (30 percent); ten years ago there were 14 (6 percent). In the Law School, 157 (30 percent) women were enrolled; ten years ago, there were 14 (3 percent). In the Medical School, 84 (20 percent) women were enrolled this spring; ten years ago there were 13 (5 percent). In the Owen Graduate School of Management, 88 (32 percent) women were enrolled this spring; ten years ago there were eight (14 percent).

The presence of women in the councils of the University has grown. The Vanderbilt Board of Trust elected its first female member in 1964, Vanderbilt graduate and national civic leader Mary Jane Werthan. Today, seven of our trustees are women. One of them is an officer of the Board and over the years many Board committees have been chaired by women.

The year of her election as Vanderbilt's first woman trustee, Mary Jane Werthan chaired the University's first estate planning institute for women. . . .

Later I spoke of the significance of women in the history of the University from its very start.

The origins of the University can be traced to the judgment and vision of a woman, Mrs. Cornelius Vanderbilt, who was decisive in 1873 in persuading her husband to found a university in Nashville, Tennessee. Since that happy day more than 108 years ago, private generosity has been the principal moving force behind all that Vanderbilt University has achieved. Wise and generous women have done much to determine the shape and quality of our university. A tour of the campus gives testimony.

Regard the trees. Bishop McTyiere planted many of the trees that even today shade the campus. Trees are highly valued and protected at Vanderbilt. The widow of alumnus James Mapheus Smith endowed a fund in his name to label the trees on the campus they both loved. Some seven hundred trees—eighty-six different species by last count—are labeled by their scientific and popular names, thanks to the initiative of a thoughtful woman who once worked among us and is forever a friend of Vanderbilt.

Furman Hall, built in 1907 to house the Department of Chemistry, was made possible by a bequest from the widow of Nashville merchant Francis Furman. It served chemistry students for nearly sixty years. Handsomely remodeled in 1967, it now serves the humanities and foreign language departments.

Neely Auditorium was built in 1925 and for decades was the University's chapel and principal student assembly hall. The funds to build the auditorium were given by the widow of former University trustee and Treasurer George M. Neely. Remodeled to serve the dramatic arts in 1976, Neely Auditorium is among the region's most innovative theater facilities.

Calhoun Hall was built in 1928, one of two new buildings erected at that time to ensure the continued strength of the liberal arts and humanities. It is named for William Henry Calhoun, Nashville businessman who died shortly after the Civil War. Half the funds were bequeathed to Vanderbilt by his daughter, Mary Ella Calhoun Foote.

More recently, and of enormous value to Vanderbilt and the community, is Langford Auditorium. Opened in 1978 as part of the new Medical Center, Langford Auditorium serves the whole campus and honors the memory of Nashville business leader Lilburn C. Langford. Mrs. Langford provided the major portion of funds required to build the auditorium.

Women touch every aspect of the University's mission and have given many kinds of leadership and service to the University. We recognize them in special ways.

Branscomb Quadrangle, where we are now, built in 1962, honors Vanderbilt's fourth chancellor, Harvie Branscomb, and his wife, Margaret. (No one knows the vital and inadequately recognized contributions of a chancellor's wife better than a chancellor.) Branscomb Quadrangle embraces four residence halls.

Lupton House was named for Kate Lupton, who in 1879 became the first woman awarded a Vanderbilt degree. Remember the story of Kate Lupton. She was the daughter of Vanderbilt's first professor of chemistry and had actually satisfied requirements for a certificate of graduation in the Department of Latin in 1877. The Board of Trust, however, notified by Chancellor Garland of Miss Lupton's eligibility for the certificate, postponed action. Miss Lupton continued her studies nevertheless, and in 1879 presented herself for the degree, master of arts. The Board of Trust appointed a committee to study the question of conferring degrees on women and the possibility of their graduation without receiving degrees. The committee found nothing by reason of sex in the University's charter or by-Laws to inhibit conferment of degrees.

With respect to diligent Miss Lupton, the committee did find that she had "completed with distinction the entire course for graduating in ten schools [as they were then called] of Latin, Greek, Mathematics, English and Modern Language, History and English Literature, Physics and Astronomy, Chemistry, Moral Philosophy and Natural History and Zoology, being two more than are required for young men for the degree of Master of Arts." The committee then recommended that the trustees "give their consent to the Faculty to confer the degree of Master of Arts on Miss Kate Lupton." The diploma was awarded in decent privacy, some say given to her father for discreet delivery to her.

Miss Lupton studied in Europe, became a college professor and author, married a professor and reared a son. Events moved swiftly in those days. Within only eighteen years, by 1897, women were admitted to Vanderbilt on the same basis as men. I said at commencement in 1979 that all the thousands of women who have graduated from Vanderbilt since then owe Kate Lupton a nod.

Vaughn House was named for Stella Scott Vaughn who was graduated with the Vanderbilt class of 1896. She grew up on the campus, daughter of the head of the Mathematics Department, William J. Vaughn. She originated Vanderbilt's first physical education program for women and was unofficial dean of women before that position was established in 1925.

Stapleton House was named for Ada Bell Stapleton, first woman member of the Vanderbilt faculty, from 1925 to 1947, and first official dean of women, from 1925 to 1940.

Scales House was named for the 1905 Vanderbilt alumna who became Mrs. Andrew Bell Benedict. She was a leader among the University's alumnae and led the movement that gave Vanderbilt its first dean of women.

The importance of women in the University's life grows each year. So, too, do the ways in which the energy, affection and generosity of men and women alike affect all that Vanderbilt does and seeks to do.

For some of us, any commencement speech in any year is a challenge, even more for the speaker than for the audience. If a reckless fate vouchsafes the need to address more than one graduating class in the same season, the same great thoughts are likely to recur. My remarks to departing seniors at Vanderbilt on May 15, 1981, had evoked an unusual number of appreciative comments—especially from Texans—so I drew on some of them again when addressing the Hampden-Sydney

College Commencement in Hampden-Sydney, Virginia, on May 24.

As I was thinking about my own Vanderbilt commencement earlier this month, I was struck by language in a report on the attitudes of college youth made by the Carnegie Council on Policy Studies in Higher Education. It said, "There is a sense among today's undergraduates of being passengers on a sinking ship, a *Titanic* if you will, called the United States or the world." The report concluded that college students in general are fatalistic about the decline of America, but "There is a growing belief among (them) ... that, if they are doomed to ride on the *Titanic*, they should at least ride first class." I know no reason not to assume that the "they," as a group, includes you.

The striking feature of this appraisal of the outlook of recent American undergraduates is not that they want to go first class. I find that a wholesome stimulant. The important conclusion from this report is that many college students are not sure that we humans on the planet called earth have a future that we can look forward to with confidence and enthusiasm, that we will look forward to with a sense of purpose and a sense of responsibility.

The real questions are, of course: what kind of future shall we have, and how will your Hampden-Sydney education help to shape it?

Those questions constitute a charge to educated minds—to know what threatens our future, to identify the nature, size and location of those icebergs that lie in the path of our ship. Those questions also constitute a charge to informed values—to be able to choose wisely among the prices to be paid and the goals to be served in avoiding disaster and in advancing the human condition, a human condition that in the end includes the welfare of all people, among them ourselves, and our children, and their children, and *their* children. It will take massive knowledge, acute thought, discerning judgment, and resolute virtue—all those qualities are necessarily among this college's goals for you—to comprehend and cope successfully with the threats to our future.

Let me illustrate.

We hear, read, and speak much about the future of the world's energy supplies. Prospects of energy shortages and of ultimate exhaustion of some types of energy properly haunt many forecasts. But it seems likely that there is another prospective shortage even more serious to the future of life on our planet. That more serious prospect is an inadequate world supply of water. One person has hypothesized, for dramatic emphasis I dearly hope, that one day we will need to pipe water from the Mississippi River to consumers elsewhere in the nation, the way we now pipe gas and oil from Texas to other states.

Two weeks ago, newspapers showed a picture of a huge sinkhole in Winter Park, Florida, caused by the lowering of the underground water tables. At first report the sinkhole was 1000 feet wide, 170 feet deep, and growing. It had swallowed one camper, five cars, one house and was threatening more. That is one tiny symptom. Since then, reports have appeared of other sinkholes in Florida, testifying to a growing condition of much more than isolated significance.

One of America's major underground reservoirs that serves farm life on the high plains in the middle of our continent—some 156,000 square miles of underground water—is estimated to go dry within fifteen or twenty years. And this is at a time when the world requires increasingly large amounts of water to meet agricultural needs for feeding the rapidly expanding world population.

The world also requires increasingly huge amounts of water to satisfy the omnivorous demands of industries that are expanding virtually everywhere. I saw the other day that people require on the average less than one cubic meter of drinking water per person per year, but the annual industrial use of water per person in the United States is 2300 cubic meters.

Speaking of the University

There is doubt that the world's future supply of water will be sufficient to sustain us. Even in the United States, threats of "desertification" in the decades ahead are before us.

Having an adequate supply of water, vital matter that that is, is far from the only water problem we have. Water is intimately connected with the use of land, and the use of land is intimately connected with the growth and expectations of population. Uncontrolled water and improperly used water do great damage in many parts of the world through, for just three examples, erosion, unwise irrigation practices, and stream pollution. William Styron spoke here at commencement last year with deep frustration about the murder by poison of his childhood river, the James.

Invoking problems of water is my way of saying to you that more is required to make our personal future possible than competent performance of daily duty. The charge to your educated minds is to know and understand and anticipate whatever threatens our future.

All the skills and information and capacity for straight thinking that the faculty would have had you acquire here will be insufficient if there is not also a tenacious determination to look at the consequences for tomorrow of what we do today, with an unrelenting resolve to avoid the icebergs, rather than silently to assent to the inevitability of hitting them.

I also invited the attention of the graduates to the usually complex and sometimes painful choices that conservation of any resource entails. Consequences of measures are usually different for different population groups. I read a long litany of others among our country's difficulties, and emphasized that our diverse and economically unbalanced world of many cultures is truly one world in matters of resource need, use, and conservation. I cited past calamities that individual nations and world civilization had survived, and ended with what seemed to me always to be the necessary injunction:

Many Constituencies, 1980–1981

Democracy is dependent for its success on citizens of foresight, insight, self-restraint and moderation, on educated minds and informed values. And so is a successful world. . . . The whole of our being, the whole of our world, and the future as much as the present are the proper concerns of all citizens. Please address those concerns in ways that glorify yourselves and that glorify Hampden-Sydney College.

Good luck, always.

❧

The last time I spoke to incoming first-year students was on August 29, 1981—as usual in Memorial Gymnasium. After the customary welcome, invitations, and injunctions, this followed:

In the next few minutes I shall state four facts. I ask you to remember those four facts. I just might ask you at that picnic next Wednesday what the four facts are. That would be your first pop quiz at Vanderbilt and it would be a bad beginning to fail your first pop quiz when the answers are given four days in advance.

The first fact: Commencement 1985 will be here before you know it—sooner than seems humanly possible tonight, at the start of the great adventure. That is an unlikely thought on this first night, but in May 1985 you will find it to have been true.

This first fact means you need to move swiftly during the next three years and nine months. There is much to do—to learn, to enjoy, to accomplish—and for every seat you members of the class of 1985 occupy, there are sitting somewhere else tonight several other persons who would like to be where you are tonight but to their disappointment are not. You have an obligation to make the most and best of the fleeing time between now and the spring of 1985.

So that is fact number one: Commencement 1985 will be here before you know it.

Speaking of the University

Fact number two is this: You are important to others. You are very important to yourself, but you are also important, and at times more important, to your family, to your friends, to your neighbors, to your fellow citizens, to the whole of American society and beyond. This fact that all of us are important to other people says clearly that we have a responsibility to other people in what we do (and fail to do).

Where you now sit on this first Vanderbilt night others have sat before who have become important, constructive, contributing Vanderbilt women and men of the world, on whom their communities and fellow human beings have depended for sustaining and advancing important dimensions of our joint welfare. Vanderbilt students have become governors—the present Governor of Tennessee is one; Vanderbilt students have become senators—one of Tennessee's two present United States Senators is one; and Congressmen—we currently have more than one of those; Vanderbilt students have become great athletes; great singers; celebrated jurists; presidents of large banks and corporations; missionary leaders; religious leaders; civic leaders; famous physicians; prominent lawyers; inventive engineers; profound scientists; pioneering nurses; influential educators—in fact, individuals who have sat where you sit tonight throughout all Vanderbilt's history have contributed their toil, courage, merit, genius, and educated talents to improve the human condition. You are important to others, and thus have obligations to those others. . . .

Important people can have a sense of humor, a sense of proportion, modesty, and they can have a good time, too, so don't let the fact that you are important unduly weigh you down. But remember it.

At past University convocations I have frequently declared the third fact that I invite you to remember: that at Vanderbilt our first concern is the human intellect, but our main concern is the human being. That is the third fact I ask you to remember, and its main meaning is: you are here to educate your whole self.

Many Constituencies, 1980–1981

Four of Vanderbilt's schools offer undergraduate degrees—the College of Arts and Science, the School of Engineering, George Peabody College for Teachers, and the School of Nursing. The faculties of these schools strive to maintain in their curricula sufficient diversity of courses and coherence of purpose to assure students a chance to get what in the faculty's judgment is a liberal education. At the same time, the faculties strive to send forth graduates equipped with the training and professional development they need to work effectively and with reward in our high-technology, fast-changing society.

The liberal education that we have traditionally extolled in the United States, and that we cherish at Vanderbilt, seems steadily to be becoming a smaller and smaller part of the nation's total formal educational offerings. This is so significantly because our emerging post-industrial society has enormous and varied needs for specialized and sophisticated professional and technical skills. But some colleges and universities, Vanderbilt being one of them, believe that the chances for civic virtue, personal wisdom and, if you will, individual happiness, are enlarged by an education of breadth and diversity to accompany development of sharply focused intellectual capacities. That is why there are curriculum requirements—certain courses and types of courses that must be taken, and elective courses that must be taken in precisely defined academic areas.

The objective is to help a determined student attain two goals: desired and needed competencies and, simultaneously, enrichment of a wise, compassionate, whole self. Alas, the market for competence is usually more immediate than the demand for wisdom. Moreover, it is easier to produce comprehension of even complex phenomena than it is to stimulate intellectual inventiveness, undeviating integrity, integrated personalities, and universal outlook. The advocates of liberal education hold that learning new processes of mind and learning to master intricate equipment, scientific formulations, and quantitative manipulations are not enough to protect and generate values by which people can prosper safely together. A sense of the whole and loyalty to values essential to a viable world culture are also needed. So, the third fact again: Our first concern is the human intellect, but our main concern is the human being.

The *fourth* and last *fact:* College is just the beginning of mature education.

Increasingly, formal instruction is required for virtually all vocations and avocations. The cumulative consequences of five centuries of invention have assured that.

Formal education is also increasingly being sought in all age groups. Greater length of life, the changing occupational aspirations of women, especially, but also of men, and great occupational mobility assure that.

And all activities of any sophistication or difficulty will require recurring education for a person to stay productive and competitive. The rapidity of technical development assures that.

There are many ways by which knowledge is acquired, information is transferred, skills are developed, habits are disciplined, intellects are trained, insights are stimulated, curiosities are satisfied, pleasures are derived, and values are shaped. All those educational processes occur at Vanderbilt. But education will steadily become ever more dynamic technologically. Cable television, computer aids, video disks and a wide range of other innovations will alter modes of instruction more rapidly and radically than in the past. And many college graduates—including many of you, after you finish at Vanderbilt—will study, as many graduates now do, in educational programs offered by financial and business and industrial concerns, by the armed services, by civic centers, churches, art galleries, museums, publicly financed institutes, private proprietary institutions, and a wide variety of other organizations.

The vehicles for conveying educational opportunities beyond college will in the future be even more numerous and diverse than in the past. Our post-industrial society will become increasingly information-loaded, science-driven, technically sophisticated and socially complex, increasing the need to "keep current" in whatever activity one works.

Here, then, are the four facts I invite you to remember: *first*, commencement 1985 will be here before you know it; *second*, you are important, often more important to others than to yourself; *third*, at Vanderbilt our first concern is the human intellect, but our main concern is the human being; and *fourth*, college is just the beginning of mature education.

We are glad you are here. Good luck always.

❧

The meeting of the Vanderbilt Faculty Assembly on September 3, 1981, was the twenty-first since the Faculty Senate was reconstituted in 1967. The assembly convened in Langford Auditorium on Garland Avenue, the first session held outside of Underwood Auditorium. As earlier selections from assembly meetings have indicated, reports on much standard business were routinely made, including a report on completion of the new stadium. (It was really new, despite taking as much advantage as possible of the underpinnings of the old one. Of the new structure I said, "At least one person has expressed the hope that the new chancellor will be as much an improvement in looks and function as the new stadium.") Toward the end I spoke as follows:

President Fields kindly suggested that he yield the time at this year's meeting of the Faculty Assembly that in the past four years has been accorded him to speak. I am grateful to him and shall use the occasion to give you my view—or, you will be grateful to hear, part of my view—of where we stand, now, at the conclusion of Vanderbilt's Centennial Campaign, and of what lies ahead.

The general state of Vanderbilt's welfare in 1981 must be judged good . . . but by policy, taste, and international standard, none of us at Vanderbilt should ever believe our state to be good enough, and surely I do not. This is my attitude toward all reaches of the University's life and work and it will be reflected in my report to you on the Centennial Campaign. . . .

We are far from realizing our full ambitions to increase, more than we already have, the presence of minority students, faculty and administrative officers on the campus. We are far from realizing our full ambitions to increase, more than we already have, the presence of women students in our schools where their enrollment is not already satisfactory, and the presence of women faculty and administrative officers in those parts of the University where their representation is not already satisfactory. Viewed from the perspective of the past, substantial changes have occurred; viewed through the eyes of aspiration, not enough changes have occurred. We have, however, policies, procedures and people of good faith and good will at work. All institutions in our society, educational and otherwise, confront similar conditions. As the basic educational and training patterns of the society continue to evolve, the presence of minorities and women in sectors of activity where they are now, as we say, under-represented, will inexorably increase, and Vanderbilt and our country will benefit.

What I want to say about the Centennial Campaign has eight themes running through it.

First, in its totality, the campaign was an enormous success, raising $181,400,000—with more yet to come as a result of the campaign—against the original goal of $150 million.

Second, many specific goals of the campaign, set in advance by the schools and officers of the University, were achieved.

Third, some of the objectives of the campaign, set in advance by the schools and officers of the University, were not reached.

Fourth, a very large portion of the campaign's proceeds is in the form of deferred gifts, which is one reason—for those who wonder—why the University's budget officers have been this year just as searching and, one might say skinny, as ever in examining proposals for expenditure.

Fifth, the aggregate of identified and articulated financial needs of the several schools and other educational components of the University—as set forth in the series of printed "case statements"—far exceeded both our original campaign objective of $150 million and the sum actually raised of over $181 million, meaning that the campaign's success did not reap a surplus of unspoken-for millions of dollars that are up for grabs.

Sixth, the increased level of giving to Vanderbilt that was achieved among alumni, supporters who are not alumni, parents of students, corporations, foundations and other contributors constitutes the platform on which rests Vanderbilt's private fund raising for the future.

Seventh, already in place and in action is the new, revised Vanderbilt fund-raising program for the years next ahead—with modified structure, revised staffing, adequate funding and a clear sense of mission. The campaign is over; the campaign has begun.

And eighth, ultimately Vanderbilt's financial strength, as well as its educational quality, depends on the strength and excellence of the faculties of the University in whose judgment and merit, always and inescapably, are rooted the University's missions and its ability to accomplish them.

Vanderbilt has always depended on private philanthropy. It was founded with a gift of $1 million from Cornelius Vanderbilt and the philanthropic energies of Methodist churchmen and laymen. Members of every succeeding generation of the Vanderbilt family have contributed to the University, some with extraordinary generosity. Since the separation of Vanderbilt from the Methodist church in 1914, the University has conducted a series of fund-raising drives, each in its context major and important.

Since 1938 the annual Living Endowment appeal has brought

significant resources to Vanderbilt and during the past two decades three major campaigns have been successfully completed: one for $30 million, built around a matching grant of $4 million from the Ford Foundation, in 1960–62; one for $55 million, built around an $11 million matching grant from the Ford Foundation accompanied by an $11 million matching grant from Harold S. Vanderbilt, in 1966–70; and the campaign recently completed, grounded in no foundation incentive but stimulated before the formal launching of the campaign in the fall of 1977 with advance commitments from Vanderbilt trustees and others exceeding $51 million.

On each of these occasions the goal has been set with a weather eye to the University's ability to meet the goal as well as with deep realization of the University's needs. That the Centennial Campaign exceeded its goal by more than 20 percent does not reflect, simply, a poor judgment of our capacity. Rather, and more important, it is authentic evidence that the professional staffing and conduct of the campaign, led by Vanderbilt's Executive Director of Development David R. Jones, joined by an extraordinary volunteer corps, succeeded more than, in my observation, Vanderbilt has ever succeeded before in discovering new donors and new incentives for enlisting their support of the University.

The strategy, tactics and trench warfare of the solicitation campaign were brilliantly led by Centennial Campaign Chairman David K. Wilson, who is now chairman of the Board of Trust. David Jones is not here, and I am going to ask Mr. Wilson to stand on behalf of himself and also on behalf of the large cadre of our able and devoted Vanderbilt development staff colleagues without whose talented labors the campaign could not have succeeded.

We were all aided mightily by Trustee Sam M. Fleming, who, during all but the last two months of the campaign, served as chairman of the Board of Trust. Although Mr. Fleming is not with us today, I will say that in Mr. Wilson's and my view Mr. Fleming has directly and indirectly raised more money for Vanderbilt over the years than anyone else in the University's history.

I then pointed in some detail to several additional consequences of the campaign, more sophisticated "concepts and capacities for program and financial planning" being among them. I gave a lengthy, detailed report of the salubrious effects of the campaign on space available to the several schools, as well as other comments on the extent and form of the campaign's benefits. The broad results were as follows:

Total cash received by June 30, 1981, came to slightly over $70 million, about two-fifths of the total raised. Total deferred gifts committed by that date totaled slightly over $111 million, about three-fifths of the total raised.

Of the cash received, $19 million was given for endowment and $52 million for current operations, some of the latter resulting from normal, on-going faculty fund-raising activities to support their own work.

Of that cash received—totaling slightly over $70 million—some $51 million was given for restricted purposes and some $19 million for unrestricted use by the University.

Three categories of deferred gifts account for the $111 million coming to the University after July 1, 1981.

Planned bequests—that is one category—totaled $63 million.

Trusts—that is another—totaled $18 million.

Outright pledges, normally payable within five years or less— that is a third—totaled $31 million.

Those add to $111 million.

A major objective of the campaign, explicit from the outset, was to build the future financial strength of Vanderbilt. We would, of course, have been happy to receive the full $181 million in cash on the barrel head, but the fact that the $111 million, or three-fifths of the total, will flow to the University in the years ahead—in addition to other monies Vanderbilt raises pursuant to its future solicitations—is a strong, heartening element in our future.

There were about two thousand more words about financial resources, followed by:

What are Vanderbilt's most important resources? We of the University know that you are—not chancellors nor presidents nor development officers, not even trustees and generous friends, not even students, but the faculties of the University. Vanderbilt has been built by insight, imagination, courage, energy, talent, love, loyalty, and leadership of the faculties who have served it across eleven decades. They have taught the students, they have performed the research, they have rendered the public service. You are the essential central being of the University.

Vanderbilt is a university of the future and you are the University's life of the future. Nineteen eighty-one is not to be remembered as the year the Vanderbilt Centennial Campaign achieved a glorious success. The academic year that now begins must be remembered as the year we moved forward with magnified resources, invigorated ambition, unrelenting energies, and unbending resolve to make Vanderbilt the best university that can possibly be.

Thank you, now and forever more.

❧

During 1980 and 1981, in many of the occasions when I was asked to speak I had a particular personal interest, including the dedication of the new Vanderbilt stadium on September 12, 1981; an Appreciation Dinner in the University Club on October 29, to thank the many persons responsible for the success of the recently ended fund drive; and the Homecoming Lun-

cheon two days later at which I had the pleasure of awarding
the Chancellor's Cup for the nineteenth—it would be my
last—time. I was happy that the winner was a member of the
Peabody faculty, recently joined to Vanderbilt: Paul S. Redel-
heim, assistant professor of special education.

A ceremony formally inducting Eamon Kelly as president of
Tulane University was held in New Orleans on October 10, 1981.
I had known his three immediate predecessors, among them
Vanderbilt alumnus Sheldon Hackney, and had known Mr.
Kelly as a member of the staff of the Ford Foundation. I was
happy to be asked to speak on the occasion, and did so, in part,
as follows:

If the most important obligation of a university is to look ahead,
three questions arise: How does it do so? What can it do about what
it sees? What can its president do? . . .

An American university has a special obligation to do this. We
here in New Orleans today, but also all in America, live in well-
insulated isolation from many dangerous, offensive, profound realities. We read, hear, and speak about much that is real, much of deep
and painful significance, but our comprehension and responses are
restricted by the inordinate difficulty of feeling the actualities of our
existence. It's the difference between reading crime statistics and being mugged.

By comparative standards—what other standards are there?—
we in the United States lead comfortable, secure, well-protected,
materially well-rewarded lives of authentic meaning to ourselves. By
a roll of cosmic dice, we are the world's chosen people. Measured
by material welfare, Americans, including those in our urban ghettos and rural slums, are a privileged minority among the world's
masses. We here today are a further tiny minority of the world's
privileged. But most of us accept our good fortune as a matter of
course and then go on to other worries. We do not . . . look on our

good fortune as an unearned miracle [which it is]. But unearned miracles breed complacency.

Soedjatmoko, the rector of the United Nations University and former Indonesian ambassador to the United States, said last July at Rockefeller University: "The whole globe has become a very small island."

Our very small island is an island of multiplying population densities, of revolutionary technologies of communication and transport, of complex interactions of conflicting cultures, of growing destructiveness of the means of violence, and of increases in the numbers to whom the means of violence are available. Our small island is an island of physical wasting by consumption and erosion—wasting of the very planet itself, an island beset by other forces that have combined, in Soedjatmoko's words,

> to make the only [remaining] frontiers available those of communication and communion with our fellow human beings.
>
> Unless we learn to love our fellow human being—whatever his culture, color, ideology, relative strength or social status—we may all very well perish.

That does not sound much like the Garden District of New Orleans or the Belle Meade section of Nashville, but it is a glimpse of reality that makes me feel that we are living our blessed, lucky lives in cocoons of anesthesia.

At a symposium at Syracuse University last January, Andre van Dam, of Argentina, speaking from "A Third World Viewpoint," made the overarching statement that the developed nations, and particularly the United States, cannot expect the future to be fashioned as was the past, that is, only in light of their own needs and opportunities. The existing distribution of the world's energy sources, raw materials, capital surpluses, labor supplies, potential markets, and national aspirations make that expectation a thing truly of the past.

The recent president of the World Bank, Robert McNamara, declared in assessing two decades of development:

> Between the two populations of the planet, that of the developed part and that of the undeveloped part, there is a seismic rift so deep that it can produce terrible splits causing everything to explode.

These comments address the disparity in material circumstances and sense of satisfaction between the world's developed and less well developed nations, between what for shorthand have come to be called the "North" and the "South." Kurt Waldheim, secretary general of the United Nations, warned at a recent session of the U.N.'s Economic and Social Council: "Mind the Third World's despair, world chaos can come out of it." Realistic and wise people know there is no way that we of the North can ignore them of the South except to our infinite peril. For starters, think of all that oil, all those minerals, all those markets and all those people that they have.

These global dislocations are glimpses of reality and they are accompanied by other realities that we will ignore at mortal risk. Trends within the United States should challenge our traditional self-confidence. In 1972 the United States had the highest standard of living in the world. I read that we now rank ninth. The fall in economic growth and American productivity has now continued long enough for it to be recognized as a new continuing condition, not a temporary aberration. Somewhere I saw that this year for the first time the Japanese will make more motor vehicles than Americans will. We are much aware of our inflation, unemployment, unbalanced federal budget, impaired ladders of upward mobility for important sectors of the population, and other inequities in American society.

Speaking of the University

I offer these lugubrious observations to suggest the demanding responsibility that universities, as the central thinking organs of our society, have to know the future, to know where we are going and to help steer the best course. University research, invention, training and teaching are the principal sources of the dynamism that propels our civilization into the future.

There is an interesting article in the last issue of *Fortune* magazine on "The Next Industrial Revolution." It discusses computer-aided design and computer-aided manufacturing—CAD/CAM. The article says that CAD/CAM,

> if wisely and widely applied, . . . could overcome the productivity stagnation that has led to questions about the ability of American industry to remain competitive on the world scene. . . . Says a leading CAD/CAM specialist: "Revolution is an overused word, but that's what's going to happen here."

CAD/CAM advocates say it "has more potential to increase productivity than any other development since electricity."

A Frenchman named Jean Jacques Servan-Schreiber argues that there is extraordinary potential for increasing human productivity by applying revolutionary developments in computers and transistors and in the "microprocessor—a wonderful device from which the three basic elements of all wealth converge: information, matter, energy." In other words, what a layman might call computer power can be brought to bear on the deprivations and aspirations of all the world.

Christopher Evans, an Englishman, writes about computer power, saying,

> Most important of all . . . will be its application to education. . . . Of all the barriers that divide the world . . . the biggest and most intractable is ignorance. Education and knowledge have enriched men's lives from the beginning of time and

affluence has only sprung up where ignorance has been conquered. The cycle is self-perpetuating, for the more affluent the society, the better it educates its members, and so, in turn, its affluence increases.

Servan-Schreiber argues that computerization is to an exhausted industrial society what the latter was to agricultural society—a fundamental transformation, not only in methods, production and consumption, but in ways of living. . . .

In addition to developments in microelectronics, one hears that there are on the horizon developments in biotechnology freighted with many potent consequences, including the promise of a second "green revolution."

These things are viewed by some with optimism as enabling humankind to address successfully its pervasive shortages of water, food, and energy and to solve the accompanying problems of education, transportation, and resource management.

Yet the realist knows that the world's diversities and complexities are too great for a hope as simple as that. There is probably equal chance that disparities among nations, and within them, will be exacerbated by the new technologies originating from the already developed industrial nations. There is a prediction that average per capita income in sub-Sahara Africa—an area of 150 million people, already abjectly poor—will decline over the next ten years, while average per capita income goes up in some other, richer, parts of the world. The average American consumes twenty-five times more commercial energy than the average inhabitant of India, yet the latter consumes forty times more than his neighbor in Nepal. Microelectronics and biotechnology and other wonders will need to develop and spread quickly to satisfy the multiplying expectations of the world's populations for material equity.

The specter of a post-democratic world appears in which issues of survival take precedence over the values we cherish and have contested over for centuries, such as social justice, civil liberties, and national independence.

These fragmentary references to the realities of our future make a hard course for university people, if the obligation is inherently theirs to bring the resources of the human intellect to bear effectively on the difficulties, hopes, and opportunities of humankind. Sir Winston Churchill once wrote that as an old politician he had long experience in making decisions about matters he did not fully understand. All citizens, including citizens of universities, are required all the time to make decisions about matters they do not fully understand. But the decisions will be made one way or another, and our obligation is to increase the understanding of the matters about which they are made.

What can the president of a leading American university of world outreach, such as Tulane is, do? He will recognize the starting point, which is that a university is more a family than a hierarchy, and that keeping the house in order, and bringing in the students, the faculty, the friends and the money, is a collaborative enterprise.

It is so much a collaborative enterprise, and there is so much important housekeeping to be done, that one in President Kelly's position, or mine, often asks himself what can a university leader really do to lead—to see the future, to address the future, to improve the future?

Surely two things we can do: Know that the real work of the university is done by others, and that therefore in their motivation lies more than anywhere else the university's future; and second, know that no university duty is more precious than lifting the eyes of all whom the university touches to the distant horizons of peril, hope, opportunity, and greater happiness for all humankind.

Mr. President, your colleagues in higher education congratulate you and wish you every blessing and good fortune in the adventures ahead.

Many Constituencies, 1980–1981

During my last full year as chancellor, the Board of Directors of the Alumni Association asked me to address it with reflections about Jean's and my years at Vanderbilt. Give us, they said, a "review of twenty years in twenty minutes—disappointments, successes, what you would have done differently." I protested the impossibility of doing anything other than summoning a potpourri of incomplete recollections and reflections whose only authenticity would spring from their spontaneity. Nonetheless, I barged forward, on October 30, 1981, in Room 118 of the Sarratt Student Center, saying in part:

> It is important to recognize that in a university, especially a developed university of quality, the institutional development of the university and the personal leadership of the chief executive are not coincidental processes. A university is a highly decentralized institution in the dispersion and location of authority, and consequently the leadership of the chief executive officer is limited, or absent, in such matters as curriculum, course content, degrees earned, appointment of faculty, and admission of students. A university's sources of funding provide many diverse sources of control and independence. And there are many diverse constituencies, each of which has or may have influence, independence, and sanctions. These include faculty, students, alumni, trustees, staff employees, the United States government, foundations, and others.
>
> A university also has much more stability in continuity and momentum and inertia than any other type of major institution, with the probable exception of the church. Even a giant's crowbar sometimes bends instead of lifting. Yet there are intersections when leadership, or lack of it, vision, or lack of it, energy, or lack of it, influence, or lack of it, skill, or lack of it, good taste, or lack of it, sound

instinct, or lack of it, experience, or lack of it, good judgment, or lack of it, rigid integrity, or lack of it, sound educational values, or lack of them, do become decisive—not often, but often enough to impose heavy responsibility, and welcome opportunities.

So, a university chief executive, though understandably ever conscious of the limits on his initiative and his authority, cannot truly say, "I could never make a difference." The only worse error she or he could make would be to believe that the chief executive could ever make all the difference. The sources of university merit are multiple. And they are rooted in time—time that runs back long before any current individual began his part.

How is Vanderbilt stronger now than twenty years ago? It is a more nearly complete university, fitted for our times not only through the addition of the Owen School, and Peabody, and Blair, but through significant strengthening changes within the other schools as well—at a time when many universities are cutting back. Vanderbilt has a broader financial base than formerly and relative to its missions is probably stronger, especially in the present financial climate. Its intellectual freedom is accepted. That was confirmed in the time of troubles through which we went with virtually no damage to the fabric of the institution. That was not so in many other places. Respect for political, religious, and intellectual freedom is established. There is present a climate and practice of actual diversity.

Vanderbilt is now a more nearly national and international institution, as reflected in its enrollment, its alumni, and its visibility and recognition.

The physical plant is substantive itself, but it is also symbolic of educational and extracurricular programs. There have been many additions: among them, completion of the Stevenson Center, construction of the Student Health Service, multiple additions to the old Medical Center, a new hospital, Light Hall, Langford Auditorium, the remodeled Neely Auditorium, additional parking lots and garages, the McGugin Center, the new track, additional playing fields, a new stadium, the gym balconies, many fraternity and sorority houses completed under a program already underway, the remodeling of Furman Hall, reconstruction of the old chapel area of Kirkland Hall, four Carmichael towers, Mayfield Place, Chaffin Place, indoor tennis courts, the University Club, Olin Hall of Engineering, Sarratt Student Center, the Bryan Building, the Flowers addition to the library, the underground addition to Godchaux Hall, the whole Peabody campus, the new Owen School building, the Law School addition, and many acres acquired since 1963 through the property acquisition program that was begun in 1956.

The important matters are what goes on inside the physical plant. The quality of undergraduate extracurricular life has become more active, diverse, and healthy as represented by student initiatives and organizations, such as Orientation, Impact, Parents Weekend, undergraduate department associations.

The quality of teaching, research, and service is hard to measure and demonstrate, but one can point to new or changed administrative or educational structures—Vanderbilt now has overseas programs in Leeds, Madrid, and Regensburg, to supplement the program established earlier in Aix-en-Provence.

Here I alluded to a number of new programs of recent years, in the Department of Molecular Biology, the Institute for Public Policy Studies, the European Studies program funded by an Exxon grant, the Environmental and Water Resources Engineering program, many in the Medical Center, and many within individual departments in all the schools.

It can be said that we have a tradition of high quality undergraduate instruction that has been maintained or enhanced and that the quantity and maybe the quality of research have gone up, but be it acknowledged that so have [almost] everybody else's. The relative standing of Vanderbilt in a community of high quality universities, most of whom also have been getting better, is hard to change. But the trends are with us: The academic strength of a university depends more in the long run on its financial strength than on any other single factor.... and Vanderbilt has healthy constituencies among those who prosper.

What would I have done differently? One is tempted to say everything (or nothing). No one is more conscious of the sins of commission and omission at Vanderbilt these last two decades, I can assure you, than this chancellor. And, also, no one knows better than this guilty party how and why they were committed, and their reasonableness at the time of action or inaction, and the lack of a desirable alternative. It is more fruitful to look ahead—to ask what among the many tasks and challenges and frontiers ahead come first to mind. There are seven general, generic ones.

First, always, increased distinction of faculty. That requires money, present or promised quality, and more general institutional appeal—an appeal often dependent on nuances, gestalt, style, subtleties.

Second, always, a better qualified and more diversified student body. We need increased qualified minority enrollment and continued strengthening of enrollment of women. And we need greater geographic spread among our students. These goals also require money, promise, and appeal.

Third, larger participation of minorities and women in all reaches of the institution where they aspire to have more participation.

Fourth, accommodations to changing national, Tennessee, and Nashville government policies, the ones that are largely financial in impact—and a better community understanding of the nature of universities and of Vanderbilt.

Fifth, financial resources always.

Sixth, enhancement of the unity of community—including alumni. Cohesion, mutual confidence and understanding.

Seventh, and most important, the improvement of Vanderbilt University in the discharge of its missions—teaching, research, service—and in its performance as a citizen of the city, the state, and the nation. This seventh is dependent on the previous six. . . .

My view is like that of Mr. Branscomb's when he left office in 1963. Harvie said, "I am now going to watch how easily my successor does all those things that I have been trying to do for years and could never get done." That was a charitable view, and I plan to emulate Mr. Branscomb's generosity and perspective.

ELEVEN

Leaving
1982

THE FIRST SIX MONTHS OF 1982 were my last in office. The Alumni Office kindly arranged farewell meetings with Vanderbilt clubs in nine cities: Memphis, Chattanooga, Houston, Dallas, Atlanta, Chicago, Louisville, Birmingham, and Washington. Jean accompanied me when possible. The faithful turned out and we were grateful. During the spring I also spoke on something over twenty other occasions, the remarks for four of which are included here.

Sam M. Fleming had been a Vanderbilt trustee for thirty years when I retired as chancellor in 1982. The year before, he had completed six years as president of the Board of Trust. (The title chairman was used during four of his years.) The president and past presidents of the Vanderbilt Alumni Association gave a dinner in his honor at the Belle Meade Country Club in Nashville on March 2, 1982. Members of the Fleming family were among those present. I spoke toward the end of abundant tributes.

Sam Fleming of Vanderbilt: alumnus of fifty-four years; trustee of thirty years; chairman of the Board of Trust for six years.

You know from knowing Sam, and from what you have been

reminded of tonight, that Sam Fleming has had a demanding career in banking and business, spiced with energetic civic activities, active social entertainments, vigorous times on the golf links, excursions into reading and writing history, and travel to foreign lands. But, with all that and more, over the decades he has without lapse held at the center of his energetic attention the interests of Vanderbilt University.

It is easy to be misled. Across the years, Sam Fleming has directly and indirectly raised more money for Vanderbilt than anyone else in the University's history. Yet that extraordinary feat is not the source of his greatest service to Vanderbilt, nor of our greatest indebtedness to him. But let me emphasize that he is the most effective money-raiser in Vanderbilt's history since Commodore Vanderbilt's founding gifts in 1873.

In 1960–62, he was vice-chairman and the crucially important leader of the $30 million Campaign for Vanderbilt. He was national chairman of Vanderbilt's over-subscribed $55 million campaign between 1966 and 1970. He was the closest collaborator of the chairman of the $150 million Centennial Campaign that ended last June 30 with a total raised of $181.4 million. He has been significant in enlisting support of members of the Vanderbilt family, and in all the years I have been Chancellor, and no doubt before, he has been central in choosing goals, in designing strategies, and in soliciting donations. His effectiveness has been partly a consequence of his extraordinarily wide range of friendships in many sectors of society—in Nashville, throughout the region, and over the United States—and partly a consequence of his powers of persuasion, of his unflagging energy, and of his own personal generosity, consistent and substantial.

Sam Fleming is the best trustee of a private university in the United States—as you will see: keep reading your mail—but not because he gives and raises money.

Of all his many contributions to Vanderbilt, the most important has been his far-sighted, fertile vision. He has preferred—over standards of region or habit or convenience—world standards, convinced that Vanderbilt deserves the best, can achieve the best, and that the first duty of its people is always to strive for the best.

He has brought robust imagination to enlargement of the University's academic and public service missions. The creation of the Owen Graduate School of Management and the merger of George Peabody College for Teachers into Vanderbilt were in significant measure dependent on his vision, insight, skill and spirit. He was chairman of the Board of Trust during the years the Blair School of Music grew closer to Vanderbilt, and he championed the merger of the two.

At least in my time, Mr. Fleming was the first trustee to point to the educational, clinical, and financial importance of building a new hospital. He was the most persistent trustee, although always tactfully persistent, in expressing the need for a new hospital. He sensed the need and played a critically significant role in achieving other improvements—in academic buildings, in student housing, in auxiliary facilities, in athletic facilities, including all the gymnasium balconies and the new stadium.

Mr. Fleming has understood, instinctively, the effective roles for trustees to play. Through authentic generosity in friendship, he has helped mightily to strengthen the unity of the Vanderbilt community.

As a trustee, Sam has served on an abundance of standing and ad hoc committees, being at one time or another chairman of several, including the three most important, the Executive Committee, the Budget Committee, and the Investment Committee, and president (or chairman) of the Board itself from 1975 until 1981.

In the Board's deliberations, he has brought his extensive business and banking experience to the University's service without inappropriate intervention in the University's internal administration. Some of you may know that Sam is a person of strong impulses. Yet he has never wavered in his receptivity to a better understanding of the special characteristics of university higher education. He has been perceptive and patient in addressing the expectations and assumptions of faculty and student constituencies, not always familiar at the outset to lay trustees, and by example and explanation he has helped other trustees to be patient and understanding, too.

Sam Fleming has understood that the academic merit of the University requires more than formal instruction and physical facilities. He has stood firm when attacks from outside Vanderbilt, and sometimes from within, have been made on its policies of educational freedom. He has helped strengthen the University significantly by his sober steadiness in the face of criticism, sometimes even criticism of himself. He has understood the necessary allocations of authority within a front-rank university, and has respected with good cheer the autonomy accorded to faculty and students and, most understandingly and compassionately, to the Chancellor.

No one could possibly be more grateful to Sam Fleming tonight than the Chancellor of Vanderbilt University.

On April 18, 1982, the Association of Governing Boards of Universities and Colleges, meeting in Denver, Colorado, gave its annual award for Distinguished Service in Trusteeship of independent institutions to Sam Fleming. The committee making that nationally significant selection comprised the president of New York University, the president of the Exxon Education Foundation, the chairman of the board of the Equitable Life Assurance Society of the United States, the chairman of the Board of Trustees of Howard University, and the president of the New York Times Company Foundation, who was also that newspaper's principal writer on higher education.

On November 6, 1987, Fleming Yard, beside Rand Hall on the campus, was named in honor of Sam Fleming. I expressed many of the same sentiments I had felt five years before and concluded:

Sam Fleming was always available. I consulted him freely. I indulge the notion that we were a team. Time after time, in issues simple and complex, familiar and unfamiliar, he listened, probed, speculated, suggested, offered, and in the end would conclude by saying, "Well, all right, do what you think is best for the University"—and that would be better than it would have been without him.

❧

In my first two years at Vanderbilt I spoke to the Vanderbilt Aid, on March 27, 1963, at the home of the Vernon Sharps, and on April 21, 1964, at the home of the William Earthmans. The third time came on April 8, 1982, at the home of Dudley Morgan, a Vanderbilt trustee. Alice Mathews presided, and took proper note that this was the first meeting of the newly combined Peabody and Vanderbilt Aids. Mrs. Morgan made the introduction. I called the remarks "Before and After." Reconstructed from notes, they went as follows:

In 1963 the Vanderbilt Aid was in its seventieth year. Now it is in its eighty-ninth. It is now strengthened by the merger on January 15, 1981, with the Peabody Aid—itself with a long and important history—to become a single organization.

Since its beginning, the Vanderbilt Aid has made loans to over 5,500 students. Prior to 1980–81, the last academic year, the amount lent annually was $20,000 to $30,000. And the amount of new money added to the loan fund was around $5,000 each year. Last year, $9,300 was added, and because of changes in the availability of other sources of student financial assistance, in 1980–81 $132,000 was put out in 105 loans.

Leaving, 1982

Many students who later became significant citizens have been helped by the Vanderbilt and Peabody Aids, including: famous newspaper columnists, a large number of physicians, several star athletes, including at least one All-American, several bishops, numerous ministers, several judges, many lawyers, many officers of financial, industrial, and banking firms, a goodly number of faculty members at Vanderbilt and elsewhere, a number of Vanderbilt trustees, and here and there among others a dean and the wife of a United States senator.

What you do is important, Vanderbilt is grateful for it, and I urge you to do more of it.

I am also grateful for the very kind and charitable introduction I have been given by Dudley Morgan. Last night much tribute was paid to Jean Heard by the Friends of the Library in an evening of music at the Blair School of Music. It was a much deserved recognition in her husband's detached opinion. From such generous expressions, there is a danger that one could be misled—even persons close to Vanderbilt like yourselves—as to the full nature of the chancellorship and what a chancellor and the chancellor's spouse actually do. In fact, what a chancellor and spouse are most likely to remember, first, about the time in office is—let's call it the human side of being chancellor.

The greatest source of wonder is the telephone. It rings, and what the rings bring is often amazing. There was the call one evening from the Kentucky mother about her son. The son had run out of gas on the edge of town as he was leaving for Birmingham during spring break. He had no way of getting his car or himself to a filling station and, as our caller assured us we must know, the gas shortage then afflicting the nation made it almost impossible to get gas anyway. Moreover, her son's Vanderbilt dormitory had been closed for the holiday and unless he went to Birmingham he would have no place to sleep. Jean Heard called faithful Vanderbilt alumnus Jimmy Armistead. His filling station and truck came to the rescue.

357

Speaking of the University

I had an irate call one night from a furious lad complaining about the ants that infested his dormitory room, 218 Barnard Hall. He had moved out for several nights, was told the exterminators had done their work, had carried his belongings back in the dark of night, and found the ants still there. What did the Chancellor plan to do about it? I called Dean K.C. Potter and reported the distress of one of his students. K. C.'s reply: "The boy's right. There have always been ants in that room."

One night I had a call from a member of the Fine Arts faculty about a person said to be improperly held in jail. I inquired whether the poor fellow was an undergraduate or a graduate student. He was not a student at all, the faculty member said, just an acquaintance of his.

One night about eleven o'clock the phone rang, rousing me from a comfortable bed.

"Is Alex there?"

"This is he."

"This is Roger."

"Roger? Roger who?"

"Roger May. You called me."

So I gave my full name and explained to our football star that a prankster had obviously been at work. I assured good Roger that I was glad to hear from him anyway. It was a standing reminiscence between us.

I remember with some clarity a telephone call at 1:25 A.M. on Friday, February 5, of this year. "What time does the gym open tomorrow?" was the question.

Think you not, however, that the telephone is the only means for invading privacy. One morning I was having a meeting with some Vanderbilt associates in a sun room of the University house where we live. There were consequently a number of automobiles parked in front. Good Jean Heard had been away and when she returned and entered the front hall she observed some ladies examining the

Canton china in a breakfront, and otherwise inspecting the place. She introduced herself in what the visitors must have thought was an excessively proprietary way. They responded that they were pleased to meet her and continued their surveillance. Eventually one asked, "This is the Belle Meade Mansion, is it not?"

One day we noticed a family picnicking by the stream that runs through the yard. They had come on a bus, climbed the wall separating the property from Harding Road, and were having a picnic. A child in the group had cut his foot and a parent came up to the house seeking medical help.

A contrasting episode occurred when a very nice man from Alabama drove up to the front of the house, said he had seen the healthy stand of bamboo growing on the property down by the stream, and asked whether there would be objection if he cut the bamboo and took it away.

Once the front doorbell rang and I answered it. There stood a thin, worried young woman about thirty years old. Behind her in the driveway was an automobile with her family, including her husband. She explained that they were in dire family and financial straits and were having to move from Michigan to Alabama. She hoped help could be found in Alabama. They had no money with which to buy gasoline. I gave the poor lady what I thought would be a useful sum of money.

I had the ambition that while in office we would so conduct ourselves that we would never be sued, and certainly not sued successfully. I learned a lesson, however, on October 4, 1963, the day I was installed as chancellor. One of our personal guests from Alabama, an elderly lady who was the mother of a friend, tripped on burlap webbing that covered an area to which she was driven by a University driver. She broke her hip. There was a fairly clear intimation that if the University had been running its affairs properly she would not have tripped. The Vanderbilt Medical Center came to an admirable rescue.

Speaking of the University

What I remember most, and most distinctively, are the marvelous times with students. Over the years Jean and I have entertained large numbers in the chancellor's house. We have had the great pleasure to have eaten many meals and attended many social events in the rooms of students. Recently, this year, six splendid young men invited us to dinner in a suite in one of the Carmichael Towers. Ten splendid young women invited us to an entertainment in a Chaffin Place suite. On February 11 we were invited to a great "Crush Party" at the Tri-Delt House, to which I understood it was appropriate to wear a red vest. On March 16 we had dinner in a Carmichael suite with six students who were mountain climbers. They had climbed Mount McKinley and Mount Rainier, among others.

I reported to the ladies that for the previous five years or so a tradition of Halloween visits had begun and that during the 1981 Christmas season a group of students came voluntarily to sing Christmas carols at the house, and that

two years ago I was invited by a group of students to have lunch. Four males and four coeds had organized a lunch on the roof of Kirkland Hall, appropriately elaborate and umbrellas at the ready against the drizzle that threatened.

I told also at some length about the Wild Bunch, a vigorous and attractive group of undergraduates in the class of 1977, of its origin and of their kidnapping me in the spring of their senior year. And I also reported the annual softball game that was held for eight years between the "Administration All Stars" and the ZBT fraternity.

These accounts were followed by reflections on the more conventional educational developments of the previous nineteen years (akin to comments made on other occasions in my last year before retirement): doubling of the student body, tripling of the faculty, increase in the budget by ten times, addition of three dozen new or radically expanded buildings on the old Vanderbilt campus, the addition of Owen, Peabody, and Blair schools, improvements in the quality and vitality of the educational programs ("the fact that cheers me most"), the confirmation of educational freedom ("in all its ramifications"), the strengthening of the University's financial base, and the quality of all categories of Vanderbilt's people, closing with reminders of future Vanderbilt responsibilities and renewed gratitude to its many supporters, especially the Vanderbilt Aid.

❧

On April 17, 1982, I spoke at a dinner in Branscomb Quadrangle during the first Black Alumni Reunion Weekend held on the campus. I was introduced by Bill Campbell. He had been an exuberant Vanderbilt undergraduate, had graduated from the Duke Law School, and in 1993, with the 1996 Olympics looming, was elected mayor of Atlanta, that largest Southern city east of Texas. I thanked him and also indefatigably loyal Walter Murray, who was serving as the reunion chairman, and Bill Meadows, director of Alumni Relations, and the officers and directors of the Alumni Association, who had initiated in 1979 a Committee on Minority Relations and in 1980 had adopted the committee's proposals.

I am grateful, most of all, to you who have come back, for we have much work to do together, work that will not be done, that cannot be done, unless we undertake it together. It is important work, important to each of us here, important to our university, important to Vanderbilt's missions and to the thousands of people Vanderbilt serves, and to the thousands more it must, can and will serve in the decades ahead. And the work will not be done without you. You are decisive to the future, as you have often been decisive in the past.

Waverly Crenshaw, class of 1978, made suggestions to the Board of Directors of the Alumni Association in October 1977 that led by a direct line to this first reunion that you, that we, are attending this weekend.

Eileen Carpenter and others, in the spring of 1967, meeting on the second floor of Alumni Hall, took initiatives in expressing explanations and expectations, as felt and understood by black undergraduates, that led in September 1967 to my declaration of personal understanding, and of Vanderbilt policy, that to treat our minority students equally we would have to treat them differently.

Perry Wallace in his way, and Larry Wallace in his; Walter Overton in his; the Brown twins in their way, and Ramona Bell in hers—each of you here, and all other black students who have come to Vanderbilt in these years of remaking America, in these years of overcoming, have been doing a part of the work we have done, and laying the foundation for the work we have yet to do together. More than two-thirds of the black students who have come to Vanderbilt have earned their degrees. Each of them was getting an education, but also each of them was helping to build a more nearly universal university. And those who did not finish, whether by their own choice or not, made contributions, often painful contributions, to enlarging the comprehensions, and to enlightening the spirit, of this university.

Walter Murray pioneered in organizing a program of specially designed academic assistance for students with what I think it fair to call specially designed academic needs. And in the earlier years most black students took part, and all were welcome to take part, in the deliberations of the Human Relations Council, a forum for exchange of information and ideas—quite literally for the exchange of education.

Leaving, 1982

Vanderbilt University—we all together are part of Vanderbilt University, we and others are, in fact, Vanderbilt, but here I mean the formal, legally chartered entity that is The University—Vanderbilt University, out of its own unique heritage and circumstances has made its contributions, too, to the overcoming in which we together here are engaged.

Vanderbilt's initiatives with foundations and individuals and its own monies have led to some one and one-half million dollars in undergraduate black student financial aid alone in these last eighteen years. I wish it had been ten and one-half million. Vanderbilt has adapted operating policies to needs and realities. And it has with consistency addressed persons inside and outside the University who did not agree with its policies and actions, converting some and resisting the rest. Too little, to be sure—too few black students, too few black faculty, too few black administrative officers, too few black admissions counselors, too little understanding, too little interaction across the lines, too little progress toward the goals set forth by the Alumni Association Committee on Alumni Relation—too little, but not too late. No university is perfect, no person is perfect, but we are better than we once were, we are better tonight than we have ever been before, and next year we will move forward again.

Over the years, in welcoming new students at the opening of the fall semester, I have often said that once you join Vanderbilt, you join not just for four years, you join for life. By saying it is so, I hope to help make it so. It is not true for everyone. Some white students—some majority students, shall we say—leave Vanderbilt unhappy, or, though contented, leave Vanderbilt apathetic toward the University. Some never come back to a reunion. Some of those majority alumni, who, I would think, should feel grateful and obligated to the University, feel alienated and are antagonistic. Yet, whether they acknowledge it or not, Vanderbilt is part of them and has helped them to be what they have become. So it is with all for-

363

mer students, including all Vanderbilt's former black students. You here, especially you here, are a part of Vanderbilt in a way that I, for example, who never attended Vanderbilt, can never be. You are part of the living body of the University and you can influence its future in significant ways. You can help to increase the black presence in Vanderbilt and to bring the benefits of Vanderbilt to black people in ways that no one else—in ways that *no one* else—can.

I think Vanderbilt has now entered a new stage, has climbed to a new institutional plateau from which it can mount still higher. The increasing body of black alumni of experience and achievement enables you to influence the University in new and effective ways— toward the goals we hold together for a better life for all, in a better nation for all. When I sometimes think that the road seems long, and the time interminable, I then remember the young black man who came over to Vanderbilt from another part of town, in the deeply discriminating, inflexibly segregated year of 1939, looking for work, and was hired to rake leaves and bundle them into gunny sacks. [I then recalled, as I had done before, that] he told me once of his sense of awe at being on the Vanderbilt campus, and his simultaneous feeling of separation from it. That young black man later became the first black student to enter Vanderbilt, the first black student to earn a Vanderbilt degree, the first black student to earn a Vanderbilt Ph.D. degree, and the first black man to be elected a trustee of Vanderbilt on the Board of Trust's own nomination. Bishop Joseph A. Johnson, Jr., traveled a long road, and yet he made a short journey, both at the same time. There are many short journeys that Vanderbilt and its people, with your help, can take in the months and years ahead. Let us take them together.

❧

I gave my twentieth and last remarks to Vanderbilt graduating students on May 14, 1982, on Curry Field.

364

Leaving, 1982

Ladies and gentlemen of Vanderbilt: My wife, Jean, and I are deeply grateful to Chairman Wilson for his generous remarks, to you for your generous response, to our trustees for our long, privileged association with them and their wives and husbands, to the Board of Trust for its formal conferring of emeritus rank, and to President and Mrs. Fields for their service beside us these last five years.

We especially thank our faculty and staff colleagues and their families for stout comradeship and many kindnesses over many years, and particularly for their abundant expressions of friendship and appreciation in recent weeks. Students on the campus and former students in places near and far—and often their families, too—have been movingly thoughtful to us both. All who compose this university will ever have our abiding gratitude and affection for the enormously rewarding privilege accorded us these past two decades of being, with them, a part of this marvelous university.

At Vanderbilt commencements—we have only one each year—we give main attention to the persons being graduated. We do not have a visiting speaker, but it is the chancellor's privilege to say a few words to our new graduates. At the last nineteen commencements I have spoken of the obligations and opportunities of educated women and men, of changes in the world that impose those obligations and offer those opportunities, of values important to foster, of requirements for our common survival, of the nature of knowledge and the nature of America. Speaking today from this platform for the last time, I shall do so about Vanderbilt, our university.

You who are being graduated here have been part of the living Vanderbilt, contributing to it as well as drawing from it. As former students you will continue to be part of the living Vanderbilt. Since last October, I have attended eighteen Vanderbilt meetings across the nation, from Los Angeles and Phoenix to New York and Atlanta, from Houston and Dallas to Chicago and Washington.

Vanderbilt lives vibrantly in those places and in most places in between. Many of you will be vigorous in Vanderbilt's life during the next half century, perhaps some as faculty members, maybe more than one as trustees, no doubt many as parents of Vanderbilt students, certainly many as watchers of Vanderbilt teams and many as shakers of Vanderbilt tambourines in our inevitable solicitations, still more as participants in affairs of the alumni. Your future is partly Vanderbilt's future.

Because Vanderbilt's future is important, I speak about it to you who will influence it much.

Thomas Jefferson in 1816 wrote a letter to Samuel Kerchival about the process for amending the Constitution of the United States. Vanderbilt does not have the kind of constitution the United States has, but it has the equivalent in its trustee by-laws, in its faculty and administrative rules, and in the habits, conventions, and traditions by which it lives. What Jefferson said about the nation applies to Vanderbilt.

He wrote:

> I am certainly not an advocate for frequent and untried changes in laws and constitutions. . . . But I know . . . that laws and institutions must go hand in hand with the progress of the human mind. As that becomes more developed, more enlightened, as new discoveries are made, new truths disclosed, and manners and opinions change with the change of circumstances, institutions must advance also, and keep pace with the times. We might as well require a man to wear still the coat which fitted him when a boy, as civilized society to remain ever under the regimen of their barbarous ancestors. . . . Let us . . . [not] weakly believe that one generation is not as capable as another of taking care of itself, and of ordering its own affairs.

Vanderbilt will have a new chancellor later this year, and all of us of Vanderbilt must heed Mr. Jefferson's meaning: a new generation is as capable as a previous one of taking care of itself and ordering its own affairs.

A university's first concern is the human intellect—reason, knowledge, understanding, and their applications. Modern universities are thus the seedbeds of the modern world's pervasive dynamism, the world's irresistible compulsion to change. Yet universities are ironically suspicious of proposals to change themselves, their own structures and habits, traditions and preferences, whether proposals to do so come from within or without. But universities, too, must change—not their primary values, but their ways of living—and those who will help make Vanderbilt's future under its new leadership must have the insight and fortitude to remember Mr. Jefferson's realism.

The great danger always in the development of institutions is timidity. Alfred P. Sloan, Jr., who built the General Motors Corporation into the world's largest private industrial enterprise, concluded at the end of his career that while he always believed in planning big, he always discovered after the fact that he had not had the imagination to plan big enough. The only limits on Vanderbilt's true greatness will be imposed by Vanderbilt itself.

Vanderbilt is not an abstract idea, a disembodied spirit, with a future somehow independent of Vanderbilt people. You Vanderbilt people will join with the new chancellor and his colleagues to determine the new destiny of your university.

Albert Einstein many years ago wrote that "Communities tend to be less guided than individuals by conscience and a sense of responsibility." He was asserting that the responsibility for a community's welfare, such as Vanderbilt's welfare, rests ultimately in individuals.

And that means all individuals. Albert Camus, writing on the duty of the artist, concluded, "We must simultaneously serve suffering and beauty." He was saying that not even artists, no matter how rare their talents, can be excused from community service, let us say university service.

Speaking of the University

Last Tuesday night I saw several of you graduating seniors being interviewed on television about your plans for the future. Your comments revealed joy and achievement in the past, hope and confidence in the future. I was glad. I also reflected that the privileges we here today enjoy are so extraordinary, compared with the realities of the world's vast majority, that you and I could easily be trapped into believing those privileges are normal and permanent.

You and I were fortunate before we came to Vanderbilt. We were fortunate that we came to Vanderbilt. What can we do now in return? Madison Sarratt, for whom the student center is named, always had a response to that question. It was: "Love Vanderbilt."

We can love Vanderbilt by supporting our new chancellor in leading Vanderbilt across new thresholds to create a better university, better in its educational distinctions, better in the range and value of its public services, better in the richness of spirit and daring imagination with which it looks forward. You especially can love Vanderbilt by remembering that you, as single citizens of our university, can use your influence, too, to make a nobler Vanderbilt future.

On February 5, 1963, five days after assuming the office of chancellor, I spoke for the first time to the faculties of the University. I said that day: "I propose that you and I shall have a good time during these coming years."

I have had a good time for two decades. I hope you graduates have enjoyed your years here. You take something of Vanderbilt, and a bit of me too, away with you today. Good luck always, and may the common Father of us all ever bless this university.

Index

Index

Index

Index

Index

Wilson, Anne, xiii
Wilson, David K., xiii, 294, 338, 365
Women's Advisory Committee, 161
Women's Panhellenic Council, 37,
 41
Women: status at Vanderbilt University. See Vanderbilt University: and status of women

Wray, Cecil, 210
Wyatt, Joe B., xiii

Yale University, 227, 244
Young, Mary, 186
Young, Norvel, 109

Zald, Mayer, 187

SPEAKING OF THE UNIVERSITY

was composed in 13.5 on 15.5
Centaur type
by Graphic Composition;
printed on 60-pound, acid-free,
Natural Smooth paper,
with 80-pound Rainbow endsheets
and dust jackets printed in 3 colors,
and bound over 88-point boards in
Roxite B-grade cloth, by Braun-Brumfield, Inc.
Both book and jacket design are the work of Gary Gore.
Published by Vanderbilt University Press,
Nashville, Tennessee 37235.